Social Welfare

718 857 6066.
weds. 5p. Home
Thurs. 2³⁰ pm at School
Tues. 2³⁰ pm. "

Nelson-Hall Series in Social Work

Consulting Editor: Charles Zastrow
University of Wisconsin—Whitewater

SECOND EDITION

Social Welfare
Policy and Analysis

Andrew W. Dobelstein
University of North Carolina

Nelson-Hall Publishers
Chicago

Project Editor: Laura Weber
Illustrator: Bill Nelson
Typesetter: E.T. Lowe
Printer: Capital City Press
Cover Painting: Kathleen Eaton, "Moon over Wabansia"

Library of Congress Cataloging-in-Publication Data

Dobelstein, Andrew W.
    Social welfare : policy and analysis / Andew W. Dobelstein. —
    2nd ed.
        p.   cm.
    Includes bibliographical references and index.
    ISBN 0-8304-1428-2
    1. Public welfare—United States.   2. United States—Social
policy.   3. Human services—United States.   I. Title.
HV95.D62   1996
361.6 1 0973—dc20   96-4578
    CIP

Manufactured in the United States of America

10 9 8 7 6 5 4 3 2

CONTENTS

v

Chapter Two

THE PROCESS OF POLICY-MAKING   28

Chapter Three

POLICY-MAKING AT THE LOCAL LEVEL   50

Chapter Four

METHODS OF POLICY ANALYSIS   67

CONTENTS

Chapter Nine

CHILD WELFARE   212

Chapter Ten

OLDER ADULTS   244

PREFACE TO THE SECOND EDITION

For sixty years American social welfare policy flourished under the framework of the Social Security Act of 1935. Beyond the many social programs created under its authority, the Social Security Act, as part of its genius, has also provided a national system for participation by all levels of government in America. The federal government, the states, and localities, have all had a hand not only in carrying out a vast array of social welfare programs, but also in developing a national agenda for these programs' purposes. Thus, while America has never approached a comprehensive social welfare agenda, as might be found in Western European "welfare states," the Social Security Act has provided the blueprint for the ongoing development of nationwide social welfare policy objectives. For example, America has created a nationwide program to assist retired adults maintain economic integrity. Other developed programs include a framework of health care for the poor, financial support for needy children, income protection in times of unemployment, and numerous policies and programs that minimize social risks to children.

The 1995 welfare reforms would provide yet another assault on this majestic legislation. Not only would these reforms have reduced social spending and eliminated familiar programs, but the Congress would have also shifted the initiative for social welfare policy away from a responsibility shared by states and the federal government. Much of the intergovernmental, "federated," welfare structure developed during the past sixty years would be replaced by a system of block grants that will allow states far-reaching flexibility in setting their own social welfare policy agendas. Instead of national social welfare policy objectives, America would have a collection of state policy objectives.

Programs that now carry an entitlement to their use for all who qualify will disappear as social welfare programs would come and go as states and localities determine how to best spend their welfare dollars.

As American social welfare policy stands on the cusp of momentous change, it is too soon to chart how the pending welfare reforms will affect social programs and, most importantly, the structure of American welfare policy itself. Indeed it could be several years before the seeds of the 1995 welfare initiatives become noticeable products. There are both positive and negative aspects as we try to visualize the future of welfare reform. American social welfare policies and programs have been long overdue for an overhaul. Clearly the reasons why people are poor today are quite different than the reasons people were poor sixty years ago. More and more, the many grant-in-aid programs have failed to address such changing conditions. Additionally, states have developed considerable capacity to plan and implement programs to address local problems of poverty. For many years states have reshaped federal social welfare policy mandates to meet their own needs, and recently a flood of "waivers" from federal regulations have been requested by and granted to states. In this way, block grants reflect changes that have already taken place. The challenge for social welfare policy now will be to use these changes to ensure that social welfare policy continues to benefit both individuals and the American system, as well.

As with the original text, this edition is indebted to many whose thinking, knowingly or otherwise, has been influential. Constant questions from my students have increased my clarity on many subjects, particularly with respect to policy analysis. Dr. Ron Haskins, now Senior Staff Director House Ways and Means Committee, Subcommittee on Human Resources, contributed significantly to understanding the shape of present Congressional welfare reform activities. Janet Hartnett, Deputy Director, Office of Policy and Evaluation for Administration for Children and Families, Department of Health and Human Services, often sharpened my thinking about the processes of administrative decision making. Vee Burke, Congressional Research Service, Library of Congress, generously shared her analysis of the 1995 welfare reforms, as did Lee Cowan and D'Arcy Phillips. Jeannie Newman, my research assistant, helped revise the statistical tables. Leslie M. Baker also helped me appreciate the need to speak in everyday language about these complex social policy subjects. These are only a few of the people who took an interest in this second edition. In spite of their helpful efforts, any misrepresentations of their ideas, the ideas of others, or errors of fact, remain with me.

Writing in 1945, the noted social work educator Charlotte Towle captured the vitality of the Social Security Act when she wrote,

PREFACE

The Social Security Act established a framework for the partnership of the Federal Government and the states in providing financial assistance to large groups of individuals who temporarily or permanently lack the means to that livelihood. . . . The Social Security Act bespeaks this country's commitment to a set of values beyond the sole value of economic self-dependence. Depletion of the personality and pauperization of the spirit are evils to be avoided as well as economic pauperization. The administrators of the Act are committed to the principle that man does not live by bread alone nor is he to be valued solely by his bread-winning capacity. (*Common Human Needs.* New York: National Association of Social Workers, 1957. [Introduction])

Unraveling the Social Security Act raises the troubling question of whether any commitment to the values Towle saw in the act remains today. Welfare reform should be a way to raise the human spirit. Hopefully, the acrimonious debate over welfare reform does not reflect an underlying American repudiation of, in Towle's words, "a concept of democracy as a way of life [governed] by a faith in man, in his worth, his possibilities, his ultimate dependability." It is only as our present social welfare policy students chart the course of continuing welfare reform that we will be able to tell.

PART I

Theories and Methods of Policy Analysis

D iving this text into parts provides the opportunity for students and teachers to divide their attention between theories and methods of policy analysis and America's major social welfare policy subjects. In many ways this is a division between theory and practice. Part I contains information that will provide a theoretical foundation for understanding how policy analysis fits into America's policy-making system and some methods by which policy analysis tasks are accomplished. Part II applies these theories and methods to familiar social welfare policy areas, or sectors, that are continually examined as America searches for new answers to long-standing domestic problems.

Part I of this text seeks to help the student understand the place of policy analysis in the vast complex of public decision making in America. Public decisions are a product of political processes which depend on a variety of information. Sometimes we think of information about constituency preferences, interest group programs, and the influence of the powerful—"political information"—as less important in policy making than the facts and figures of a particular issue under consideration—"scientific information."

Policy analysis provides a good deal of the information necessary for political decisions. Policy analysis must take into account both "political" and "scientific" information, and as it does so, policy analysis often provides a bridge between the two kinds of information, giving decision makers a more firm decision foundation. Chapter 1 provides some ways of understanding policy analysis that show the different purposes policy analysis may serve in decision making processes.

Chapters 2 and 3 provide a framework for understanding how policy decisions are made in the American system. Knowing where decisions are likely to be made is very important to knowing what kind of information policy analysis must supply. Some decisions are made in different branches of government. Others are made at the state or local levels of governance, while still others may depend on forces that interplay between public *and* private sectors of activity. Each decision center has somewhat unique information requirements.

Chapter 4 provides three models of policy analysis that can be adapted to the specific information requirements of the various policy decision centers. Chapter 5 describes a number of techniques of data collection, analysis, and presentation.

Part I provides a theoretical orientation to policy analysis that shows the wide variability in its application. Variability, however, can be managed when clarity exists about what kind of information is required in specific policy-making settings. Once this orientation to policy analysis is understood, the actual tasks of policy analysis within the context of specific policy problems, the substance of part II, become more clear.

Chapter One

UNDERSTANDING PUBLIC POLICY

Introduction

Wednesday afternoon, March 22, 1995 bells sounded in hearing rooms and all over the U.S. House of Representatives office buildings announcing a roll call. With some impatience, and with much anticipation, members began entering the floor of the elaborate House of Representatives. A buzz of conversation filled the air as representatives milled around, waiting for the House to be called to order by the Speaker.

"What is it?" One freshman Republican legislator asked of a colleague as he rushed toward the House floor.

"House Resolution 119 on Welfare." His colleague informed him.

"What's [Majority Leader Dick] Armey (R.-Texas) say?"

"Yes!"

"What about the Christian Coalition?"

"Leadership says we just eat it, Frank. That's it. Period!" Both legislators made their way to the House floor.

Speaker Newt Gingrich called the House to order, and debate began on H. Res. 119. After vigorous and often vitriolic debate, H. Res. 119 passed, 217–211, largely along party lines. But fifteen Republicans voted against the rule, and three Democrats voted for it. Most of the Republicans who voted against the resolution did so because of their antiabortion position and the pressure brought by antiabortion groups. The abortion issue had become deeply divisive among Republican House members. Essentially, the welfare reform legislation (H.R. 4) under consideration would deny cash assistance to teenage mothers and reward states for reducing out-of-wedlock births. These elements of welfare reform could prompt unmarried mothers, and particularly teenagers to have more abortions according to anti-abortion foes such as the National Right to Life Committee and the U.S. Catholic Conference. Thus anti-abortion foes sought to amend pending welfare reform to have these provisions removed, while traditional anti-abortion groups, such as the Family Research Council and the Christian Coalition supported these provisions of the bill as providing the means to take a strong, traditional, conservative stand against out-of-wedlock births and teen pregnancy. The Christian Coalition was particularly active and was "score-carding" members (i.e., keeping track of how members voted).

The issue of abortion deeply divided Republicans, and had become a source of embarrassment as the strong differences threatened to tear the fabric of the Republicans' "Contract with America" over one of its centerpiece promises—welfare reform. Wrangling over the abortion provisions in welfare reform had gone on for weeks with different bills being introduced, and volumes of amendments offered on H.R. 4. Weeks before, confusion and chaos over welfare reform appeared so strong that some observers believed no welfare reform would be possible in this session of Congress, much to the delight of Democrats who hoped to see the "Contract with America" fall apart.

Majority Leader Dick Armey had been lobbying Republicans to stick with the conservative position of denying assistance to unwed teenage mothers and women who had out-of-wedlock births and support the leadership on H.R. 4. Yet every day the Republican coalition seemed to come apart more and more. Finally Armey went to Speaker Gingrich and asked for a "rule" on H.R. 4, but Gingrich told Armey to go to the Rules Committee himself.

The Rules Committee holds a special place of authority in the House of Representatives, since rules govern how decisions are made. The Rules Committee is a powerful and "independent" committee, except that it is very much under the influence of the Speaker. Armey was well aware of how the Rules Committee operated. He was also aware that Representative Solomon, chair of the Rules Committee, had strong anti-abortion views himself, had had conversations with a well-known Catholic bishop about welfare reform, and, as a result, was not strongly supportive of welfare reforms with the existing provisions. Speaker Gingrich said he would speak with Chairman Solomon on Armey's behalf. Later Armey went to the Rules Committee and got his rule.

The rule for a vote on welfare reform was essentially that current approved amendments would be packaged into the bill, and no separate vote on those amendments, or the addition of new amendments, would be allowed when welfare reform was voted on. This meant that the conservative views supported by the Family Research Council and the Christian Coalition would be part of welfare reform and there would be no opportunity to amend H.R. 4 to remove these provisions when it came to the floor for its vote. Republicans who were concerned that the harsher provisions would promote abortions vowed to fight the rule, and Majority Leader Armey, counting votes carefully, believed that he could prevail on H. Res. 119. He knew there would be some losses that he could not prevent since the split was more a matter of sincere opinion among some Republicans, not merely political posturing.

The tension mounted as the roll was called on H. Res. 119. Speaker Gingrich, himself, voted "yea." Still it looked close. But when all the votes were in H. Res. 119 was approved by 217–211, an eight vote margin; a victory, but a close one.

"After the vote on the House Resolution," one House staffer remarked, "it was all over. We knew we had welfare reform, and we knew that the 'Contract with America' would hold together."

"It might have been closer, and we might even have lost," another staffer commented, "if six or eight Democrats had not been at the White House for some briefing, and had been here to vote instead."

Two days later, March 24, 1995 H.R. 4 passed the House of Representatives by a vote of 234–199. H.R. 4, the 1995 welfare reform, one of the most significant pieces of welfare legislation, perhaps since the Social Security Act itself was passed in 1935, was on its way to the Senate, and hopefully, the House believed, to the American people.[1]

Yet as dramatic as this vote proved to be, much less dramatic activities had gone on well before March 22, 1995, that if less dramatic, were perhaps even more unusual than the vote on H. Res. 119. H.R. 4 began its odyssey during the 1991–92 presidential campaign when candidate Clinton pledged to "end welfare as we know it today." Exactly what he meant by this campaign promise was not clear, although he talked frequently about his experiences as governor of Arkansas, and of putting people to work instead of giving them welfare. It seemed to matter very little that the country was digesting "welfare reforms" created by Congress in 1988, the Job Opportunity and Basic Skills Program (JOBS), and that this latest welfare reform had fallen far short of its political objectives, repeating the dismal history of welfare related, work mandated, programs going all the way back to the 1967 Work Incentive (WIN) program. Nor did it seem to matter much that Congress had amended welfare programs in significant ways in every session of Congress since the Social Security Act was created in 1935. Still, it seemed, we failed to get it right.

At about the same time of the presidential campaign, a group of House of Representative Republican staff members began to get together to think about and study welfare in America. Although informal, the group of staffers who began to meet was encouraged, if not led, by chief minority council of the House Ways and Means Committee, Dr. Ron Haskins. Haskins developed considerable academic experience in social welfare policy analysis before coming to work for Congress. And, as an ex-marine, he knew how to lead, as well as how to follow, and when it was right to do one or the other.

The interesting feature of this informal group was that the staffers who met and talked came from different committees or subcommittees, all of which had some authority over one or another welfare-type program. Perhaps it was the fact that Republicans were not in control of either Congress or the White House that emboldened this group, or perhaps it was the information that they began to collect with the help of the Congressional Research Service on the range, complexity, and cost of social program spending.[2] Or maybe they were driven by partisan politics, as some later suggested, but one fact emerged from these meetings: if welfare was ever to get beyond unworkable "reforms," committees had to give up jurisdiction over some of their programs, just as the federal government would have to give up its direction of social welfare programs it had guarded so jealously for the previous sixty years.

Neither giving up committee program jurisdiction, nor backing out of federal dominance in social welfare development would be easy, but it could be done through the creation of block grants. Now there are many reasons why congressional committees want to maintain jurisdiction over specific programs (see chapter 3). However, the most difficult hurdle is political: political constituencies develop around specific programs and these constituencies help congressmen get reelected as congressmen refund and expand programs they control. Block grants would lessen jurisdiction as well as erode political support for committee chairs and members. Looking on themselves as a form of the "loyal opposition" this group of staffers had little hope of achieving the kind of welfare reform they envisioned, and so they could be expansive in their proposals. For example, they even envisioned wresting the Food Stamp Program away from the Agricultural Committee and making it part of the income maintenance block grant, an effort that finally sank the welfare reform proposed by President Carter some years earlier.

In all fairness, some committee members themselves were less reluctant to give up jurisdiction over programs than would often be the case. For example, the House Committee on Education and Labor had jurisdiction over the JOBS program, which was not doing well and in need of serious reformulation. So one by one, programs were identified that could be stripped from committees and included in a welfare block-grant package for the states.

Then the unexpected happened. The 1994 Congressional elections put the Senate and the House of Representatives in Republican control, placed more Republicans in governorships, and a large number of state legislatures changed from Democratic to Republican control. The 1994 elections were the most stunning in the past thirty years, and, many conceded, the outcome was due to the "Contract with America," which Newt Gingrich introduced into the campaign itself. From the state house to White House, Republicans boasted that the contract was what turned the political tide, while Democrats grumbled that the contract was a political ploy that could not be carried out.

One element in the "Contract with America" talked about reforming welfare by denying welfare benefits to unmarried teenagers, denying welfare to children born out of wedlock while their mother was receiving welfare, and putting people to work. The Clinton staff was in a difficult position inasmuch as it was proposing a welfare reform that was remarkably similar to the "Contract with America." But the real surprise came to the staffers in the House of Representatives who had been working on their block-grant proposals.

"All of a sudden we were ahead of the power curve," one staffer commented. "We had a well-thought-out welfare reform proposal and tentative agreements from the committees about program jurisdiction. I couldn't believe it. We were in the driver's seat and far out in front."

Another staffer commented. "Here we were, in control of the House, and leadership pushing to implement the Contract while it still had currency among House Republicans. We turned to Ways and Means, and they said, 'I think we have something you might like.' And like it we did."

But there was still much work to do. Staff crunched numbers and showed how the proposal would reduce spending. Governors, many of them newly elected, grabbed at the opportunity presented by the block grants. State flexibility had been the cry of most governors since the small social service block grants were created in 1984.

Not everything ran smoothly. Agriculture balked at putting food stamps into the block grant, even though the new chairman was somewhat favorably disposed to the idea.

"Agriculture needs an urban base," one staffer commented. "Farming makes up such a small portion of agriculture spending today, and that of our constituency, that without urban spending, agriculture would be lost. And you need to remember," the staffer continued, "welfare is big business, not so much in the amount we spend for benefits, but who carries out the programs. In agriculture, grocery stores are big beneficiaries of food stamps, as are those in the computer industry who are developing 'debit card' type spending mechanisms, and those who are constantly investigating fraud. Food stamps is big business, and agriculture had to hang on to them."

Table 1.1 shows the scope of H.R. 4 with respect to program coordination and the way new spending might be carried out. It is too soon to say exactly what this latest welfare reform will look like exactly; some expect the Senate to change it considerably, and a conference committee will likely be needed to harmonize differences the Senate may pass. The president may continue to

Table 1.1: Summary of the 1995 welfare reform changes as contained in H.R. 4.

Title I: Block Grant for Temporary Assistance for Needy Families Title I creates a single cash welfare block grant to provide assistance to needy families with children. States will have to maintain 75 percent of their current spending levels. This block grant will replace:

Aid to Families with Dependent Children
Emergency Assistance
Job Opportunities and Basic Skills

Title VII: Child Protection Block-Grant Program and Foster Care Adoption Assistance This is a complex title that consolidates 18 existing child protection programs into two "open ended" entitlements and two block grants.

Foster Care and Adoption Maintenance will remain as open ended entitlement programs for poor children
Designated for poor children who cannot remain in their own homes as presently set forth in federal law.

Child Protection Block Grant
Two streams of money are provided—entitlements and discretionary—covering the following programs:

Foster Care Administration
and Training
Adoption Administration and Training
Independent Living
Child Welfare Services
Family Preservation

Child and Family Services Block Grant
Replaces programs authorized under the Child Abuse Prevention and Treatment Act including:

Abandoned Infants
Family Resource Program
Missing Children
Family Unification
Child Abuse Grants
Adoptions Opportunity
Child Abuse Investigation
Crisis Nurseries
Child Abuse Reasearch
Family Support Centers
Children's Advocacy

Title VIII: Child Care Block Grant Available for low income parents whether on a welfare program, a mandated work or training program or not, as long as the parent meets state criteria for "very low income." This block grant will eliminate the following existing day care programs: (Note: Some of the funding is mandatory, some is discretionary.)

Child Development Scholarships
Native Hawaiian Family Centers
Dependent Care Planning
At-Risk Child Care
AFDC Work-Related Child Care
Title X of Education Act (child care)
Transitional Child Care

Other Significant Features of H.R. 4.

Title II: Supplemental Security Income (SSI) Reforms changes eligibility rules for "drug addicts" and "alcoholics" and changes the eligibility determination process for children.

Title III: Child Support (Enforcement) changes the rules for state child support enforcement by program tightening. Sets different distribution formulas for child support collections to improve motivation to pay child support and establishes a framework for a national reporting and collection system.

Title IV: Restructures Welfare and Public Benefits for Noncitizens

Title V: Reductions in Federal Government Positions requires a 75 percent reduction in federal positions in program areas now coverd by block grants.

Title VI: Public Housing Benefits would not be permitted to compensate for losses due to failure to participate in mandated programs such as Temporary Assistance.

Title IX: Child Nutrition Seven states will be granted experimental block grants. The rest of the programs remain intact.

Title X Food Stamps and Commodity Distribution States given flexibility to harmonize food stamps with other block granted programs.

Source: U.S. Congress, House Ways and Means Committee, Subcommittee on Human Resources, July 1995.

veto the legislation, as he has threatened to do. There is question whether Congress has enough support to override a veto, and the process may have to start all over again. Some fear that the block grant will place expectations on states that they will be unable to meet, and in the final analysis will use their new block-grant flexibilities to do "more of the same—a risk we have to be willing to take," one congressional staffer commented. It will be years before the impact of H.R. 4 will be fully known.

Yet, even in its incomplete state, H.R. 4 represents a great change in the direction of social welfare policy and programs. Throughout the following chapters some of these changes will be discussed from the perspective of how the income maintenance provisions of H.R. 4 will affect existing policy debates and program activities. Even though the details of the income maintenance and child welfare block grant may not be known for a considerable period of time, it is clear that grant-in-aid program consolidation will take place, and one, two, and maybe even more block grants will emerge from this consolidation.

Beyond the details of H.R. 4—what it will look like exactly, how it will be carried out, and how programs will change over time—the development of H.R. 4 offers important lessons not only in how social welfare policy is made in America, but also provides important insights into what exactly social welfare policy is, and the purposes social policy serves in the American political system.

The Idea of Public Policy

When the House of Representatives created its 1995 welfare reform it created public policy, and the preceding pages illustrate many of the themes that comprise an understanding of public policy as it is experienced at a single point in time. Welfare has existed as part of the Social Security Act since 1935, and it has been changed almost every year since then. The 1995 changes are more important than some of the other changes, less important than others. All these changes created public policies, and these public policies were related to other public policies; thus, present policy builds on previous policy. No public policy stands alone.

Any single public policy serves a number of specific and general purposes. The 1995 welfare reform made changes in who will get benefits and how benefits will be provided. Additionally, the vast network of agencies that now provide these services will be changed as the 1995 welfare reforms are put into place. For example, many congressional representatives support block grants for welfare precisely because they believe these welfare changes will reduce the influence of federal and state administrative bureaucracies in providing welfare benefits. Such combinations of specific and general purposes of public policy vary from policy to policy, and the 1995 welfare reforms were no exception. While specific purposes for public policy satisfy specific constituencies—like families that need welfare support—the general purposes satisfy expectations for the larger community. In general, public policy satisfies one or another of five purposes, all of which can be found in the 1995 welfare reform. The 1995 welfare reforms: (1) solved a social problem; (2) located the public interest; (3) identified and legitimized special social goals; (4) provided a context for resolving conflicting values; and (5) established the direction for future social activity. A closer look at each of these five general purposes should expand an understanding of public policy.

Solving a Social Problem

The words, "social problems" conjure up vivid images of street violence, abused and neglected children, prostitution, and homelessness. To suggest that public policy solves these problems overstates the case. It may be more precise to say that public policy "addresses" social problems, or that social policy *tries to solve* social problems. In reality America's social problems, particularly the big social problems like crime and homelessness, are seldom "solved" in the sense that once policies are created, these problems cease to exist. Yet it is still important to think of public policy as actions that solve or try to solve social problems.

There are several reasons why public policy does not "solve" social problems as problem solving is usually understood. In the first place, not everyone sees problems in the same way. Often what one person thinks is a problem may seem completely normal to another person. Problems emerge when values are applied to existing life conditions. The room you may be sitting in is not a problem. It may become a problem if you feel hot, for example. Then you may say the room is a problem because it is too hot. Yet your friend may feel perfectly comfortable in the room until you turn down the heat. Then it becomes a problem for her.

Since different people place higher or lower values on life circumstances, different people often understand a problem from different perspectives. For some the room may be too hot; for others it may be too cold. Solving a problem for one person may create a problem for someone else with different values. In this sense, a problem may not be solved. Values drive problem identification, just as values drive the solutions we seek in the form of public policy. From identifying the problem (the beginning), to selecting a policy to deal with the problem (the ending), the whole of public policy development is driven by values.

Social problems come in various forms and sizes and do not necessarily mean that a society is in serious trouble. American society is highly complex, a diverse mix of people. The economic system that energizes America, and the political institutions that order it are founded in the belief in individual choice and maximum participation, which foster increased diversity. U.S. society operates pretty well most of the time. Public activities are undertaken to enhance private interests. But this picture of success emerges from a context of constant change, adjustment, readjustment, and accommodation. Some of these changes create problems, such as the need for a constant supply of decent housing, that involves large social and geographic sectors. Some problems, such as relocation of displaced textile workers, are small, involving discrete sectors. All are important. The idea of a dynamic society constantly dealing with problems through public policies is important to an understanding of the purposes of public policy.

This complexity of American society is yet another reason why public policy does not solve a problem in the usual way one understands problem solving. For example, social relationships among racial and ethnic groups in American society constitute a serious, continuous problem. In the 1960s, the Civil Rights Act and the Voting Rights Act were public policies developed to ease social tension and improve social relationships. But despite the importance of these policies, black and white populations have not reconciled their differences. Though some progress has been made, blacks remain largely segregated socially, economically and geographically—a source of serious conflict as the black population continues to receive so little of the total public resources. This is a serious problem that remains an agenda item for public policy.

In the Southwest large numbers of Spanish-speaking people are migrating to the United States from Mexico and other South American countries. Hispanic Americans are the largest growing population in America today, making Southern California, in particular, a bilingual culture. The influx of Spanish-speaking immigrants, both legal and illegal, caused such a strain on California's public resources, that Californians approved a 1994 referendum that prohibited spending public resources on illegal immigrants, with the threat of denying public services to thousands of people. California's courts ordered a delay in implementing that particular policy. Thus a public policy designed to resolve a problem brought about by American diversity appears to make the problem worse by withholding resources from those who may need them.

Solutions to problems may range from conservative to liberal policy choices, depending upon how the problems are perceived. In reviewing health care delivery, Alan Shostack, a sociologist, has demonstrated how the problem of inadequate care might be resolved by different approaches depending on how the problem is understood. If, for example, inadequate care is viewed as a result of too many people asking for too many services because public and private insurance companies will pay for it, a policy to restrict access to health care by raising fees might seem to resolve the problem appropriately. On the other hand, if the problem is seen as the inability of the health-care industry to provide basic care to the average person, one might conclude that the health industry has too many interests competing for high profits—drug companies, large hospitals, equipment manufacturers, nursing homes—and thus suggest that the government regulate the costs and profits of health care providers.[3]

Solutions to problems may also take the form of policy choices aimed at specific groups in the population—for instance, women, minorities, children—or they may prompt policies that enhance the well-being of everyone, including special groups. The first of these types of policies has been called *residual*. Residual policies are created on the assumption that although political, economic, and social systems operate effectively most of the time for most people, residual problems remain that have to be accommodated by public policies.

The second kind of policy is called *institutional*. These assume that solutions to problems have to be applied universally and usually are accomplished through some change in existing institutions.[4] The differences between institutional and residual policies can be illustrated by comparing the Social Security Retirement program (OASDI) with financial assistance to the aged, Supplementary Security Income (SSI). OASDI is based on the assumption that protection of income in retirement requires a universal restructuring of our economic system; in this case the government taxes everyone and reserves these funds for everyone's use in retirement. SSI, on the other hand, provides limited financial resources to older people when their equity in OASDI is so marginal that they need additional financial resources.

In sum, public policy resolves problems, but the way each problem is understood becomes important for how that problem is resolved. In many cases, the particular view taken toward a problem is a normative position: one in which a standard for viewing the problem has already been established. This standard is often one based upon values or ideology, and policy analysis usually accepts these values as facts leading to a decision. However, for any problem a number of conflicting normative views may exist. Poverty, for example, is a social problem for which many policies have been established—in fact, many of the policies discussed in this book were designed to deal with the problem of poverty. Some people take the position that poverty is the fault of the individual; others see poverty as a problem of the social system (as when blacks or women are discriminated against in employment); still others may see poverty as the result of an inequitable distribution of money and power. And although these views reflect personal ideologies and beliefs about poverty, they are advanced as basic facts in debates over policy. They constitute "normative positions" on poverty.

Policy analysts and policy choice must come to grips with normative positions, because the prevailing or public views on a subject often reflect values held by the larger society. Sometimes these prevailing views reflect deeply held religious convictions, as with the abortion issue. Sometimes they reflect the particular values of a policy analyst or the values of the method of analysis itself. Sometimes they reflect the values of the decision maker. Thus normative positions are evident not only in the way problems are identified, but also in the ways policy alternatives are examined. Chapter 4 presents three models of policy analysis; each also includes recognition of normative issues. In subsequent chapters that examine specific policy subjects, the normative orientations to each problem are stated as clearly as possible so that they can be considered in the analysis itself.

Locating the Public Interest

The public interest is an elusive but extremely important concept in policy development. The whole purpose of democratic government is service to the public. The acts of such a government are presumed to reflect the preferences of the governed. When they do not, the governed attempt to bring the government into line with public preferences, through a range of available political activities such as voting, decrease in public support for government, and, on occasion, civil unrest.

Charting the public interest is extremely difficult in a complex society. Different people and different groups of people usually want different things—another example of the influence of normative issues. People also want change, which reinforces the idea that the public is "fickle." In the 1960s, for example, the American public seemed to be asking for greater freedom of choice over the termination of pregnancy. By the 1980s, the American public seemed to be asking government to restrict the choice. By 1995 abortion has again opened old debates, and confused policy, as seen by the 1995 welfare reform debates.

Public opinion is very hard to measure. Public opinion polls provide some gauge, as do statements from major public actors, but these may be superficial or fleeting reflections of the public interest. For example, after winning election to a second term of office, President Reagan talked about his victory as a proof of positive public support for his policies—yet his popular vote was less than one percentage point greater than that of his opponent, Walter Mondale, and opinion polls showed that a majority of the electorate disagreed with his policies, even though they liked him.

Public opinion translates only crudely into public policy. Public opinion is an expression of the masses, but policy is shaped by elites. Thus public opinion may not always be converted into results that reflect broad public interests. For example, public opinion may favor an equitable tax system, but tax policies leave tax systems inequitable.

Nevertheless, public policy does provide an important focus of public interest. A number of publics will be involved in the creation of any public policy. A president or a governor may initiate a policy proposal after a number of individuals and groups associated with an issue have come to some conclusion about the dimension of the problem, its normative orientation, and proposed solutions. A legislator may undertake an effort to develop policy. Many publics, many individuals, and many groups interact in the policy-making process. All policymakers have to be sensitive to a variety of public orientations. Thus in the process of developing policy a considerable amount of public consensus is achieved, so that by the time a public policy is developed, it offers a pretty good indication of how the American public is oriented toward the issues at stake.

By locating the public interest, public policy freezes public thinking and public action on an issue at a particular point in time. Because the processes of policy development are complex and time-consuming, public policy is not likely to be on the cutting edge of new issues. In any dynamic society the circumstances that give rise to an identifiable problem are changing constantly, as are the political institutions that reformulate public interests into public products. As a result, it often seems that no sooner has a public policy emerged than there are pressures to change it. In this dynamic environment, the public is frequently apt to question whether government and public representatives in government are responding to public wishes.

Whether or not publics should be involved in policy development is undebatable: publics *are* involved, often in complex ways. When a public policy process has been completed, public interest is reflected in the policy; the public interest in the issue emerges from the process and becomes clear.

Identifying and Legitimating Social Goals

Because it is closely associated with locating the public interest, public policy identifies and legitimates social goals. Although we visualize policy development as a progression from problems to goals, such may not always be the case. Goals may preclude problems or may exist independent of them, and social goals frequently determine the framework of normative discourse that surrounds most policy debate. Goals are most frequently thought of as desired states of affairs. A goal is an image of the future, which provides a guiding framework for many actions that follow. Goals also provide a measure of social progress, which can be gauged by how much has been achieved with respect to the vision set forth by the policy. Public policy serves to identify goals and confer legitimacy on them. Thus through the development of public policy a particular set of ideas become formalized goals, and movement toward or away from these goals can be charted, as the following example illustrates.

On January 8, 1964, President Lyndon Johnson went before Congress with his state of the union message. Reporting on the state of the union is required of new presidents, and these messages frequently state the policy objectives (social goals) of the new administration. In this particular address, Johnson introduced a bold new goal: the elimination of poverty in America. "This administration today, here and now, declares unconditional war on poverty in America," he proclaimed. "Our aim is not only to relieve the symptoms of poverty, but to cure it, and above all, prevent it."[5] This statement inaugurated an effort later called the "War on Poverty," a centerpiece of the Johnson administration's "Great Society." This announcement and the activities that followed formed the administration's public policy. They were goals, and they were also public policy.

President Johnson's declaration of war on poverty provided a context for a number of specific policy proposals. He asked Congress to develop and expand eleven major programs: (1) Appalachian development, (2) youth employment, (3) expanded food stamp distribution, (4) a national service corps (VISTA), (5) more stable unemployment insurance, (6) extension of minimum wage coverage, (7) federal aid to education in impoverished communities, (8) construction of more hospitals and libraries, (9) hospital insurance for the aged, (10) expanded public housing, and (11) federal aid for mass transit.

This cornucopia of policy initiatives was an astute summary of the direction of the nation under the Kennedy administration. The general mood of the nation had suggested that poverty was unacceptable. In 1959 Michael Harrington had exposed the ravages of poverty in the United States, and public opinion seemed to support efforts to deal with it. For example, President Kennedy had managed to initiate a limited food stamp program, but many of his social initiatives could not find their way through an entrenched Congress.[6]

President Johnson's message to Congress set forth policy objectives that reflected a buildup of broad interests in dealing with poverty systematically. On August 20, 1964, he signed legislation that further clarified the social goal of the policy initiatives presented in his state of the union message: America's objective would be to afford the poor some security and to enable them to "move with the majority along the high road of hope and prosperity."[7] This legislation was the Economic Opportunity Act, which created a range of programs that were used for the next twenty years to reduce poverty in the nation. Thus a diffuse goal—reducing poverty—was legitimated through the policies of Great Society programs.

Creating a Context for Resolving Conflicting Values

Public policy is designed to solve public problems, and the resolution of a problem often depends upon the normative orientation of the problem solver. The solution of a problem for one group of persons may raise problems for another group. Johnson's proposals to eliminate poverty provided opportunities and support for many people with low incomes, but they also burdened state and local governments with complex federal programs, causing political backlashes that have endured ever since. In 1981, for example, President Reagan proposed to reduce the burden of federal programs on states by creating block-grant programs that would allow states flexibility in dealing with social problems. In exchange, he solicited agreements from governors that they would accept reduced amounts of federal funding in exchange for relief from federal regulations. The resulting reductions in funding, combined with a severe recession, brought thousands of people back into poverty and ill health, and the percentage of citizens living in poverty reached the level that had existed before Johnson's policies were instituted.

Again in 1995 governors sought more freedom from cumbersome federal programs and Congress answered with more block-grant programs. Sometimes these adverse or conflicting elements of policy are identified as "unintended consequences" or "unanticipated events" of policy choices. Unintended consequences represent efforts to even out competing value positions among different groups. Most commonly the competition is between those who have and those who do not. The long-held idea that America is a "community of publics," and the concomitant notion that this community will express itself in a democratic policy that at least satisfies the greatest number, if not the greatest good, is increasingly under fire. One analyst, C. Wright Mills, who has focused his attention on the divisions among groups, claims that American society has never been a community of publics, but is instead severely stratified : "At the top, members emerge as elites of power. The middle does not link the bottom with the top. The bottom is politically fragmented and increasingly powerless."[8]

Understanding public policy thus requires understanding power. Power, and "power elites," as Mills terms them, are extremely important to the analysis, development, and realization of public policy. Power has been defined as "the capacity to overcome part or all of the resistance to induce changes in the face of opposition."[9] In this view, power itself has no value exclusive of its expression; the purposes to which power is put give it value.

In the policy-making process, once questions of value are decided, few conflicts arise over using power to implement policy. Power struggles are more apt to transpire over agreements about the values themselves. In other words, power struggles concern values and the choice of normative positions. Mills and others who discuss American society as elitist argue that power in the hands of a few gives those few a great advantage in determining the normative orientation toward an issue; consequently this elite exercises great influence in the direction of public policy.

Amitai Etzioni distinguishes between *power assets* and the *exercise of power.*[10] Possession of the potential to act confers power assets, which may be converted into *expressions of power*, but are not necessarily used in this way. Groups or individuals who hold power assets tend to calculate whether to exercise power or not. Consequently expressions of power are often made even when power is not exercised outright. For example, an individual or a group, perhaps a small labor union, may choose not to act (that is, not to exercise power) because it calculates that the power that could be exercised by another group, for example, management, would be greater; hence by exercising its power in a strike the union would lose the struggle. However, the threat of exercising that power (a power asset) might force management to some concession. This distinction between the assets and the exercise of power is extremely important in policy analysis, since power influences normative debates, or the "policy agenda," as many analysts call it.

Because American society is composed of many groups, representing a variety of values, a constant ferment stirs the policy agenda. In fact the number of goals on the agenda is so great that resources are insufficient to realize all of them. Consequently, groups moving toward realizing particular goals will tend to resist any perceived competitors. Cooperation under these circumstances is difficult to achieve, and conflict is more likely to be the dominant mode of interaction. When cooperation is achieved, as it often must be when dealing with complex public problems, it is frequently imposed by another party. For example, cooperation between labor unions and management may be achieved because the Department of Labor also has power assets that can be brought to bear to compel cooperation on policy matters. This type of cooperation is often engineered by mediators who bring the parties to the bargaining table. In Etzioni's words, "Power and cooperation are, thus, not a

17

mutually exclusive pair of concepts; cooperation often has a power base, and power is exercised through cooperation."[11]

In this view, public policy development provides an environment in which power exchanges can take place either cooperatively or through conflict. Since power assets are not equally distributed, and since changes in power relationships take place through the application of power, public policy development provides the framework in which power can become restructured.

An example of the restructuring of power through policy-making can be seen in Edward Banfield's and Martin Myerson's study of the development of public housing policy in Chicago in the 1950s. The city had decided to expand considerably its public housing. Once that decision had been made, the real and continuing struggles—for control of land and money—began in earnest. A variety of conflicting claims over site selection, occupants of the proposed housing, and construction had to be resolved. The ensuing scramble was a competition for shares of city resources and, eventually, the authority to give the city itself control of the process by which resources would be distributed: "The 'Big Boys' could get and keep power enough to run the city only by giving favors for the maintenance of [their power] base. The people of Chicago probably did not fully realize the price that was being paid to assemble enough power [to build the housing]."[12]

Setting the Direction for Future Social Action— Policy and Planning

Policy builds on policy, and in this incremental form, public policy sets the course for further social development. In America at least, public policy appears as a process of changes leading to a better society. Some may want to protect the environment, others may want to improve housing or health care, still others may want to redistribute income and wealth. Yet these different actions only *seem* separate. In fact they constitute a single process. Human urgings for a better society are deeply imbedded in the American ideology, and Americans believe that a systematic, orderly process of policy development will lead to good for society. This belief stems from a positivist ideology that originated in the writings of Auguste Comte, the founder of sociology, and in the literature of utopias. The influence of positivist thought in policy analysis is examined in great detail in chapter 4, but it is important here to understand the essential support that positivism gives to public policy. The very idea of policy, a committed direction, in contrast to uncoordinated activities, attests to the positivist belief that society can be improved, and positivism gives compelling vitality to the idea that social policy leads, eventually, to social reform.

The close connection between public policy and future change, and the underlying belief that changes will produce a better society, explain in part the close historical relationship between the activities of social planning and social policy. The application of scientific knowledge to practical problems marked the beginning of the systematic study of why social change takes place, or how social change can be managed and directed. This planning tradition emerged from the American city planning movement and the social and municipal reform efforts of the early 1900s.

This spirit of reform was consistent with the ideological orientation toward positivism—the belief that science could and would create a better society— and was so far-reaching in its influence on American social institutions that any consideration of policy analysis owes some debt to this early history. Largely because of increased pressure for change from settlement-house workers and other social reformers, state legislatures and municipal governments began to set aside portions of land for parks and other public purposes. As far as the cities were concerned, developing parks and other public facilities was consistent with efforts, already underway for several decades, to ensure safe water supplies, adequate waste disposal, and public safety and fire protection. In Chicago, the philanthropist William Kent gave land to Jane Addams' Hull House. The great landscape architect Frederick Law Olmsted conceived New York's Central Park as a place in which city dwellers could experience "a day in the country," based on the ideal of humanizing the urban experience.

To achieve the objectives proposed by the reformers, municipalities had to develop plans not only for new parks but also for the many other community resources believed to be essential to a decent life in urban America. This planning required not only information about what might be possible, but also reform in the structure and character of local government, for municipalities needed additional staff to execute these new projects. Moreover, reformers sought to protect these public accomplishments by insisting that the increasing number of public officials be chosen by popular elections rather than through patronage, thus giving further authority to the rational, as opposed to political, nature of this form of policy development.

As the twentieth century progressed, this blending of scientific information with social reform and city planning led to the emergence of social planning as a defined discipline and specific sector of activity. Herbert Hoover created the President's Research Committee on Social Trends in December 1929.[13] Among its members were the political scientist Charles E. Merriam of the University of Chicago and Howard V. Odum, a sociologist at the University of North Carolina who had helped to establish its school of social work. Although the committee was commissioned to develop plans to guide the country through the economic calamity of the Great Depression, Hoover gave only nominal support to this work, perhaps because he underestimated the impact of the worsening economic circumstances. The depression, however, did reveal the serious flaws in the American economic and social structure, and Hoover's Research Committee provided intellectual energy for President Roosevelt's "brain trust," which eventually did help create the social plans that lifted the nation out of the depression and led the way to establishment of the federal role in policy development under the Social Security Act.

The origins of the science of policy analysis are much too broad to be examined here, but briefly it may be said that the emerging base of social knowledge fused with ideas that a better social order could be planned and realized. "It was in this context that applied social science, first in the form of statistics and demography, and later in the form of established disciplines of sociology, economics, political science, and public administration, rose as a challenge to the practical problems of understanding and controlling the complexities of society."[14]

The close association between policy analysis, policy-making, and various forms of social and physical planning has continued to the present day. Policy documents are often called "master plans." Nearly every local community in America—cities, counties, and even multi-jurisdictional organizations—has its planning boards or planning councils. The purpose of these planning groups is to develop policy, usually about necessary land use. These policies eventually became incorporated into something called a "comprehensive plan." For example, recently the small town of Carrboro, North Carolina, adopted a policy that stated, in part, that for purposes of land use, mobile homes would be treated in exactly the same way as homes permanently constructed on a site. This policy became part of Carrboro's land-use plan. Now, when an individual or a corporate group contemplates using land in Carrboro, the treatment of mobile homes must be considered along with many other planning factors. The mobile home policy sets the agenda for further policy development and therefore remains in close association with an ongoing process of planning.

Similarly, the Social Security Act, along with the many amendments to it over the years, is both a policy document and a planning document. For example, as public policy Title II provides federal support for a public retirement program. As a planning document, Title II requires the anticipation and implementation of sophisticated financial provisions for retirees, including the projection of national economic performance as far as fifty years into the future as well as a series of population projections so that economic guarantees can be supported over this period of time.

Classifying Public Policy

Diversity of public policy prohibits general statements about how public policy is analyzed and developed. Policy is categorized most frequently according to who makes it and to the purposes it serves. Such classification schemes are useful insofar as they provide common points of departure for thinking about policy proposals, but public policy as a concept must be defined before classification can be discussed reasonably. Throughout this text, public policy is understood in the following way: *Public policy is an action (or in some cases, an inaction) usually undertaken by government, directed at a particular goal, and legitimated by the commitment of public resources.* A detailed discussion of this definition introduces the next chapter, but for the purposes here of classifying public policy this definition restricts our consideration of public policy to *activity of government.* On the basis of this definition, public policy can be categorized and its different purposes can be explained by identifying those who make it.

Administrative Policy

Administrators most frequently make public policy. In general, administrators are persons who work in government agencies that have responsibility for carrying out programs. Thus they make policy within the context of a particular program, or policy, or problem. For example, Donna Shalala, Secretary of Health and Human Services in the Clinton Administration, and her administrative staff, never made policy about airports or interstate highways because these policies were made by the Department of Transportation. Administrative policy-making may be restricted further by the function of administrators. Because their primary responsibility is to implement programs (and policies), administrators cannot make policies that would create new programs or change the policies that established the existing programs. As a result of this narrow frame of reference, administrators are required to develop policy that is carefully measured against established program mandates.

The "Baby Doe" regulations of 1985 demonstrate the limited scope of administrative policy-making and the consequent need to apply scientific knowledge to the policy-making process.[15] Congress included a provision in the Child Abuse Prevention Act of 1984 that failure to provide treatment to disabled newborns would constitute abuse and neglect; doctors could be held legally accountable for failing to provide needed medical treatment. The Department of Health and Human Services (DHHS) was required to implement this program within the framework of a format unique to administrative pol-

21

icy-making: regulations. These regulations required DHHS not only to stay within the bounds of the Child Abuse Prevention Act but also to avail itself of highly technical information in developing its policy. Answers to questions such as, "What constitutes imminent danger?" and "What is medically indicated treatment?" had to be extracted from detailed expert knowledge.

Legislative Policy

The legislative process of policy-making or, in more common terms, the development of statute law, is a human labyrinth. Figure 1.1 shows how an idea is translated into statute law in Congress. The process is similar in the states, although some of the elements, like the number of times a bill may have to be read, will be different. It may be relatively obvious how a proposal begins the legislative process, but the twists and turns of the process frequently change the character and substance of the proposal, and indeed it may become lost altogether along the way. The intrigue of the legislative process, not reflected in figure 1.1, is legendary. A more complete explanation of the significance of policy analysts for the legislative process is a major focus of chapter 2. For the moment it is important to consider a few ideas about legislators as persons who make policy.

Legislators are a diverse lot. They are elected from geographically defined districts: 535 of them to the United States Congress, and often more than 100 to each state legislature. These districts—urban, rural, rich, poor, Anglo, African- and Asian-American—are as diverse as the country itself. Legislators are thus to bring to legislative forums widely divergent views about problems and what should be done about them. Most legislators are educated as lawyers, but many are "professional politicians"—they see law-making as their vocation, and they want to keep their jobs. All, except one hundred senators in the U.S. Congress, stand for election every two years. Legislators have no job tenure. For this reason, and others related to their working environment, legislators are very sensitive to the concerns of their constituents.

Legislators create statute law. Because of the authority behind it and the general deference given to it, statute law establishes our most formidable public policy. And because of the wide diversity of the viewpoints of the participants and the complicated legislative process, it is also the most difficult to create. Yet precisely because it is so formidable, legislation is sought most frequently in the development of public policy. Legislation is a good example of policy that fixes future courses of action. When a law is made, all the other policymakers—administrators, executives, and judges—are brought into action.

Figure 1.1: A model of how Congress makes a law.

Committee Action	HR 1 Introduced in House	White House	S 2 Introduced in Senate	*Committee Action*

Referred to House Committee

Bill goes to full committee, then usually to specialized subcommittee for study, hearings, revisions, approval. Then bill goes back to full committee where more hearings and revision may occur. Full committee may approve bill and recommend its chamber pass the proposal. Committees rarely give bill unfavorable report; rather, no action is taken, thereby ending further consideration of the measure.

Referred to Senate Committee

Referred to Subcommittee

Referred to Subcommittee

Reported by Full Committee

Reported by Full Committee

Rules Committee Action

In House, many bills go before Rules Committee for "rule" expediting floor action, setting conditions for debate and amendments on floor. Some bills are "privileged" and go directly to floor. Other procedures exist for noncontroversial or routine bills. In Senate, special "rules" are not used; leadership normally schedules action.

Floor Action

Floor Action

House Debate, Vote on Passage

Bill is debated, usually amended, passed or defeated. If passed, it goes to other chamber to follow the same route through committee and floor stages. (If other chamber has already passed related bill, both versions go straight to conference.)

Senate Debate, Vote on Passage

Conference Action

Joint Committee

House of Representatives

Once both chambers have passed related bills, conference committee of members from both houses is formed to work out differences.

Senate

◄— Compromise version from conference is —► sent to each chamber for final approval.

VETOED

White House

SIGNED

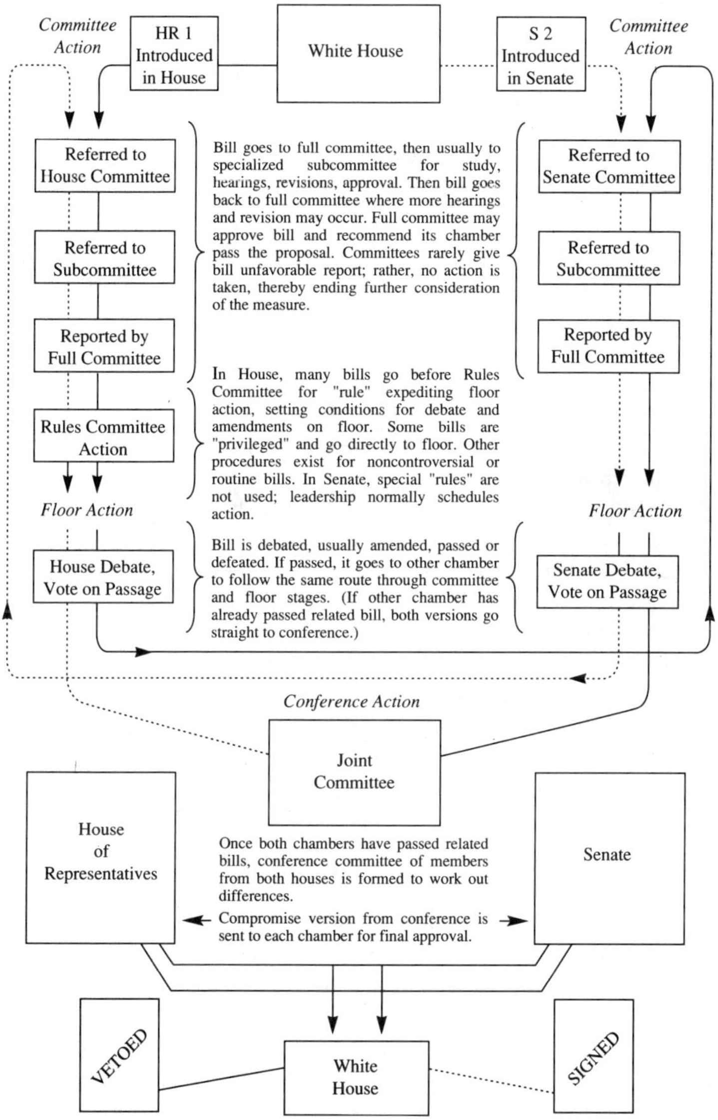

Compromise bill approved by both houses is sent to the president, who can sign it into law or veto it and return it to Congress. Congress may override veto by a two-thirds majority vote in both houses; bill then becomes law without president's signature.

Source: Adapted from U.S. House of Representatives, "How Congress Makes a Law" (1987).

In contrast to administrators, legislators have almost no limitation on the scope of their policy-making. The only limit on legislators as they make policy is that they must not make unconstitutional laws, but often the constitutionality of a legislative action is not decided until after the law has been implemented. Much legislative activity takes place within committees; these are intended to address different subject areas but are not strictly limited forums of discussion. Just about anything is open to legislative policy-making, and creating new policies is as much a part of legislation as modifying old ones. Social science knowledge, an administrative asset, is not very useful to legislators, because the legislative process is so complex and because the legislators' actions are so closely connected to the desires of their constituents (or interest groups). In other words, legislative policy-making is highly politicized.

Executive Policy

Political executives make policy, but their policy-making is limited by their primary responsibility of carrying out policy made by others. In most cases political executives are elected officials such as the president, governors, and mayors. Others, such as heads of administrative agencies, may be appointed. The secretary of the Department of Health and Human Resources, for example, is not elected to the post, but chosen by an elected official (the president) and confirmed by other elected officials (the Congress). The superintendent of a local school system may be elected by the citizens of the school district or may be appointed by the school board that is elected by the citizens. Thus administrators and executives share some limitations in their activities as policymakers. Both operate within a limited scope, and both are forced to rely heavily on technical information, because their primary policy-making responsibility is in relationship to carrying out or implementing programs.

The overlap between executives and administrators is best exemplified by the Reagan administration's expanded use, in its second term, of the Office of Management and Budget (OMB) to direct the policy-making of administrative agencies. Because the president has considerably more executive control over OMB than over administrative agencies, OMB has increasingly been asked to review proposed policies to determine if they conform to guidelines set down by the president. Before Reagan was elected president, reviews were made of issues in a very general way. This approach was exemplified most clearly by President Ford in 1974, when he required only that policy with inflationary implications be reviewed by OMB. Reagan expanded this authority in 1981, when he created the Task Force for Regulatory Relief to review the propriety and necessity of policy-making (regulations) in the other administrative agencies. In 1981 he also issued an order giving the director of OMB authority to "designate any proposal and rule as a major one" (and thus subject it to OMB review) and to "waive sections [of proposed regulations] involving [Regulatory Impact Analysis]." [16] As one commentator put it, "There is no doubt that the February 17th order [EO 12291] developed a centralized review mechanism in the White House with power to 'crack the whip' to bring agencies in line with Reagan's objectives . . . a power play that shifts power from the regulatory agencies to the OMB." [17] This illustrates that a wide range of action by administrators may receive careful scrutiny from executives and may even require their approval. The implications of this trend in policy development are discussed in chapter 2. At the very least, this trend has increased the need for social science information among executives and administrators.

Judicial Policy

Judges' policy-making activities differ from those of administrators, executives, and legislators. Traditionally, judges are expected to restrain their personal values in deference to precedent and tradition. In other words, judges read existing law (statute and case law) and make policy based on their interpretation of whatever policy already exists. It might be said that judges do not make policy so much as they affirm and clarify policy on the basis of what other policymakers have already done.

This traditional view of judicial policy-making has received considerable examination since Theodore Becker's pioneering analysis of the judiciary. Many have viewed the actions of judges as political (an "objective application of a political law" in Becker's words), but Becker himself attempts to locate the judicial system within the larger political framework of American government. In his view the political actions of judges are not aberrant forms of judicial behavior, but an integral part of the system of checks and balances in the American system. Specifically, he argues that in "a bargaining type of policy formation which is highly sensitive to pressure, courts allow for unimprovised solutions as conflicts reach high levels." [18] This view of judicial policy-making would correspond with the function of public policy as a means of resolving conflicts over allocation of resources.

There are many outstanding instances where judicial policy-making has broken with the traditional view of judicial behavior. *Baker vs. Carr* (1964) forced reapportionment in the states. *King vs. Smith* (1956) forbade the states to deny aid to children by questioning the moral fitness of their homes. The greatest example of judicial policy-making will probably remain *Brown vs. Board of Education* (1954), which overthrew racial segregation in this country by deciding that separate schools did not constitute equal schools.

Despite its wide-ranging authority in terms of subject area, judicial policy-making is circumscribed by the limits placed upon judicial authority: issues must be brought before the court, and they must be issues about constitutionality. Because judges must rely more on legal information than on social science, the courts are perhaps not as much partners with social scientists in the policy-making process as are legislatures.

Conclusion

Although public policy seems to be an elusive concept, it becomes clearer as the purposes it serves are examined. Public policy represents a social benchmark, showing where American society stands on specific matters. Thus, Americans are concerned about abortions: *Roe vs. Wade* and the Hyde Amendment summarize where the nation stands on this matter. Americans are concerned about the welfare of children: the Social Security Act and resulting regulations identify how Americans respond to these issues. Americans are worried about clean air and water: the "Super Fund" and the EPA state the nation's position on the environment. For housing concerns there is the Housing Act and tax credits for home mortgages. The list goes on and on; for every issue there is some policy that identifies the position of America's citizens.

Within this litany of public policy, policies often overlap one another both in time and in substance. Public policy is like an elaborate mosaic of American society. Change one part, and the entire mosaic changes. For this reason it is difficult to discuss the major social policies, how they are developed, and how they are analyzed, without giving some consideration to the whole picture of public policy.

The 1995 welfare reforms, as important as they are, only represent another piece in America's constantly changing social fabric. Denying welfare benefits to children born out of wedlock may seem more like a social policy a foreign country, not America, might produce. Such a policy only makes sense when seen in the context of the whole of American social welfare policy directed toward children and their needs. In this context a small policy change, a new piece added to the mosaic, makes the whole *look* different when in fact the "new look" is very much a product of all that has gone on before.

By understanding the purposes of public policy it becomes more evident that public policy is an expression of the whole citizenry. Public policy represents a collective choice (not always evident as an overt choice) made through the instruments of governance. If these instruments do not work well, the policy will not adequately address the issue put before it. People within the institutions of government make policy, and consequently there is a public process by which policy is made. Policymakers need information and a method for making policy. An understanding of policy analysis, therefore, becomes important.

These subjects are discussed in subsequent chapters. Chapters 2 and 3 examine in greater detail the processes of policy-making and the interaction in that process of those who make policy. Chapter 4 discusses methods of policy analysis and identifies the kinds of information that are important for the type of analysis that may be undertaken. Chapter 5 discusses how this information is examined—what analytic procedure is most used with which kind of information. Once this framework for public policy analysis is developed, part 2 of this book, an analysis of some of the most evident public problems of the day, can be seen as an applied study.

Chapter Two

THE PROCESS OF POLICY-MAKING

Introduction

The process of policy-making may seem as difficult to understand as the idea of policy itself. Policy-making usually begins when a problem is identified and suggestions are made about what to do about it. However, the rest of the policy-making process may be hard to follow. Diverse actions are involved in policy-making, spanning many different policy decision centers. Policymakers differ widely as well. The activities involved in passing a law and the individual policymakers who are involved in making a law are quite different from the activities that produce regulations to implement the law and the persons who develop regulations. Information is as varied as the policy process. All policy analysis needs information that will lead to a decision, but the kind of information that the policy analyst uses depends upon the point in the policy process at which analysis is expected.

Generally, policy analysts are engaged in collecting and evaluating information about serious public problems in order to suggest the best courses of action to policymakers. Successful policy analysis depends upon how the policymakers use information as well as on the kind of information they have. Some policymakers rely heavily on detailed information; others find this relatively unnecessary. Understanding policy analysis thus entails a clear perception of who is making the policy, when information is likely to be needed, and what kind of information is likely to be required. Although a detailed examination of the policy-making process cannot be undertaken in this book, some understanding of the process is necessary to determine what kinds of analysis are appropriate at different points.

The Policy Development Spectrum

Chapter 1 offers a basic definition of public policy: *A public policy is an action (and in some cases, an inaction) usually undertaken by government, directed at a particular goal, and legitimated by the commitment of public resources.* Yet this statement, and others like it, belie the complexity of public policy and its development. The action may be taken in the public sector by any unit of government, or several units of government acting together. Statutes enacted by legislatures and decisions made by courts are public policies, as are administrative rules and regulations and the actions of chief executives and their staffs. Usually governmental units must act together to produce a public policy, as when the legislature passes a law that an executive must approve. Sometimes governmental units act alone, as when administrative agencies change regulations. Such complexities in public policy-making are repeated at the federal, state, and local levels of government, all of which have authority to develop public policy, independently or cooperatively with one another.

Policy-making might also take place in private, nongovernmental sectors. When an automobile manufacturer decides to close a factory, or when the Chase Manhattan Bank raises its prime interest rate, or when the AFL-CIO decides to call a strike, public policy has been made. Similarly, for-profit firms and nonprofit corporations at the state and local levels make public policy. For example, a metropolitan hospital may decide not to take Medicaid assignments, or a local Salvation Army may set policy that would exclude homeless people with children from one of its shelters because of lack of space. Private sector policy-making is public policy when it engages public problems. Knitting together the strands of public- and private-sector decisions and actions adds another level of complexity to the policy-making process.

Public policy development is further complicated by *interlocking goals.* As appealing as it may be to think that public policies address single goals, it is virtually impossible to identify policy goals that do not interlock in one way or another. Improving secondary education, for example, involves raising teachers' salaries, using schools as a community resource, and promoting stable families with adequate incomes. Achieving each goal contributes to realizing the others. Deciding which goals to address requires a decision process that may precede systematic analysis of the problem itself. Because even individual goals are understood differently, concentrating on a single goal may compromise policy analysis and policy decision making. For example, in 1987–88, policy analysis of welfare reform concentrated on the single goal of putting people to work. But policymakers understood the goal differently. Should all have to work, or could some be excused? Welfare reform faltered over disagreements over this goal. Welfare reform in fact has several goals that must be sorted out before policy analysis can begin.

Committed resources legitimates public policy. Resources can be committed in a variety of ways, including both present and future commitments, and resources are committed from varied governmental and private sector units. Categorical grant-in-aid programs, for example, commit resources of the federal government, but only if state governments adopt federal policies and commit their own resources as well (see chapter 3). Through the commitment of resources, public policies have power over distribution that, for policy analysis purposes, must be examined in terms of those who gain from the distribution and those who lose. Even though the resources may be directed at an agreed-upon goal, the implications of distribution often spread well beyond specific policy goals. Consequently, a public policy undertaken to achieve one objective may in fact achieve the opposite because of the way resources are provided. Few would have guessed, for example, that a federal policy granting accelerated depreciation for business investments during 1981–85 would actually inhibit capital investment because corporations "sold" tax credits to each other.

The wide scope of public policy-making suggests the complexity of attempts to analyze it. The type of policy analysis called for in most cases is determined by the point(s) in the policy development process where a particular policy decision is likely to be made. Table 2.1 is a simplified model of the stages in a particular public policy process. Notice how the character of policy analysis might differ between stages one and four. At stage one, a variety of possible social goals might be examined, with prospective policies accompanying each. Stage four might include policy analysis of program implementation, as, for example, when considering the impact of regulations on different populations. At stage four, analysis might be confined to a single goal, but the distributional impact of alternative implementation strategies could receive considerable attention. Examples like table 2.1 suggest that there is no clear center point in the policy-making process, and likewise that there is no single strategy or technique that can be applied in policy analysis (a problem that receives detailed attention in chapter 4).

Table 2.1 shows how at the beginning of a policy process a problem or issue takes on a public character and policy actors are excited into action. The process of policy-making does not end with a specific policy event, however. Public policies must be translated into products in the form of programs that are carried out by professionals. Policy-making also takes place in the implementation process, usually by administrators who have considerable knowledge of existing programs. Finally, professional people implement programs, usually in face-to-face contact with the citizenry in the environment where the issue or concern was first raised.

30

Table 2.1: Paradigm of the policy development process.

Stage 1	*Stage 2*	*Stage 3*	*Stage 4*	*Stage 5*
Normative issues	**Policy processes**	**Policy transitions**		**Policy execution**
Public problem, issue, or concern	Policy-making units: • Executives • Legislatures • Administrative agencies • Courts • Private-sector organizations	Public policies	Public programs	Professional activities
Example: Financial security in old age	• President • U.S. Congress • Federal courts • Employers	Social Security Act, 1935 (as amended)	Social Security (Title II) employee retirement programs	Local Social Security offices

Table 2.1 is a linear model, but in reality policy development may be initiated at any of the five stages and may end at any of them. Sometimes a policy action will create a policy that is not implemented. In 1962, for example, Congress and the president created the Mental Health Services Act, designed to develop community-based care for persons with psychiatric problems. But no public programs were developed until 1964, mostly because financial commitments to the policy were limited and the states were slow in developing their own resources to implement the policy.

The Mental Health Services Act also illustrates the incremental nature of policy development across the whole policy development spectrum. It is not unusual for policies to take several years to develop. The 1988 social welfare legislation that created the Job Opportunity and Basic Skills program (JOBS) was first proposed in 1987 by the Ninety-ninth Congress, and completed 2.5 years later by the One-hundredth Congress. The speed with which Congress created the 1995 welfare reform, in a period of less than a year, is the exception to the way Congress usually proceeds with respect to social welfare issues.[1] Discussions that appear later in this book of specific policies present a good picture of the length of time it takes for policies to mature. For now, it is important to trace in greater detail the policy development activities schematized in table 2.1 and table 2.2.

Table 2.2: Policy decision-making units and information needs.

Policy-making unit	Decision-making environment	Type of information needed
Executive (presidency)	Single action, leadership	• range of alternative policy situations • dealing with policy substance
Legislative (Congress)	Negotiation, compromise	• nature of group(s) affected (constituents, interest groups) • who "wins" or "loses"
Judicial	Courts, very formal	• legal aspects of policy • litigation management
Administration	Staff meetings	• policy-specific data • program-specific data • who "wins" or "loses" • values involved
Policy transition	Negotiation	• values involved • processes
Policy execution	Day-to-day exposure to problems	• program-specific data • values involved • settings for services

Policy-Making Units

Two important assumptions about policy analysis underlie the discussion that follows: first, policy is made at all the five stages represented in table 2.1; second, the kind of policy analysis required depends upon the needs of the policymaker. Because all policy units in the American system do indeed make policy, both independently and in concert with other policy-making units, it is important to understand the operating context of each unit in order to determine its policy analysis needs and tailor the analysis to the policy-deciding tasks. Thus some grasp of the various constraints on policy analysis that affect these units is necessary. Table 2.2 summarizes some of the main aspects of each of those units.

Executive Policy-Making: The Importance of Initiation

As discussed in chapter 1, the executives of public policy are governors, or the president, or high-ranking officials who, in the national government, compose the cabinet. In the private sector these are corporate presidents or executive officers. In theory, the legislature makes law, the judiciary determines its constitutionality, and executive policy is made as law is implemented. In practice, however, the executive often initiates a policy process. The executive speaks with one voice. Consequently a clear message is communicated about what problems need attention and how they can be resolved. The executive is close to program implementation, and consequently is close to the problems. Because most policy is built on existing policies, and because the executive is charged with implementing policy, the executive is often forced to seek changes in policy or to initiate policy, rather than respond to it. This is particularly true of the president of the United States.

The political strength of the American presidency has varied over the nation's history. The United States Constitution defines exactly the powers of Congress, but it specifies only five powers for the presidency: (1) command the nation's armed forces, (2) authority to grant pardons for crimes against the United States, (3) power to make treaties, subject to Senate confirmation, (4) power to appoint Supreme Court justices and foreign ministers, and (5) the right to fill vacancies in the Senate. These five powers seem modest and almost irrelevant to the observer of modern government, which seems to place so much authority in the president. The stature now enjoyed by the American presidency in the exercise of domestic power is not a product of a strong institutionalized commitment to formal power, but a result of the vagueness with which presidential power is defined. In short, the power of the presidency depends upon the leadership ability of the individual president. John Kennedy complained of a "deadlocked democracy," but his successor, Lyndon Johnson, created public policy of enormous proportions. Richard Nixon was accused of initiating an era of "imperial" presidency, but under his successor, Gerald Ford, the phrase shifted to "imperiled" presidency. When Jimmy Carter was frustrated at every turn in attempts to achieve his policies, such as comprehensive welfare reform, his vice-president called the presidency "the fire hydrant of the nation." President Reagan had complete success in realizing his policies during his first term in office, yet, to the contrary, President Clinton had little success with his showpiece legislation, health care.

The first term of the Reagan presidency demonstrates particularly well the importance of leadership in presidential policy-making. Reagan achieved outstanding legislative and administrative success that realized several policy changes of great magnitude.[2] The Omnibus Budget Reconciliation Act (OMBRA, 1981) and Reagan's Economic Recovery Tax Act (1981) both achieved significant new policy goals by cutting taxes and slowing the rate of growth of domestic spending. OMBRA not only reduced domestic spending but also forced the consolidation of a number of domestic programs into block grants, thus transferring considerable authority to the states. This process of devolution, or passing of authority, from the federal government to the states also assisted in the reduction of the number of federally supported domestic programs by almost one hundred, reducing the federal labor force by 92,000 persons, and restricting the amount of federal regulatory activity. The block-grant legislation also centralized administrative policy-making in the Office of Management and Budget, over which the president exercises more control than he does over individual administrative agencies.

The quality of presidential leadership, however, disguises the institutional problems inherent in presidential policy-making. The president has virtually no control over the resources necessary to implement policy. For example, when President Eisenhower issued Executive Order 12646, requiring nondiscriminatory hiring practices in government contracts, he had no funds to establish an administrative organ to implement that policy. And although the presidency is the only political office designed to speak for all the people, it is fractured by competing interests and compromised politically in frequent contests with Congress. The system of constitutional checks and balances of power greatly restricts the capacity of the president to act decisively in policy matters. As administrative agencies develop increased independence with Congress, presidential authority over the administrative bureaucracy continues to weaken. Perhaps even more significantly, Congress appropriates the funds needed to carry out all executive activity. Under such constraints, without strong leadership the presidency can quickly be gridlocked into inaction.

Executive policy-making requires special knowledge about the issues under consideration (table 2.1, stage 1). More than any other policy-making unit in the American system, the executive must take into account a comprehensive range of policy alternatives. Unlike legislators, who must represent varied interests, the executive is expected to represent the full range of public concern on any issue and consequently must take the very largest view of a problem and its solution. The executive is expected to lead, and, therefore, must have available the widest range of possible alternatives in order to minimize the institutional danger of deadlock when the time for decision making comes. The policy problems of the executive are illustrated by the pressure constantly brought on a president (or on a corporate executive) to take some position or make a stand—and by the frequency with which these positions must be abandoned. Not taking a position communicates weakness and uncertainty; yet sticking with a position, once taken, that has proven defective after a period of public scrutiny, gives an impression of inflexibility. However, abandoning a position may be seen as vacillation, which cuts deeply at the executive's leadership stature. Without knowledge of a full range of alternatives, and without systematic analysis to determine the best range of policy alternatives, executive policy-making degenerates quickly.

Legislative Policy and the Quest for Statute Law

Unquestionably, legislation is the foundation of all public policy-making. The product of legislation is statute law, the most forcible of all public policy. (In the private sector, articles of incorporation and corporate bylaws represent a somewhat similar consensus and force within the individual organization.) Legislators are the center of policy activity. They possess considerable political power to make policy, but the legislative process is a fragmented one. Legislators exist at the federal, state, and local levels of government. At the federal level, and in every state except Nebraska, legislatures are composed of two bodies chosen from diverse constituencies; both these bodies must agree before a position can become a policy. And legislators themselves are diverse. Repeated studies have shown that legislators who continue in office are likely to possess characteristics similar to the constituencies that elect them—a sobering revelation, considering the diversity of American culture.[3]

Legislatures operate within both extremely formal and very informal structures and hence involve complex procedures. As suggested in chapter 1, creating statute law is a time-consuming and complicated undertaking. Legislators frequently make policy by inaction. Because it takes so much power to steer an initiative through the legislative process, it is easier to defeat a proposal than to bring one into law. Thus much legislative energy emphasizes defeating legislation. Compromise often is the alternative to defeat; this is what gives most legislation its "watered down" flavor.

Legislators are handicapped by their formal structure. The U.S. House of Representatives is composed of 435 members, elected locally from districts of relatively similar size. These representatives must consider wide-ranging policy proposals, and a majority of them must agree before a proposal becomes law. As most of us have discovered, it is hard to get a majority of three out of five ordinary people to agree on something controversial; it is virtually impossible for 435 persons, all attuned to the fine points of an issue, to meet in a single room and try to accomplish a task without some organization. Hence Congress and other legislatures observe very formal rules of order for final discussions and votes, and establish committees to do the preliminary work on proposals for legislation (bills). The committees are further divided into subcommittees, and staff members become very involved in moving things through this committee process. Thus although the floor vote may be the deciding event in legislatures, the policy-shaping work is done in the committee phase.

> Committees are the instruments by which Congress defines public problems and shapes policies. Here the political soundings are taken, the delicate compromises

worked out and the technical language of the bills drafted and redrafted. Floor debate may illuminate problems and crucial questions may even be resolved in the clash of voting in the chamber. However, it is quite impossible for a large body of legislators to write a complex piece of legislation during floor debate.[4]

The committee process is like the tip of the iceberg—most of the whole cannot be seen. Even the public part of the process is often too dynamic to capture in a summary statement. Usually the public record of committee hearings provides only a general indication of the political forces at work in the committee process of shaping the proposals that become ratified (or are defeated) by floor votes.

Unlike the executive, which speaks with one voice, legislatures speak with many voices. Consequently, without leadership, either from within the legislature or from outside (as when a president provides leadership), the legislative process is likely to result in stalemate. The many voices of the legislature have varied origins, and the policy analyst must be aware of the different forces that shape legislative behavior. Legislators may act as delegates of the people, or as party members, or as statesmen. When acting as a statesman, a legislator may be acting from personal convictions about an issue, perhaps from personal preferences, or because he or she is motivated by a larger view of what would be best. Even though Americans tend to dislike the idea that legislators vote their own views about what is best, a strong case can be made for doing this, and most decisions are made on the basis of this concept of legislative independence.

A more popular view of legislative behavior suggests that actions are motivated by the legislator's responsibility to act on behalf of those who elected him or her to office. The legislator may identify as a constituency (1) the whole district from which she or he is elected, (2) the registered voters of the district, (3) those who actually vote in the district, or (4) the voters who voted for the representative. Legislative behavior can vary greatly depending on which of these "constituencies" seems most important at a particular moment.

Policy analysis must especially take into account legislative representation of special interests. Concerns about special interests are as old as the U.S. Constitution, and they were addressed frequently by James Madison.[5] For example, the Constitution was constructed to assure fair representation of the states in the federal union. But as the nation has grown, it has become increasingly difficult in more complex issues to separate public officials from their constituents' interests, and the contemporary proliferation of centers of interest—frequently called "interest groups"—has become a fundamental feature of democratic government as we know it in America. Special interests are represented in legislative decisions, most frequently through the influence of paid representatives of interest groups—lobbyists.

It is through these interest groups that private-sector policy choices most frequently affect the public policy-making process. Preference for the rich and powerful, disenfranchisement for the poor, single-issue politics, graft, deception, and callous disregard for the general welfare are a few of the evils inherent in interest-group politics. Often overlooked, however, are the advantages that interest groups can bring to the legislative process. Interest groups can translate private sector problems into clear and fair recommendations for action. They can present, with great accuracy, the existing or desired policies of the citizens and organizations involved. This kind of information is extremely important to policymakers, and it is not likely to be obtained except through lobbyists. To represent private interests in an accurate way, solid and reliable information must be provided to support the position of the interest group. Hence the legislative process (or the policy analyst) is often supplied with a rich array of such information, which has to be sifted, evaluated, and reevaluated in terms of interlocking interests.

Interest groups also serve the legislative process by providing linkage between legislators and constituents. A legislator may find it difficult or impossible to remain in touch with large numbers of people. Interest groups represent what large groups of people are saying and thinking. The legislator, in turn, can respond to people through the interest groups, often through their newsletters.

Interest groups further assist the legislative process by helping adjust differences among interest groups over policy outcomes. A legislator may play one interest group against another to promote further clarification of facts and issues. For example, the legislator may indicate that on a certain issue the position of the U.S. Chamber of Commerce is different from the position of the American Public Welfare Association. This leads to discussion between the two groups; one or both may then court sympathetic allies as a means of strengthening the case before the legislator. The Chamber of Commerce, for example, might seek and gain support for its position from the National Association of Manufacturers. Thus a coalition begins to build, helping the legislator resolve policy conflicts that may stand in the way of making a decision. Even groups with diverse orientations to an issue may form a coalition to support a particular policy proposal. This strategy may backfire, however; the legislative environment often prompts policy decisions based on marginal considerations that have more to do with satisfying claims of interest groups than with the substance of the proposal under consideration.

The context of legislative policy development—a diverse group of people, a complex structure, and special ties with constituencies, usually through interest groups—dominates stage 2 of the policy process as shown in stage 2 in table 2.1. Legislatures require special kinds of information to facilitate policy decisions. They need information about who is likely to be involved and affected in the policy choices under consideration. They need information about "winners" and "losers" with respect to alternative public decisions. They also need information about how the private sector is likely to respond to the possible public policies. They want information about how to balance competing interests in order to make a decision *now* more than information about long-range implications. In other words, they are more concerned about the ability to make a choice than they are about the nature of the choice—more concerned about the substance of making a decision than they are about the substance of the decision itself.[6]

Administrative Policy: Regulation and Program Implementation

Next to statute law, administrative policy attracts the most public attention. Because administrative agencies are charged with implementing policy mandates, and because these policy mandates are expected to be carried out in certain ways to achieve their purposes, administrative agencies have been responsible for fashioning policy analysis as we know it today. This form of policy analysis features the use of social science knowledge and social science research in its analytic work. Administrative policy-making exists in both the public and private sectors and is likely to be concentrated in the transition phases of the policy-making process (table 2.1, stages 3 and 4).

To understand administrative policy analysis, one must first understand the administrative activities of the large public bureaucracies and the complexities that such administration raises for the American system of governance. Public administrative agencies as we know them today were completely unforeseen by the founders of American government, so that the system of constitutional checks and balances was designed without taking them into account. The institutional checks on administrative behavior that now exist have developed through ever-changing political alignments with the other branches of government. Because they have no constitutional basis, clear theories of administrative policy-making have been difficult to develop.

Administrative agencies emerged in their present form as part of the professionalization of social science, and as a way of applying science to the acts of governance. In 1887, Woodrow Wilson published "Public Administration," an incisive essay that sought to explain how the rationality of the new social sciences could be brought to bear on the rapidly expanding activities of the executive branch. "Public administration," he stated, "is detailed and systematic execution of public law."[7] This scientific approach to government administration developed around the beginning of the twentieth century, contemporaneously with professional planning, industrial management in the private sector, and the social and political reform movement.

Public administration matured after World War II, as both public- and private-sector management became influenced by the rediscovery of Max Weber's political and social explanations for the development of modern bureaucracy. Herbert Simon in particular provided a synthesis between the new science of management and the earlier science of administration through his emphasis on the rationality of both. He established a foundation for the classic definition of both public- and private-sector administration: a scientific, "value-free" activity isolated from the surrounding politics of government activities. Simon understood formal organizations as human enterprises characterized "by a high degree of rational direction of behavior toward ends that are objects of common acknowledgement and expectation."[8] In his analysis, administration was a means of achieving agreed-upon goals. Thus Simon distinguished between policy-making and implementing policy, and he studied the two as different, yet rational, activities. This stance reinforced the dichotomy between politics and administration that had been suggested by Wilson so many years before. Simon deepened the distinction by arguing that rational decision making and rational administration, as in public administration, were the expression of the new social sciences, whereas politics (at its best) was an expression of art. Implicit in this view, however, were (1) the belief that public administrative agencies, through the election of the executive, were clearly under popular control, and (2) in accord with Wilsonian tradition, an understanding that administration merely carried out decisions made in the political process.

This orthodox view of public administration was seen by others as ill-suited to the realities of administration in the years after World War II. In 1949 Paul Appleby observed that public administration was clearly a political process.[9] Shortly before that, Dwight Waldo had illustrated the value-laden, culture-bound, nonrational, incremental character public administration took on in actual practice. He was particularly dismayed by the distinction that had developed between politics and administration, and he advocated an integrated understanding of administration. "Any simple division of government-and-administration," he wrote, "is inadequate [because] it carries with it the idea of division, depicting an antagonism."[10] The traditional notion of public administration as a form of scientific management was gradually abandoned as public administration came to be recognized as a part of the political process that exercised discretionary power of its own. In a classic study published in 1953, Robert Dahl and Charles Lindblom demonstrated that public administration was in fact deeply engaged in value choices, often outside the controlling authority of the elected executive.[11] Theorist Wallace Sayre wrote that public administrators develop autonomy and express political power ". . . much as Presidents, senators and Congressmen, party leaders, and interest group leaders make their respective claims . . . achieving levels of self-direction satisfying even to their own aspirations."[12]

This digression into the origins of the activities of administration as we know them today is intended to highlight the most delicate problem in the processes of administrative policy-making in both the public and private sectors: a lack of consensus over the appropriate balance between making policy and carrying it out. The rationality of administrative policy-making activities remains a vigorously defended tenet, but few today would disagree that administration has been used to achieve political objectives, independent of strictly reasoned outcomes. To attempt to understand administrative policy-making in any other way than through this paradoxical view both oversimplifies and distorts the expectations placed on policy analysis in administrative settings.

Although it is tempting to distinguish between two groups of administrators in the administrative context—for example, the "technocrats," experts in a particular field, and the "bureaucrats," who maintain the political balance of an organization—this simplification too may only cloud our understanding further. The whole of the administrative policy-making process is involved in balancing the two, in reconciling the rational administration of the technocrats with the bureaucrats' demands for political products such as fairness, representation, and conflict resolution. To accomplish this, the administrative policymaker needs a complex blend of information. Policy analysts must provide the administrative policymaker with a wide range of alternatives for consideration as part of the process of rational choice. These alternatives include both "rational" and political products. Administrative policymakers require considerable factual information in order to project the effects of different outcomes. They are also concerned about the marginal utility of various alternatives, in order to support their decisions when the time comes for review or approval by the executive or legislature. Administrative policymakers are often forced to choose a less preferred policy that has greater potential for adoption, and their policy analysis must provide enough information to explore the entire range of policy possibilities.

Judicial Policy and the Force of Case Law

The policy products of the judiciary are often obscured by the complexity of the overall judicial process. In a certain sense courts may not initiate policy; usually they are involved in sorting out policy differences created by others. Yet, informally, courts "invite" policy debates, as when a grand jury is created, or when the Supreme Court signals whether it will or will not become involved in litigation. When the United States Conference meets, it sets an agenda for litigation, and when the U.S. Supreme Court issues a decision in a case, this may also suggest how related decisions are likely to be made. The structure of the judiciary suggests that its policy role may in fact range across the entire policy-making process in both the public and private sectors.

Judicial policy is made at the federal level, at the state level, and locally. Each of these units of governance has courts that make legal judgments on matters that fall within the purview of the specific unit of government authority. Thus the federal courts, including the U.S. Supreme Court, make judgments on national legal matters, state courts make judgments on matters that pertain to states, and so forth.

Judicial processes are complicated by "standing," meaning whether or not it is possible for a matter to receive attention in a particular court of law. Certain matters must be brought before certain courts; for example, some cases must be heard in state courts. Sometimes, however, plaintiffs who wish to bring a case before the courts may have options. Depending upon which issue of law the plaintiff may choose to engage, a choice of court may be possible. This targeting process, usually called "litigation management," may be based on points of laws that would be more favorable to the plaintiff, and represents a form of political choice.

The politics of litigation management most frequently involve choices between state and federal courts. State courts have traditionally been most sympathetic with state government and related agencies, but they have limited jurisdiction over public social issues except for issues relating to property. Historically, federal courts have generally been involved in matters of dispute between states and the federal government, but in recent years—since the "Warren Court" (so called after Earl Warren, chief justice, 1953–69)—they have become more responsive to social issues, particularly issues of personal rights and protection. Consequently, contemporary public policy has been more deeply influenced by judicial decisions than in the past. This expanded involvement of federal courts has been supported by authority given them in the First and Fourteenth Amendments to the United States Constitution and also by a reinterpretation of the Administrative Procedures Act (1946). Both the amendments deal with issues of personal rights as they intersect with

41

private-sector policies. The First Amendment guarantees freedom of religion, speech, and press. The Fourteenth Amendment guarantees equal protection under the law for all citizens. Both these amendments offered a wide latitude for the Supreme Court's involvement in policy-making during the 1960s. The Fourteenth Amendment, in particular, became a cornerstone of judicial authority in public policy. *Brown vs. Board of Education* (1954) was the landmark case; by reinterpreting the Administrative Procedures Act, the decision in *Brown* opened the floodgates to social litigation.

Litigation management provides an important means to seek policy changes through the use of the various courts. Litigation management not only involves framing an issue so as to have it heard in the most favorable court system, but also carefully choosing a plaintiff, skillfully building the facts of the case, and structuring the case to fit the existing legal theory.

Litigation management may thus be the key political issue in the policy-making role of the courts. One commentator has stated that "the federal courts have always (and correctly) been perceived by political leaders as a major instrument for control over the substantive content of public policy." He also observes that "it may make a considerable difference to the parties whether a case is to be tried in a state or national court."[13]

Presidents Reagan and Bush had unprecedented opportunity for changing the ideology of the U.S. Supreme Court as it developed during the past twenty years. With the appointment of new justices, many with conservative social views, the role of the U.S. Supreme Court is undergoing a period of political change. Given the philosophy that seems to emerge from the (Justice William) Rehnquist court, those who would seek an expanded role for the federal government in social policy have begun to steer clear of judicial policy-making altogether.

An apt illustration is *Gilliard vs. Craig*.[14] In a class action, Daisy Gilliard sued the state of North Carolina for back welfare payments. Her son, Samuel had been receiving Social Security checks from his father; her other children had a different father. In calculating the family's AFDC benefit, the state had considered Samuel's Social Security money as a resource available to the whole family. Gilliard believed this to be unfair; even though Samuel lived with the family, it seemed he must be entitled to the Social Security benefit regardless of the financial status of the other family members.

The federal district court in Charlotte, North Carolina, had developed a reputation for sympathy in civil rights matters. The state courts, however, were very conservative in matters that affected state government agencies. Gilliard argued that the case should be heard by the federal court, as the action of the state welfare agency had deprived her of due process under the Fourteenth Amendment. The state, on the other hand, argued that the case should be heard in the state courts, because the issue involved the personal property of Samuel and, as such, was not appropriate for the federal courts. Gilliard prevailed. The case was heard in the federal court, and Justice James MacMillian ruled in her favor, ordering the state to pay her, and all others like her, whatever back monies were due to them because of this budgeting practice—a total of about $135,000.

From the Gilliard case and previous discussion it is clear that judicial policy-making requires rather specialized information. The policy decision in *Gilliard* might have been vastly different had it been made in a state court. There the decision would have been made on the basis of property, that is, whether or not Gilliard had a valid claim to more public support than she was getting. Because eligibility for public support is a matter of the state's jurisdiction, she might well have lost her case. On the other hand, because the federal court was interested in protecting Samuel's legal right to the Social Security benefit, irrespective of any relationship Gilliard herself might have with state agencies, she won her case for herself and others.

As the Gilliard case shows, attorneys as well as judges need information not only about the legal aspects of any given policy and the methods by which the judicial system operates, but also about the substance of the policy subject. Information about judicial politics and judicial issues and methods may be marginal to the policy issue, but information about the policy itself and how it fits into that specific policy-making process (the legal aspects of the policy) is central to judicial policy analysis.

The legal parameters of a policy question exist whether or not the policy has the force of law, including formally executed administrative policy. Hence all policy analysis, of both the public and the private sector must be sensitive to the legal constraints that will affect any policy choice.

Though policy analysts do not need to have legal training in order to analyze a policy issue, they often seek the advice of legal experts to clarify the legal elements of a policy problem. Policy analysts would do well to carefully investigate any questions that seem to require specialized legal information as the dividing line between a legal issue and a substantive policy issue is seldom clear.

Policy Transitions

The transition phase in the policy process is hard to describe because so little attention has been devoted to understanding this important process. Obviously a great deal happens between the time a law is passed, an executive decision is made, or a court decision is reached, and a policy emerges into a program. The transition that takes place involves many forms of analysis (sometimes not specifically recognized as analysis, or alluded to as "good common sense") and the final choice of a specific program form. So while formal policy analysis may not be evident, policy choices are made by persons who have responsibility for moving the process of policy-making from one point to the next.

Usually administrative agencies play a lead role in the policy transition phase. The administrative agency usually has the task of blending varied viewpoints of not only the policy actions heretofore involved in policy-making, but reconciling these views with policy actors who will be influenced by the policy as it becomes implemented in the form of a particular program. If policy is made on the federal level, for example, transitional activities must also take into account how states will respond to the policy if and when they themselves become part of the policy administrative agency. Additionally, administrative agencies may themselves be seeking specific policy outcomes, based on their own normative views, as described above.

Thus getting from public policy to public programs requires considerable policy skill. Often the federal administrative agency provides a mediating function between federal expectations, as set out in statute law, and the specific problems found in states and localities. These different agendas constitute major features of American federalism, and it is up to administrative bureaucracies at both the federal and state levels to adjust federal policy, often developed for the general case, to the specific needs of localities.

The creation of the federal Child Support Enforcement Program (CSE) in 1975 developed from earlier efforts of the federal government in this policy field in several ways. Most significantly, the 1975 legislation offered generous federal funding to improve flagging state efforts. Consistent with Social Security Act Title IV programs, Child Support Enforcement was crafted as a grant-in-aid program that provided rich financial incentives to states in exchange for very little modification of ongoing state activities. In particular, states were permitted to keep 75 percent of everything they collected from absent parents whose children were receiving AFDC. The federal government also provided $3 for every $1 states spent on program administration. The 1975 federal law that amended Title IV of the Social Security Act slipped through Congress as the second, generally unnoticed, part of a major undertaking to create the first Social Service block grant.

The 1975 CSE legislation was passed on to states who already had statutory power to require parents to support their children, thus creating some discontinuity between existing state practices and this new federal program. The federal administrative agency, the Department of Health and Human Services (DHHS), continued to prod states to improve their collection efforts, but states showed little motivation to do so. Part of the reason was the design of CSE policy itself. While Congress saw CSE as an important way to reduce federal spending for the AFDC program, other policy actors saw the program as a way to improve the financial well being of children. Thus rich financial rewards for collecting child support from welfare cases went to the states, while child support collected on behalf of nonwelfare children went directly to those children. States preferred to spend their energy on the former rather than the latter collection efforts.

According to the Bureau of the Census, by 1985 about 39 percent of all women who cared for children parented by an absent father were never awarded child support, and 60 percent of poor women were without child support awards. Only 50 percent of women who had a child support order were receiving the amount of money specified in the support order. Approximately $26.6 billion in child support was owed in 1984 by noncustodial fathers, of which about $20 billion was uncollected.

Although the CSE program was quickly implemented, it seemed to falter after its newness began to fade. By 1984 the program was collecting slightly less than $2.5 billion, (roughly 10 percent of that which could be paid). The share of that $2.5 billion that could be attributed to the efforts of the CSE program was not clear, nor was it clear what share would have been collected without the program. After a number of efforts to improve the overall performance of this program, the federal Office of Child Support Enforcement (OCSE) decided to present Congress with a legislative package incorporating changes that would be required of states to make the CSE program effective. This legislative package was presented to Congress and signed into law August 16, 1984, PL 98-378, as the 1984 Child Support Enforcement amendments to Title IV-D of the Social Security Act.

Like many other federal social welfare policy initiatives, the implementation of the 1984 amendments was difficult. First, twenty-two new, different requirements were eventually produced from the legislation. While some states had some of the new requirements already in place, many states had to make changes in their programs. Some of these requirements could be implemented by changes in a state's administrative practices, but others could only be implemented through state-enacted legislation. The amendments also carried significant fiscal penalties for states that failed to comply. In this environment, states were given until December 1987—a full two years after the final regulations were published—to implement the amendments.

By December 1987, more than two years after the federal regulations were published, and at the deadline established by Congress, only nine of the requirements were implemented in all states, and all of the requirements were implemented in none of the states. Of the nine requirements implemented in all the states, twenty-eight states had already had one requirement (#15) in place before 1975, twenty-one states had another of the requirements in place, and twenty states were operating their program with a third requirement already in place before 1975. Eventually the federal administrative agency had to grant states waivers for regulations they failed to implement, for without doing so the programs would have been out of compliance and would have had to be shut down completely.

Rather than improve, child support collection performance actually declined following the implementation of the regulations. By 1992 thirty-five states were performing below the national average of $3.99 total collections for each dollar of administrative expense. In 1992 eleven states actually spent more money to collect child support owed to AFDC recipients than they collected. Because the federal government provides funds to administer this program, the savings to the public have gone from $202 million in savings in 1979 to $173 million in losses in 1992. This program designed to save money actually ends up costing more.[15]

Summary

This example provides some insight into the complexity associated with the policy transition phase of policy development.

First, when programs do not meet expectations, the administrative agency seeks to involve other policy actors to revise the policy; but when programs cannot meet expectations, the administrative agency finds ways to help them continue to operate. Thus, there is a constant process of policy-making through negotiation going on.

Second, policy translation not only involves harmonizing expectations of policymakers at the federal level, but harmonizing federal expectations with the realities faced by the states and localities. Administrations play a crucial role in this balancing activity.

Finally, conflicts over values regarding how resources are used are addressed and to some extent resolved during the policy transition process. To the extent that there are legitimate differences about what goals policy should accomplish, and how it should accomplish them, the policy transition phase provides an environment for resolving these conflicts. Thus policy transitions are not so much a mechanical translation of policy mandates into public programs, but a process that adjusts different views about how a policy should address a problem, harmonizing these views into useful products for those who need them.

Chapter 3 presents a full discussion of the intergovernmental environment in which administrative agencies undertake their mediating activities in policy transitions. Frustrated by the growing role of government, particularly "government by administration," Congress is undertaking efforts to simplify the transitional phase of policy-making by consolidating programs and sending funds to states in "blocks" rather than on a program-by-program basis. While block grants seem to hold the promise of avoiding the need to reconcile federal policy with exigencies of the states ("turn the matters over to the states and let them decide" remarked Majority Leader Dick Armey in the recent welfare debates), different, often conflicting viewpoints between the federal government and the states are inherent in the American system, and only time will tell whether efforts to minimize these differences are more productive than efforts to mediate them.

Policy Execution: Professional People and a New Policy Cycle

Execution completes the policy cycle. The product of the policy process is usually a program or a commitment that directs the accomplishment or fulfillment of a policy in a particular way. Execution focuses committed resources, such as money, personnel, equipment, and supplies, at the problems the policy addresses. Execution usually takes place within an organizational context, such as a housing authority, an environmental protection agency, or a business. Professional people are responsible for directing the resources at the problem for which the policy was created. Beneficiaries of the policy can be identified clearly at this point; its ineffective or unintended consequences may become apparent.

Professional people must implement and execute the policy through programs. Doctors, social workers, lawyers, nurses, and many other professionals must understand the relationship between the programs they use and the normative context from which the policy was developed. The policy continues to carry values with it, and these values are implemented as part of the policy.

The way professionals execute policy may also become a form of policy-making. Sometimes professionals are given discretion in the way a program is provided, and when this happens they are expected to shape the policy as it is reflected in the program. Often a program is the product of several policies, and it may be plagued with "glitches"—inconsistencies or inadequacies. Here again, professionals must understand the normative content of the policies they execute in order to harmonize them into a usable product for the beneficiaries. Professional people are there to provide the beneficiaries with the products of the policies, and this form of policy analysis and policy-making is as much a professional responsibility as doing the specific program task—perhaps medical treatments—with a high degree of competence and skill.

Sometimes a program may not resolve the exact problem the professional faces. This situation requires that the professional understand what policy the program was designed to address. Rather than viewing the entire program itself simply as inadequate, the professional can use selectively the features that fit the problem at hand, and recognize which policies need to change in order to develop programs that will provide better assistance. When professionals try to use a program to alleviate problems that the program policies were not designed to address, the client is not served well. These professional concerns suggest the kinds of knowledge professional people must have to play their part in the policy process. As policy executors, professional people must be extremely sensitive to the mandates of the policies that created the programs they implement, and not attempt to translate any program into something it was not meant to be.

An excellent example of the policy knowledge that professional people need is evident in the Elderly Nutrition Program, created and administered under Title III of the Older Americans Act. The program was developed in response to public concern that many older people had less than adequate nutrition because, living alone, they did not prepare proper meals. In that sense the program was created from a normative position that sought to serve older people by improving their nutrition. It provided free lunch to older people in a congregate setting and offered the beneficiaries a program of nutrition education as well. However, it was not too long before professional people became more concerned about the lunch than about nutrition, and they began to question why older persons of some financial means could come and have a free lunch, when poor people might be turned away for lack of available meals. People of means did not "need" a free lunch, they argued, while many of the poor did. The policy behind the lunch program supplies a solution to this uncertainty. This policy addresses nutrition, not financial need, and the program must be provided consistent with that policy. Other programs have to be created to provide meals for the needy.

Policy execution often becomes the point at which additional normative issues are uncovered and new policy recommendations are initiated. New policies are most commonly implemented through existing agencies and organizations. Accommodating these new policies often requires agencies to change the ways they do things. Because existing agencies already have policies that regulate their operation, their inability to adjust to new policies may result in considerable slippage between the programs prescribed by the new policies and the actuality of their execution. Until 1980, for example, public child welfare agencies placed heavy emphasis on finding stable foster-care homes for children who were difficult to adopt—children who were older, perhaps handicapped in some way, or of minority heritage. Over many years, it became clear that substantial amounts were being spent to keep these children in foster homes when many of them could be in more permanent home environments. Title IV-E of the Social Security Act was created in 1980 to encourage states to shorten foster placements and accelerate adoptive placements. This change in policy caused considerable difficulty for many child welfare agencies that formerly had provided service to children by keeping them in foster homes, rather than by getting them out.

Execution requires monitoring and evaluation. Monitoring and evaluation in turn require a decision about what will be measured. Policy products typically have been measured by elements suitable for counting the numbers of people served—for example, the proportion of total beneficiaries who use the program frequently, or who use only one of several services offered, and so forth. Less tangible results of the policy—for example, whether children get a better education, or whether public housing residents are more satisfied with their lives—are harder to measure. Choosing an appropriate strategy for monitoring and evaluating these intangible effects is an especially important, and difficult, aspect of policy execution. (A full discussion of policy analysis and evaluation is presented in chapter 4.)

Conclusion

The policy-making process is far-reaching—in the time it takes to develop a policy, in the range of institutions involved in that development, and in the diversity of activities that take place within this process. Policy analysis is thus not a single act, but a series of actions that take place frequently over a policy cycle and at various points within that cycle. This activity is defined by the kind of information that is needed at a particular point in the process. Just as there is no exact center for policy-making, there is no single method for policy analysis.

Policy may be made at any of the multiple points in the policy process. To be useful, policy analysis must be specifically sensitive to the particular policy process it serves. The products of policy analysis—from oral summaries to formal published reports—may also be wide-ranging and often must serve overlapping objectives. For example, a briefing paper analyzing a particular proposal for a legislator can seldom be longer than one to one-and-one-half pages, whereas analysis of the same issue by the Congressional Budget Office may run to one-hundred pages. Both may have to deal with overlapping objectives. It is crucial that the analyst understand exactly what is being requested and adapt the analysis accordingly.

Chapter Three

POLICY-MAKING AT THE LOCAL LEVEL

Introduction

Although the policy-making model discussed in chapter 2 offers a general picture of the policy development process, policy analysis in local policy-making activities requires some special attention. Just as public- and private-sector policy-making interlock, policy-making takes place at the state and local level in an intergovernmental environment. As suggested in chapter 2, policies made by the federal government often require complementary activities by state and local governments in much the same way that policies made by the national office of the YMCA require policy adjustments by local YMCAs across the country.

It is tempting to suggest that the policy-making model presented in chapter 2 is hierarchically organized. In other words, it may seem that problems or issues become labeled as policy topics when they receive sufficient national attention, and that the policy process then spins down to the local level. In a hierarchical model, policy processes that span policy and program development and their transitions would take place at the federal level, whereas implementation, or the policies of execution, would occur at the local level—in counties and municipalities. To some extent this is a true picture of the policy development process. For example, in 1975, after growing nationwide concern about the inadequate amounts of child support that noncustodial parents were paying, Congress passed and President Ford signed into law amendments to the Social Security Act creating the Child Support Enforcement Program (Title IV-D). States were required to develop state laws and administrative procedures if they wished to take part in this new program, and the federal program and the state policies were in turn passed on to counties that developed further policies to help parents collect child support for their children.

However, even though some policy-making is hierarchically organized, considerable amounts of policy-making take place at state and local levels, independent of significant policy activities at other government levels. This independent policy-making activity is possible because state and local governments have independent, constitutionally guaranteed bases of political authority, a fundamental element in the American system, just as private organizations have independent spheres of action.

The United States has one national government, but also contains 80,000 other semiautonomous governments, including the fifty states, more than three thousand counties, and thousands of towns and cities, townships, special districts (such as school districts), and public authorities (such as housing, port, and airport authorities). Add to this the hundreds of thousands of private organizations with independent policy-making authority within their own spheres of activity, and it becomes quite apparent that the amount of policy made at the federal level constitutes an almost minuscule portion of all the public policy created in America in any given year. States collectively pass more than 200,000 new laws each year, and no estimate is possible of the number of local ordinances enacted by municipalities—not to mention the amount of state and local regulatory and procedural policies, along with the policies made by state and local courts. These examples make it clear that the public policy analyst needs to find some context for understanding policy-making at local levels.

The Structural Context

The public context of policy-making outlined in chapter 2 carries into policy-making at the local level, but with a few important exceptions. Executive, legislative, judicial, and administrative policy-making takes place within local units of governance in a manner similar to federal and state patterns. Unfortunately for the policy analyst, however, local patterns of interaction are much more complex, because of (1) the atomized nature of local political structures, (2) ambiguities in policy-making power and authority, and (3) the lack of formality in much local-level policy-making activity.

The Peculiar Context for Social Welfare Policy

Social welfare policy-making defies understanding unless three facts about the American system are first understood. First, the federal government has almost no constitutional authority to develop and implement social welfare policy. A mere thread of constitutional authority was "discovered" by associate justice Benjamin Cardozo when the Social Security Act was found to be constitutional in 1937. Writing for the U.S. Supreme Court, Cardozo said that the words "provide for the general welfare" found in the Preamble to the U.S. Constitution were sufficient to justify the ability of the federal government to levy a tax for unemployment purposes.

Although there has been other social welfare litigation subsequent to 1937 that has further defined the federal government's social welfare authority, these cases generally limit what states can and cannot do, rather than developing a constitutional foundation for American social welfare activities.[1]

A second fact about the American system that determines how welfare policy is made is that social concerns are matters for the states. Almost all legislation that defines the context for social welfare is found in state laws. Child support, abuse and neglect, adoptions, foster care, day-care requirements, nursing and rest home standards, school attendance, motor vehicle operation, housing standards, and many other social welfare subjects are defined variously by the states. The development of social welfare in America became clear as states asserted their authority over scattered and fractured social welfare activities toward the end of the nineteenth century. This state policy context preceded the development of any federal social welfare activity as we know it today.

The third fact that must be understood about social welfare policy development is that localities are creations of the states. County governments, municipalities, various authorities, such as airport authorities—all those units of local governance listed above—come into existence through a legislative action by their respective states, making them "incorporated areas" and granting them specific legislative, executive, and judicial powers. In exchange, states require local units of governance to carry out functions as the state may prescribe. For example, a cluster of neighborhoods may petition the state legislature to become incorporated as a municipality under a given name. If the request is granted, the new municipality is given specific powers, like law enforcement, but it must meet certain requirements as well—levy taxes or perform specific services that the state may require.

Taken together, the limited federal constitutional authority for developing social welfare, the concentration of social welfare authority in the states, and local units of governance that exist at the pleasure of the states, present a striking contrast to many notions about the American social welfare system. The complexity of all social welfare policy-making is better understood with this broad picture in mind, and the significance of local social welfare policy-making becomes much more apparent in this broader context.

The structural context for local policy-making is described by the legal doctrine pronounced by Justice Douglas Dillon, often referred to as Dillon's rule: "Local governments are mere tenants at the will of the legislature." This 1868 court decision held that states may "sweep from existence all municipal corporations of the state."[2] Some years later the U.S. Supreme Court held that local governments "are the creatures, mere political subdivisions of the state" and may "exert only such powers expressly granted to them."[3] Thus localities are themselves products of federal and state policies. States create local governments by granting them charters in much the same way that private corporations are chartered (also by state authority). Within these charters the responsibilities, obligations, and powers granted to local governments are clearly written out.

A wide variety of local governmental units have come into existence. Counties, townships, municipalities, and city governments have been created to provide local governance within established geographic boundaries; many of these units now have, or share, school districts, special districts, and authorities that deal with special issues of governance, such as schools, airports, transportation, solid waste disposal, and similar public concerns. These later forms of local governance almost always overlap the older ones, usually by design, creating the first complication in local policy-making: overlapping jurisdictional authority.

But if a clear legal doctrine of local government exists, defining local governments as creatures of the state, political doctrine gives local governments independent authority in much the same way as states themselves are independent of the federal government. This political doctrine derives from Article 10 of the United States Constitution, which reserves all undefined constitutional powers to the states "and to the people." Thus individuals possess constitutional authority that they are free to exercise within their own organizational arrangements, including their local governments. This doctrine of "popular sovereignty" has given sufficient political authority to local governments so as to prevent states from exploiting their legally defined authority over the local governance they create. In practice, therefore, states define local governments and vest them with power to do specific things, but leave them free to decide for themselves how they will do these things and whether they will do other things in addition to what the state specifically empowers them to do.

Examples of this independence are abundant. One common instance is provision of the Medicaid program, created in 1965 as Title XIX of the Social Security Act to assist poor people in obtaining medical services. The federal government required states to generate plans for the kinds of services that would be provided, subject to federal guidelines. Most (but not all) states require in turn that their counties administer the Medicaid program as outlined by the individual state's guidelines and that the counties contribute to the cost of the Medicaid program through their own tax revenues. In 1978 the federal government decided that, except in unusual cases, it would no longer provide funding for abortions under the Medicaid program. As a result, several states stopped paying for abortions for low-income women. On the other hand, some states resorted to the use of state monies to make sure the policy and program of publicly funded abortions continued. In still other cases, states let counties do whatever they chose to do, and some counties supplied their own funding for these services. Counties can also make policies to provide other wide-ranging health programs and services to their populations, independent from implementing state-required health programs.

As this example shows, local governments have considerable independence in policy-making, which often exceeds their legal arrangements with states. They not only engage in policy-making activities within their own areas of geopolitical authority, but frequently enter into policy-making activities with other public governmental and private organizations. One of the most interesting types of collaborative policy activity occurs when local governmental units become engaged in policy-making somewhat independently of their states' jurisdiction. For example, under Title II of the Higher Education Act, the federal government may provide funds to local school districts that experience high rates of poverty—"impact aid." In these cases, local school boards develop policy directly consistent with federal funding guidelines, independently of state activity. The "War on Poverty" programs of the Kennedy-Johnson years were characterized by federal initiatives that sought to bypass states and develop policy alliances exclusively with local governments.

Another example, discussed at greater length in chapter 8, is that almost all policy relating to housing is essentially locally oriented. Housing codes are, for the most part, creatures of local governmental activity. Zoning, which determines the kind of housing that can be build and where it is permitted, is a local responsibility. Federal public housing policy, as in the implementation of low-income housing or rental assistance, requires not only local decisions about where such housing can be located, but also coordination with policies of the federal government. Private housing policies, such as bank mortgage policy, likewise interlocks with local public policy decisions.

Although housing policy provides the clearest examples of local policy-making, decisions about transportation, health, public safety, sanitation, and other issues that directly affect most people's day-to-day lives all have significant roots in local policy-making activities, many of which are not expressly mandated by the state government. More than likely each local policy-making unit will produce policy that is unlike that made by neighboring units. And if this varied policy-making tapestry at the local level reflects beautifully the complexity of life throughout localities across the nation, its variety also creates a completely atomized context for examining local policy-making.

✳ Ambiguities of Scope and Jurisdiction

Ambiguities in the scope of local policy-making abound. The legal scope granted to local governments by state charters barely provides the outlines of policy-making authority in those units. At best this legal structure determines what *must* be done in a few instances and what *cannot* be done in most instances, but leaves everything in between to the discretion and initiative of local policymakers. The lines of authority among local policymakers themselves are also ambiguous. For example, most municipalities are governed by an elected board of aldermen or a city council (the local legislative equivalent) and a mayor (the local executive equivalent), but in most cases the councilors and mayor deliberate policy matters together—consequently lines of decision are blurred. Municipalities and counties hire managers (the local administrative bureaucracy equivalent), who often are the only officials who manage the entire budget process for the locality and hence must confront policy issues constantly. Municipalities also have justices, usually magistrates, who deal with only the most routine issues of local justice, for example, traffic offenses; these are seldom considered as policy-making activities, but nevertheless they require policy decisions from a number of perspectives that may arise in higher courts.

The scope of local policy-making is made even more ambiguous by overlapping policy-making structures. Special-purpose structures often overlap the older, geopolitical structures. For example, it is not unusual for a school district or a housing authority to serve both a municipality and a county. The school district's operating budget in large part probably comes from local tax levies and hence has to gain favorable approval by both the municipality and the county. Similarly, the housing authority may have to comply with building code requirements and zoning regulations in both the county and the municipality. In such situations it is often impossible to determine which unit has primary authority, the special-purpose unit or the geopolitical unit. The school board has authority to set tax rates, for example, but so do the county and the municipality.

Lack of clear lines of authority complicates strictly geopolitical policy-making as well. For instance, counties and cities both may have policy authority for health care. Suppose that people in an outlying county area request health care from a central municipality that has developed more extensive services; the county accordingly offers to pay the municipality for access to these until the county can develop comparable services. Once the county services catch up, and the county withdraws its support from the municipal health services, the municipality may find itself in a financial crisis.

In recent years, as local policy-making units have matured in number and scope, multijurisdictional coordinating and planning organizations have been developed to help coordinate and focus policy-making authority at the local level in the face of increasing ambiguity. The most widely recognized multijurisdictional organization is the "council of governments" (COG). As its name implies, a COG is the creation of two or more local governments, under a charter issued by the state, in which the different local governments collaborate in efforts to reach policy positions that will find acceptance throughout all participating areas. The Triangle J Council of Governments, for example, which covers the region in and around the Research Triangle Park in North Carolina, includes representatives from six counties and twenty-seven municipalities within those counties and also interacts with other joint policy-making bodies in the same geographic area.

Multijurisdictional planning and coordinating bodies constitute one of the most unusual features of the policies and programs of the Older Americans Act (see chapter 10). Called Area-wide Agencies on Aging (AAAs), these organizations are required to coordinate services for older people across local governmental jurisdictional lines. They are administrative structures created by states, and because COGs are the most prevalent multijurisdictional form of local government, AAAs are likely to be colocated with COGs and sometimes operate as administrative units under them, as, in fact, is the case with Triangle J. Like the COGs, AAAs have limited policy-making authority that is likely to be further compromised by the authority of other individual units of local governance.

Informality of Policy Decisions

Finally, local policy-making is characterized by informal policy decisions. Partly because local policy-making structures are atomized and policy-making authority is ambiguous, many local policy decisions are made informally, or even outside structures of governance. These informal decisions may be "ratified" by a local government unit, but the decision process takes place somewhere else. This sometimes lends an aura of mistrust and deceit to local policy-making activities, but the nature of local policy-making often demands such an informal process. Take the following example.

A small, local, private, nonprofit agency serving older people saw the need for day-care services for about fifty older people who were unable to stay at home alone during hours when their children worked. The agency director decided to investigate funding sources for such a program, which she estimated would cost about $75,000 a year in additional funds. Space was available in the agency for the program, and the agency already served lunch to older people. The director talked with a private foundation that seemed interested in providing some of the funding, but only for a short period of time, as a start-up grant. The agency director presented the matter to her board of directors, who adopted a policy of expanding the agency's services to include day care. Because the foundation would only commit seed money to the project, both short-term and long-term financial commitments had to be found. The county welfare department had funds that could be directed to day care, as did the state aging office through the AAA that served the local jurisdictions in which this agency was located. The state was willing to commit the money only if old people from the whole multijurisdictional region could be included in the services, subject to the agreement of the AAA director. The county did not want to commit its funding to the project unless the service was provided only to its poor older people. The director of the agency did not want to use its facilities to provide service to these populations if it meant that the people usually served by the agency (people of all incomes, but only those who lived in the municipality, not the whole multijurisdiction) might be excluded from the services. The foundation would not give the seed money until the issues were resolved.

The agency director renegotiated the policy entirely; the agency would be exclusively responsible for deciding who got day care. Service would be restricted to the county (part of the AAA's area of responsibility). Half of the spaces would be reserved for people who were eligible for county aid, whether they were receiving county aid or not at the time they applied for day care. The county would therefore pay 50 percent of the cost. The state would pay 25 percent of the cost, which would be an amount equal to providing day-care support to this portion of the AAA's multijurisdictional area. The foundation would pay the balance for two years, at the end of which the amount would be made up from fees paid by day-care users who were not in the county's quota. The balance would be made up from the general operating budget of the agency. The foundation agreed to make a small annual contribution to the agency's operating budget after the second year, by an amount roughly equal to the amount the service would require after fees, county support, and state aid were calculated.

Complex? Extremely. The county commissioners approved the policy at one of their meetings, as did the state agency office and the local agency's and private foundation's boards of directors. The policy itself was made in an informal process for which the agency director took responsibility, and in which persons not usually in policy-making positions reached agreements that were formalized by the appropriate public and private local units. The policy was the composite agreement of each local unit. No single unit "owned" the policy process. The policy that governed the provision of service was written, but the full policy, reflecting the financial commitments, was not part of this written policy. Instead, the local agency, which ultimately provided the service, had separate letters of funding agreement with the county, the state, and the foundation. In other words, not only was the policy-making process informal, but the whole of the policy was not represented in a single policy document.

This example is not unique. Local policy-making often emerges through complex processes that span the fragmented authority of several public and private policy-making units. Because no two situations are likely to reflect the same dimensions of the problem, and because no two local units are likely to participate similarly in the complexity of local policy-making structures, this particularistic policy-making process is essential to the provision of local services.

Local Policy-Making in the Broader Political Context

Local policy-making would be impossible (instead of extremely difficult) to understand were it not that broader political boundaries give it some definition. These boundaries can be found (1) within the mechanics of American intergovernmental relations and (2) within the fiscal constraints posed by the federal system itself. Both these boundaries need brief examination before the role of state and local policy analysis can be understood.

Intergovernmental Relations

Intergovernmental relations operate in America through frequently changing patterns of interaction among the national government, the states, and local governmental units. Unlike other federalized systems—for instance, Canada and Australia—where the governmental relationships among different units are fairly well established constitutionally or legislatively, intergovernmental relationships in the American system have been left to develop as the times and issues may dictate. Hence scholars of American government have had to struggle to identify patterns of intergovernmental relations. The difficulty is evident in some of the descriptive phrases attached to the concept over the years: "layer-cake federalism," "marble cake federalism," and, perhaps the clearest metaphor of all, "rainbow marble cake" with a "mingling of differently colored ingredients."[4]

Deil Wright, a well-known contemporary scholar of American intergovernmental relations, has moved from metaphor to a six-part alliterative scheme: conflict (1930s and before), cooperation (1930–50), concentration (1940–60), creativity (1950–60), competition (1960–70), and calculation (1970–present). One feature of the current "calculative" period of intergovernmental relations has been the "increasing tendency to estimate 'costs' as well as the benefits of getting a federal grant."[5] Changes in funding relationships, increased federal regulatory authority, and increased litigation over expanded regulation have led to a more cautious and discriminating approach in cooperative endeavors. The important feature of Wright's scheme is that he sees patterns in intergovernmental relations that change over time.

Yet the interaction among the federal government, the states, and local governments is not as patterned as Wright portrays it to be. Because each governmental subunit, or each branch of government, interacts in different ways with others, interactions are likely to differ depending upon the policy area involved. Though there are formal mechanisms that link fragmented counterparts, most policy interactions take place outside these formal structures. For example, the National Governors' Conference provides formal linkages among governors, and the National Conference of State Legislatures links legislators. But a particular policy issue usually requires a particular pattern of interactions among the branches and levels of governance. Congress may pass a law that requires the federal administrative bureaucracy to issue policy that is communicated to a state governor, who in turn may ask his or her administrative bureaucracy to produce policy that a local city council may have to deal with legislatively (in an ordinance) before the local program agency can develop policy that will connect a product with the people who need it. These constantly shifting patterns are difficult to pinpoint as occurring in stages.

Wright's own research suggests how difficult it is to capture intergovernmental relations in static descriptions. On examining the kinds of interactions state administrators had within the intergovernmental framework in 1978, he found that contact with other intergovernmental officials is quite widespread. Moreover, these state-level patterns vary from one functional area to another. For example, of the units he surveyed, heads of human resource agencies had their greatest intergovernmental contact with similar agencies and clientele, as well as significant contact with federal regional office personnel and administrators of similar agencies in other states. Heads of natural resource agencies, by contrast, had most contact with similar agency personnel, and significant contact with county and city officials. Even more striking differences would probably exist between the contacts of governors and those of state legislators.[6]

59

Thus although the intergovernmental environment sets some boundaries for state and local policy-making activities, intergovernmental relations are so dynamic that little or no practical value may come from pursuing an enhanced understanding of the intergovernmental system as a whole. However, it is possible to specify the intergovernmental policy boundaries for the five policy sectors examined in part II of this book: income maintenance, health, housing, child welfare, and older adults.

Table 3.1 shows fairly consistent locations for policy-making authority for these sectors at the federal level. Notable by comparison are the variations at the state and local levels.

Money—The Glue of Local Policy-Making

Local policy-making is also bounded by fiscal constraints inherent in the federal system. The federal government may spend money *directly* only for policy purposes that are consistent with federal powers granted by the United States Constitution; these are limited, and touch only obliquely on the policy sectors that are discussed in this book. Otherwise, most of the federal government's authority to spend directly comes from its authority to regulate activities among the states and to manage the economy. Spending on transportation, environmental concerns, and communication derives from this federal interstate authority.

Funding for social programs, therefore, has to take a circuitous route. The most familiar paths are the grant-in-aid and its cousin, the block grant. (The federal government also funds some programs by subsidies, interest-free bonds, and tax incentives; all of these strategies, for example, are particularly significant for funding housing policies.) The grant-in-aid and the block grant were developed as ways to distribute federal funding for specific public policies and programs. Essentially, both these mechanisms offer funds to the states if states will provide certain programs and carry out policies in ways generally promulgated by the federal government. For purposes of discussion, we might say that the chief characteristic of both these funding mechanisms is that they give considerable latitude to states as to the standards and procedures by which the programs and policies will be carried out. The chief difference is the amount of flexibility delegated to the states; grants-in-aid are much more restrictive than block grants.

The policy significance of grants is two-sided. On the one hand, both grants-in-aid and block grants pass considerable policy-making authority from the federal government to the states and to localities. This devolution greatly complicates the policy-making process, because, as described above, no exact

Table 3.1: Intergovernmental policy environments for five policy sectors (discussed in Part II).

Intergovernmental units with greatest policy authority

	Federal			
Policy sector	*Exc*	*Leg*	*Jud*	*Adm*
Income maintenance	X	X		X
Health	X	X		X
Housing	X	X	X	X
Child welfare	X	X	X	X
Older adults	X	X		X

	State			
Policy sector	*Exc*	*Leg*	*Jud*	*Adm*
Income maintenance		X		X
Health		X		X
Housing	X			
Child welfare		X	X	X
Older adults	X			X

	Local*			
Policy sector	*Co*	*Mun*	*SpD*	*SpA*
Income maintenance	X			
Health	X		X	
Housing		X		X
Child welfare	X		X	
Older adults		X		

Abbreviations: executive (Exc), legislative (Leg), judicial (Jud), administrative (Adm), county (Co), municipality (Mun), special district (SpD), special authority (SpA).
*Executive, legislative, and administrative functions have limited distinguishing characteristics at the local level.

or specific unit in the state and local intergovernmental structure ever dominates the policy-making process. For example the AFDC program (Aid to Families with Dependent Children) has operated as a grant-in-aid in which the federal government offers funds to a state if the state will implement programs that appropriately distribute financial support to dependent children and their adult caretakers. By contrast an income maintenance block grant will give broad flexibility to states in how money for income maintenance purposes will be used. So, while the federal government sets the broad framework for social welfare programs, states and localities have considerable authority to develop social welfare policy that fills in and makes the broad policy conditions operational. In particular, states and localities determine what levels of financial support there will be. Such activities constitute large policy-making responsibility.

The other side of this grant mechanism exerts a narrowing effect on local policy-making. Participating states must move within the policy as funded, and not elaborate its purposes. For example, though states set the payment levels for income maintenance programs, they do not set all financial eligibility conditions, nor do they set financial eligibility standards for other programs that use federal funds, as, for example, public housing. And though states may exercise discretion on the types of services offered under the Medicaid plan, they have no authority to determine which foods mothers can buy with their food stamps. This narrowing of local policy-making discretion, prescribed by the funding mechanism, helps to target more specifically which state and local officials are likely to participate in policy decisions once the topics of policy are known. County commissioners will most certainly be involved in shaping income maintenance policy, whereas municipalities will be involved in shaping public housing policies, usually through their housing authorities and zoning ordinances.

In 1981 the federal government began a major refocusing of its funding; eighty social welfare, grant-in-aid programs were reorganized into nine block grants. Policy and program support for areas ranging from education to social services were affected by this change. Although a full evaluation of the impact of this change has not been made, a study by the federal General Accounting Office, published in 1985, documented a clear shift in policy-making authority from the federal government to states and local governments. The study did show, for example, the boundaries that different policy sectors set on intergovernmental policy-making activities. In general, state policies to implement the new block grants were "either derived from or intertwined with basic allocation decisions made during the states' normal budgetary or decision-making process." However, in policy areas where states had had little prior policy-making responsibility, such as community services and support for energy savings, states felt the changes from policy development more acutely.[7]

Another study of the social service block grants also suggests that block-grant funding lessened intergovernmental policy-making, putting more focus on state and local policy-making. In many situations after the federal shift in 1981, specific social services formerly provided by states under the grants-in-aid were no longer offered. In most states the actual number of different services decreased. In some states such long-standing services as day care for children were no longer being provided under the authority of the block grant, even though they had been regularly provided under the authority of the grant-in-aid.[8]

Categorical grants-in-aid, the narrowest grant funding provided for social welfare programs, permits targeting of funds to deal with very specific issues, thus making this kind of funding effective at dealing with the subject for which the program was created. However this targeting often leads to less efficiency in the use of funds as money is directed at narrow populations. Specialization is likely to take place narrowing the population further and often raising the unit cost of service. Inasmuch as there is considerable variety in those populations served, both from state to state and within states, categorical funding leads to the need for developing additional categories, or, as is more often the case, using the funding for populations that only marginally meet the categorical requirements (i.e., trying to make people fit the program).

Block grants are a form of grant funding without narrowly defined categories. Block grants may not be as effective as categorical grants because the funds can be used for a broad group of activities, but they may be more efficient since they provide sufficient flexibility to adjust the use of funding for exigencies as they may exist in the local community. Because block-grant funds can be used broadly, it is more difficult to monitor their use. Moreover, because there are fewer experts involved in program development, and less administrative oversight in programs funded by block grants, appropriate use of these funds is highly dependent on the character of those who are administering them. These persons are likely to be local administrators. Knowledge of what needs to be accomplished in each community becomes essential since there are few directions or guidelines that accompany block grants.

Clearly states may decline to accept federal social welfare funds, but the motivation to accept is greater than the disadvantages of "attached strings" in either categorical or block-grant funding.

Since most social welfare authority rests with the states, states are forced to respond to social problems, one way or another. The ability to get $2 or even $9 for every $1 a state would normally spend is a powerful incentive for states to use federal funding to support social needs. In the case of block grants there is often no matching requirement at all. Block grants appear to save states and local communities money, but savings may not be realized due to the following considerations.

States and localities are forced to comply with the political pressures that categorical grants sometimes stir up. Since certain groups are helped by certain programs (for example, the elderly in senior centers) these groups develop into constituencies that lobby directly and indirectly for programs offered by the federal government. Satisfying these constituency demands is a politically valuable activity. Refusing these demands risks political misfortune. Thus the flexibility of the block grant may be limited by constituency pressures stirred up by previous categorical funding.

Finally, administrative agencies usually respond positively to categorical programs because this kind of funding requires a certain amount of administrative capacity to implement. The more narrow the category of the grant, the more administrative activity is required in making sure the administration of the grant complies with federal expectations. Moreover, narrowly focused categories require program experts, often highly sophisticated program applications, and training necessary to ensure staff are able to carry out increasingly specialized activities. Thus administrative agencies often work in subtle ways to preserve and expand previous categorical programs within the framework of block-grant funding.

Local social policy development becomes more difficult when there is less direction from the federal government, or the state, as is likely to be the case with the increasing use of block grants. Particular program outcomes become more difficult to evaluate unless allowances are made for how funding patterns may affect expected outcomes. For example, categorically funded social programs may be appropriately evaluated for their *effectiveness* (did those who received service change in any measurable way?) while more broadly focused block-grant programs may be more appropriately evaluated for their *efficiency* (did we get good value for the monies that were spent?). The former evaluation is focused on core outcomes, while the latter is focused on marginal outcomes. Both evaluations are outcome rather than process based (how quickly was the staff able to get the program up and running?).

While outcome evaluation under categorical funding focuses on the effective use of funds, evaluation of block-grant funded programs focuses on efficiency outcomes. An efficient block-grant program must examine the following: (1) Were the right people involved in deciding the use of funds? (2) How well were resources directed at each community's most significant problems? (3) What kind of ongoing community involvement assures appropriate use of funds? (4) Are funds being used to replace funding that might be otherwise available? (5) Is good value being received for funds being spent (i.e., how do unit costs compare with spending in other sectors?

Or are there too many or too few options being offered for the amount of funds available?).

There are other "marginal program benefits" that represent outcomes that also require evaluation. "Marginal" in this sense does not mean "unimportant," but rather refers to those program benefits that may not be of central concern, such as better educational performance of children. A full discussion of marginal policy analysis questions is presented in chapter 4. At this point, however, shifting funding patterns not only place greater responsibility on localities for policy development, but increased block-grant funding will also force localities to undertake different kinds of policy development activity, like program evaluation, which have not been previously expected of local policy-making.

Conclusion

Examining subnational policy-making centers and processes gives greater breadth to our understanding of the whole of the policy-making process, but it also makes general observations about the policy-making process itself more difficult. Several factors clearly complicate local and state policy-making processes: the confusions between the legal and political autonomy of local governmental units; the great variety and number of local units, which make policy individually and collectively; and the as yet unclear patterns of interaction among governmental units within the framework of American federalism as shaped by different funding patterns. The lack of one clear center of power in the American system suggests that there is no clear center of policy-making, either. Even though some policy-making sectors are more appropriate for specific governmental units, in the completion of a policy-making process all centers can become involved, and frequently most do. When private-sector policy-making is added to this complexity, the final policy-making picture truly becomes the "black box of politics," as one commentator has quipped.[9]

Under such circumstances it is not surprising that most studies of policy-making continue to focus on case studies; general principles are difficult to develop. Research by Randall Ripley and Grace Franklin has offered some hope of detecting order in the chaos. After a first investigation of bureaucratic policy within the federal system, they and their colleagues suggested that the structures of state and local policy-making units have an important influence on the roles the agencies play in policy-making. In particular, an agency's maturity, the characteristics of its personnel, and its internal decision-making processes not only determine how it becomes involved in policy-making, but also suggest what the policy outcomes might be.[10]

In later work Ripley and Franklin have refined some of their structural theories and devised an interactional framework for understanding policy development. A chief characteristic of this framework is the activity of what they call "subgovernments": "clusters of individuals that effectively make the most routine decisions in a given substantive area of policy. . . . Since most policy-making is routine most of the time, subgovernments can often function for long periods of time without much interference of control from individuals or institutions outside the subgovernment." [11]

> Not only are the lines between governmental and nongovernmental institutions blurred by the norm of open, continual access during policymaking, but there is also a constant flow of personnel between governmental and nongovernmental institutions that further blurs the distinctions. . . . This flow of personnel enhances the importance and stability of subgovernments, and the magnitude of this type of personnel interchange is so large that subgovernments have also been called "incest groups." [12]

These observations and the discussion throughout this chapter suggest once again the importance of identifying exactly where in the complexity of the policy-making process a particular request or need for analysis is located. Seldom will a policy analysis be requested that will span the entire range of the policy-making process. Without this focus the policy analyst cannot produce a product that will be useful in the policy-making process. The discussions of policy analysis models that follow, in chapter 4, are offered from the perspective that different approaches are required for each journey into the labyrinth of the policy-making process.

Chapter Four

METHODS OF POLICY ANALYSIS

Introduction

The close association between policy analysis and social research often confuses the purpose of policy analysis with the methods used in it. The purpose of policy analysis is to provide reliable information to policymakers about a problem they must consider, in order to guide policy-making activities to appropriate conclusions. This information may include detailed assessments of a problem, careful comparisons of alternative proposals, and projections of costs against benefits to identifiable population groups, as well as suggestions about the larger social and political consequences of various proposals. The phrase "policy research" is often substituted for "policy analysis" because policy analysis draws heavily on the methods of social science research. However, although it uses the products of social science research to build the information it produces, policy analysis does not have the same purpose as social science research. Whereas social science research is free to range wherever the facts may take it, policy analysis is sought within an environment of public choice. Policy analysis is scientific, but it is not social research.

Foundations of Social Science

Social science research, especially that which requires statistical analysis of behaviorally defined information, is often called "empirical" research. A dictionary definition of *empirical* shows that it may mean basing conclusions on experiment and observation, or it may mean a disregard for science, relying solely on practical experience. The origin of the word is Greek, *en peria*, meaning "in trial"; the same root, *peri*, occurs in ex*peri*ence and ex*peri*ment. Empirical research has been called "the investigator's experiences with the person, objects, or events of the real world. In other words, the raw materials from which scientific knowledge is derived are systematic observations of reality."[1]

The beginnings of the revolution in science that ushered in our modern world help put the purposes of policy analysis in proper perspective to social science research. Understanding science as we know it today began in the seventeenth century, when Galileo publically confirmed Copernicus's theory that the sun, not the earth, was the center of the universe. Science and religion became polarized into two camps: the discoverers and the believers. Copernicus had believed that the earth revolved around the sun. Galileo, however, had proved the theory by his repeated observations, made possible with tools not available to Copernicus. It was his assertion of this proof, derived empirically, that provoked Galileo's trial for heresy; under threat of death, he recanted. The furor that continued (to this day, in fact) was not over the conclusion that he had reached, but the way in which he had reached that conclusion. Before, truth about the world was presumed to be revealed to man by God. After Galileo, truth about the world could be discovered by man without God. Out of this came modern science, an understanding of the world through knowing, rather than believing. This differentiation between faith and science has remained a challenge to Western thought.

Discoveries based on science soon abounded, leading to the development of catalogues of knowledge called "encyclopedias"—first of astronomy, then of physics, biology, chemistry, and other disciplines. It was not surprising that before long someone took the same systematic approach to understanding society as well. Auguste Comte laid the foundations of what he called "positive philosophy," in which he "discovered" a law of three stages that explained the whole of social interaction: (1) the theological stage, dominated by religious belief; (2) the abstract and philosophical stage; and (3) the positive stage, in which science prevailed. Comte's works later came to be called "sociology," the study of society by scientific discovery. Comte and those who followed him were so convinced that science, or systematic discovery, was the key to understanding that they frequently urged the methods of science for studying the entire range of human problems. This movement of science through the world of social thought was "an attempt to transfer to the study of social and human phenomena, the methods and concepts of the natural sciences in the belief that human phenomena, like physical phenomena, obey certain laws of nature which can be inductively discovered by the empirical examination of successive events."[2]

The new social science found its first and most lasting synthesis in blending with biology. Charles Darwin's *Origin of Species* (1859) posited the idea of natural selection: species fitted to their environment survive and reproduce. Offspring vary in their characteristics, and some reproduce more successfully than others. In this way species may "evolve" or change. Darwin posited in *The Descent of Man* that our present human species evolved from an inferior animal form—a scientific idea that "creationism" continues to debate. Fortified with Darwin's ideas and well read in Comte's social positivism, Herbert Spencer, a contemporary of Darwin, devised what have since been called "fantastic comparisons between biological organisms and societies."[3] Spencer argued, for example, that like species that could not adapt to the natural environment, individuals who did not adapt to the social environment would not survive. He also held that government, specifically, had an obligation to avoid any activities that would interfere with these laws of nature. From this arose the social doctrine of *laissez faire*: let things alone—the world is self-regulating. Spencer's ideas of "survival of the fittest" soon became an accepted truth in human affairs.

This digression into the origins of social science provides a background for considering appropriate uses of social science in policy analysis. In its most fundamental application, social science relies on the ability to predict expected events on the basis of experience with present events—assuming that a regularity, or a pattern, exists with respect to the observable events. The key words are *regularity, observation,* and *pattern.*

On these terms, three processes are fundamental to social science methodology. First, a pattern must be assumed. The social scientist must infer through assumption, previous experience, or previous research that some patterns exist between eating breakfast, for example, and doing well in school. If no presumed pattern existed—if the two events were seen as random, without association or order—there would be no need for the social scientist to collect the data.

Second, social science requires a systematic approach to the process of observation. A conclusion is reached by assuming that the regularity observed is systematic and consequently applies in all situations. Social scientists also try to define their observations clearly, so that they can be counted. For example, suppose you, as a scientist, decided to test the assumption that children who eat breakfast are better students. After deciding what was meant by "breakfast" and "better students," you would observe what students actually did, both at breakfast and at school. The observations would have to be gathered regularly, by some system, so that all observations could be trusted to fit the presumed patterns of association between the two sets of events. For example, all the observations of each activity (breakfast or schoolwork) would have to be made at the same time of day; the same kinds of performance would have to be observed (not, reading one day, math the next); and separate records for break-fast-eaters and non-breakfast-eaters would have to be kept. Whatever observable pattern occurred could be attributed to the association of the two events—providing they were not due to chance.

Third, therefore, some mechanism is required that will enable scientists to assert whether an association that exists between sets of events is not due to chance. An association of events can never be certain; scientists can only refine their estimates of certainty. The greater the amount of certainty desired, the greater the number of observations necessary. Suppose you as a scientist kept records on 90 out of 100 second-graders at one particular school and discovered that all 90 ate breakfast and also did well in school. You might fairly predict that at least 9 of the 10 remaining second-graders would likewise eat breakfast and do well. You might also have cause to believe that in a similar group of children, the same association of events would prevail. However, if out of 100 children only 20 were observed, even if all 20 children ate breakfast and did well in school, projecting that association to the group of 100, or to other groups of students in a similar situation, could not be done with much confidence. Thus a system for collecting sizable amounts of quantified information is an essential part of the scientific method.

Essential Elements of Policy Analysis

Though policy analysis draws heavily on social science knowledge and social science research methods, and may also contribute to social science knowledge, it has its own essential elements. These include (1) identifying, understanding, or clarifying the problem, (2) identifying the location for policy decision, (3) specifying possible solutions (alternatives), and (4) estimating or predicting the impact (outcomes) of these solutions on different populations.

Problem Identification

Policy has a number of purposes, but a primary one is to resolve problems (see also chapter 1). Sometimes it may be recognized that a problem exists, but putting some boundary around the problem may prove difficult. The way a problem is defined usually determines how it will be resolved. Any of several definitions may be appropriate for understanding and subsequently resolving the problem. Problem identification requires:

70

1. *Specifying the problem's origins.* Learning the problem's history, including previous attempts to deal with it. Specifying the origin of a problem isolates who thinks this is a problem and why.

2. *Determining the problem's scope.* Clarifying who is affected by the problem. Determining the scope of a problem clarifies the groups that interact with the problem. Some are disadvantaged; some benefit.

3. *Sketching the pervasiveness of the problem.* Determining its implications for other sectors of society. Sketching the pervasiveness of the problem identifies the social institutions that may presently be engaged with parts of the problem.

"Framing" the problem within these conditions invites putting some boundary around it, or limiting its scope. But this framing may also set the conditions under which the problem will be analyzed.

Locating the Focus of Policy Decision

Policy analysis takes place at various locations during the policy-making process, and the character of that analysis differs depending on where it is located. Moreover, each element of policy analysis may differ depending on the particular location of the policy decision. Problem identification may be quite different, for example, among executives than in courts, even when the subject matter is the same. Each set of policy actions has its own political environment in which it operates.

Determining Alternatives

Determining the alternatives available for choice is an essential part of the policy analysis process. Generally, alternatives are thought of as different ways of achieving the same objective; in policy analysis, however, the alternatives themselves frequently have policy implications of their own. The task for the analyst is to explore the alternatives and make clear any further consequences they might have if ultimately chosen as policy.

Frequently alternatives are discussed and debated as choices, not so much because they are really different ways of doing the same thing, but because the alternatives themselves address normative issues inherent in the problem. For example, America has struggled for years to reduce poverty, particularly among children. Until recently, several alternatives for achieving this objective had been incorporated into Title IV of the Social Security Act. Title IV-A provided cash to dependent children and their families; Title IV-C provided work programs in place of cash; Title IV-B and Title IV-E provided foster care and adoption services for poor children who had no natural homes. (Title IV-D still provides services to help collect child support payments.)

Each of these sections of Title IV states an alternative for reducing poverty among children, yet each is seen as a policy in its own right. Each offers a different normative solution for resolving poverty among children. Title IV-A stated that children and their families should get money when they need it. Title IV-C stated that people ought to work for their money if they can. Title IV-B and Title IV-E stated that alternative homes should be available to children who need them. Title IV-D states that absent parents should pay for their children's support. These policies do not form a unified collection of alternatives, of different ways of doing the same thing. Rather, they legitimate different and sometimes conflicting normative approaches to poverty. Thus, in practice, these alternatives may pull against each other rather than pulling together; they may not act as "alternatives" as the word is generally used.

Unanticipated effects—OMBRA

This ambiguity about whether alternatives are a means to achieve policy, or an independent form of policy in themselves, contributes to the unanticipated consequences of policy choice. Inadequate policy analysis often leaves the policymaker uninformed about the impact a particular alternative may have in other policy sectors. Perhaps no better example can be found than the unintended consequences of the Omnibus Budget Reconciliation Act of 1981 (OMBRA). The immediate problem facing President Reagan in 1981 was a depressed economy and a federal deficit. A number of alternatives were possible to resolve each problem. Put most simply, more government spending would stimulate the economy but contribute to the deficit; more taxes would reduce the deficit but depress economic activity. The Reagan administration chose to reduce spending to reduce the deficit, *and* to reduce taxes to stimulate economic activity. Alternatives that represent different normative positions often work against each other, and these were a case in point: the Reagan administration's decision to press for both choices led to a recession, causing widespread unemployment, doubling poverty, and a massive buildup of the national debt.

The 1981 Reagan budget alternatives were not particularly acceptable to many congressmen who carefully guarded important spending programs under their legislative authority. The budget director, David Stockman, a presidential appointee who was himself a former congressman, knew from personal experience that a reduction in the budget would be unlikely if specific programs were considered for cutting, because no legislator would agree to trim a favorite program. He therefore persuaded Congress to accept the president's final budget grand total and to decide later where the cuts would have to be made, instead of the other way around.

The 1981 budget alternative thus established across-the-board reductions, but congressional implementation of this policy had consequences that reached far beyond reductions in funds. As a way of minimizing the impact of reduction on any single program, Congress decided to require each committee that had program responsibility to reduce the funding request for programs under its jurisdiction by an established percentage. This meant that some committees reduced all their programs by a fixed percentage, across the board, whereas other committees chose to make deep cuts in some programs under their jurisdiction and little or no reductions in others, so that the total under each committee's control came to the correct percentage.

Also, to lessen the impact of the reductions, Congress agreed to the administration's proposal to group a large number of programs into block grants—a more general form of program implementation. The financial allocation for all the programs in that group could then be reduced; the states in turn could decide which specific programs they would reduce or, again alternatively, supplement with state funds. The unintended consequences of implementing the block grant policy began to appear as states passed along to local program administrators reduced funding for established public programs that had long been important for addressing a number of domestic issues at local levels. For example, reductions in federal funding for environmental programs not only curtailed efforts to clean up toxic dump sites but limited state-level inspection activities as well. Shifting additional authority to states also created a fragmented and inconsistent social service system, in which program benefits and eligibility began to range greatly from state to state.[4] Changes also took place that conflicted with the recognized intention of existing welfare programs. In some cases reductions in funding actually discouraged welfare recipients from working.[5] One researcher has claimed that cutbacks in prenatal care programs "contributed significantly to the [increase] in infant mortality by weakening national policies . . . for the care and protection of pregnant women," greatly increasing future medical costs.[6] The full extent of the "ripple effect" of these adverse policy outcomes has not yet been determined.

Estimating or Predicting the Impact of Public Policy

This element of the policy analysis process corresponds closely with the need to consider alternatives. Had Reagan and Stockman, for instance, estimated the impact of the particular policy alternatives they chose to implement, they might (or might not) have made a different choice so as to minimize the consequences of the policy, particularly on vulnerable populations. One of the first assessments published on the Reagan domestic policy acknowledged that "some widening of the income distribution would have taken place between 1980 to 1984 irrespective of who had been President," but concluded that "the particular mix of tax and benefit reductions that President Reagan chose accelerated the trend. His policy helped the affluent but not the poor or the middle class."[7]

The estimation process abounds with pitfalls. The real impact of a policy alternative may differ significantly from the expected one for several reasons. Because there is always the possibility that the projected pattern will not continue, or will continue in a different way from what was expected, predicting the future is risky. As we saw above, to make predictions, social science depends on observations that confirm assumptions about identical situations, but it is impossible to find truly identical situations in the social world. What might seem to be a probable outcome may not turn out to be so at all. In other words, there is no certainty that any future state of affairs can be predicted.

The actual impact of a policy also may differ from the predicted impact because values conflict and normative views differ. As discussed in chapter 2, deliberation over values may subvert the entire effort of the analysis. Much as problems are understood from normative positions, the potential effects of alternative solutions are understood in terms of existing, not future circumstances. Sometimes a policy analyst may truly prefer a particular outcome and consequently may strive to develop an alternative that achieves specific normative consequences. In this situation negative consequences may truly be intended, not unintended, policy consequences. In other cases the context of the problem itself may have changed, and the consequences are different simply because the circumstances are different from what was originally understood.

Three Caveats for Policy Analysis

As suggested in chapter 2, and also in the remarks above, policy analysis has a very broad scope. Almost any social science research has "policy implications." The diverse purposes that public policies serve, as well as the multiple centers that exist for policy decisions, propel policy analysis into far-reaching activities. Three caveats, or cautions, can help the analyst apply an appropriate method of analysis.

1. *Only problems and policy alternatives that are in the public domain should be examined.* To the extent that policy analysis is concerned with the examination of public problems and the use of public resources, this restraint seems prudent. Policy analysis is less useful for the examination of private issues when those issues do not interlock with public concerns. For example, a private family counseling center, such as a family service association, may decide not to provide service to drug users without analysis of the policy decision about whom the agency wants to serve. The same family service association might conduct a policy analysis and consider an alternative to its refusal to treat drug users if local churches would agree to provide the counseling, but this alternative is not in the public domain either. Other radical alternatives could be suggested, but analyzing obscure or inventive alternatives that are so far-reaching or so questionable that they appear "best" only because nothing much is known about their implications is not consistent with policy analysis. This caveat corresponds with views of social science that emphasize regularity as a base for predictability.[8]

2. *Different centers of policy-making require different kinds of policy analysis.* Policy analysts usually are on the staff of such centers or are members of organizations directly related to them. The analyst's task is closely related to the kind of information the decision maker needs. Each organization has a mission, and because its policy analysis is done within that organizational context, the scope of analysis, particularly the identification of alternatives, must be compatible with the mission. Thus many possible alternatives for policy choice may exist outside the realm of a particular policy environment. For example, an administrative staff charged with a policy analysis task cannot suggest new legislation as an alternative to administrative policy; the focus must remain on administrative alternatives.

3. *Policy-making is a value-laden enterprise, and the analysis always takes place within an established context of values.* Social values, organizational values, professional values, and personal values all limit policy analysis. Unscrambling the values that lie behind the definition of a problem, or the range of alternative solutions, is every bit as important as determining what type of information is most useful for examining the problem itself. The analyst must be appropriately cautious about values, but values guide the analysis. Most likely these values are not the personal values of the analyst, but values that reflect a public orientation toward preferences or values that guide the operation of the organization. Policy analysis is not a political process as such, but because values are clarified in the process of analysis, it is part of the political process that maximizes value positions.

Three Models of Policy Analysis

Developing information that is useful to the policy-making process is the whole purpose of policy analysis. Although the policy analyst uses social science information in the process of analysis, debate still continues over what kind of social science information is best in what kinds of situations. Sometimes appropriate information already exists, and it can be applied readily in the analysis. Sometimes new information has to be generated by social research. In either case, that information must be organized to connect with the particular issue under consideration. Each policy decision requires a specific mixture of information presented in a specific way. Policy analysis requires reliable, useful, purposeful information. This information is likely to be some form of social science information, but the important point is that it be presented in a relevant form.

Useful information and the methods of social research required to generate it are both determined by the type of policy problem under consideration and by the particular location of the policy decision. For example, information about the fiscal costs of one alternative over another may require more specific social science data than information about which constituency or interest group is involved with the issue and why. Each analysis requires a particular blend of a variety of kinds of information, but the following three models of policy analysis can accommodate the range of these differences.

These three models are the behavioral, or "rational," the incremental, and the criteria-based (see table 4.1). To some extent they also identify three points along a continuum of policy analysis. At one end of the continuum, in the behavioral model, the analyst requires information that can only be obtained through traditional social science methods of research. At the other end, where information for policy choice is least likely to depend upon social science data and research methods, and most likely to depend on the analysis of values, the incremental model is most useful. An incremental policy analysis is sometimes called a "political analysis," because the alternatives considered seem more oriented to the political realities of choosing than to the social realities of the consequences of the choice. The criteria-based model rests at some midpoint on the continuum. It balances the use of social science research knowledge with an emphasis on the marginal significance of criteria (values) that may be involved in choosing.

Table 4.1 describes these models in terms of procedure. In practice any analysis may contain or omit different features of the models; in some cases elements from different models may be combined. The actual task of analysis proceeds as the requirements for information become clearer, depending on the problem under consideration and who is making the policy decision. The

Table 4.1: Three models of policy analysis on a policy analysis continuum.

The Behavioral (or Rational) Model[1] *look at every possibility*

1. Define the problem in objective (behavioral) terms.
2. Devise sets of specific alternatives that would resolve the problem under prescribed circumstances.
3. Project the likelihood of achieving each set of alternatives.
4. Examine data appropriate to each alternative and determine which give the greatest benefit per unit of cost.
5. Calculate the benefits of each alternative in relation to feasibility of implementation.

some limits to investigate but operate from the behavioral but utilize the...

The Criteria-Based Model[2]

1. Define the problem with respect to policy alternatives available for dealing with it.
2. Establish universal and selective criteria (values) for evaluating the alternatives (feasibility would be one of several criteria).
3. Gather data appropriate to each alternative and determine which alternative gives the greatest benefit per unit of cost.
4. Weigh costs and benefits for each alternative against the universal and selective criteria.
5. Recommend an alternative that maximizes the criteria, or offer a range of alternatives that would maximize different values in different ways.

2 or 3 alternative. P 92 ex:
value driven universal or selective

The Incremental Model[3]

1. Calculate the marginal benefits of current choices for dealing with the problem.
2. Initiate small choices toward a solution that would achieve measurable marginal benefits.
3. Accelerate the choices that produce positive results; decelerate choices that produce negative results.
4. The combination of choices that work makes up the policy.

Pure social science research — *Policy implementation*

---

1. Herbert Simon, "A Behavioral Model of Rational Choice," in R. Gore and H. Dyson, eds., *The Making of Decisions* (Glencoe, Ill.: Free Press, 1964), pp. 124-6.

2. Developed from the policy analysis model of the University of North Carolina Bush Institute. See James Gallagher and Ron Haskins, *Policy Analysis* (New York: Ablex Press, 1984), p. 87.

3. Charles Lindblom, "The Science of Muddling Through," in Gore and Dyson, *Making of Decisions,* pp. 84-90.

following discussion of the models should be tempered by our understanding that no two policy problems are the same. Just as the process of analysis varies with the kind of information necessary for a policy choice, the method of analysis in one situation may not be useful in another.

The Behavioral Model

The behavioral model of policy analysis represents analysis that requires the maximum amount of social science information and social research methods. The model has its origins in the work of Herbert Simon, a pioneer in the application of scientific principles to management and administrative decisions. Simon was a consultant with the Rand Corporation, a think tank that during the early 1950s was principally concerned with developing new technologies for making decisions. Thus the behavioral approach to policy analysis was developed from a context of how effective decisions *should* be made. More than any other, this model depicts an orderly process by which decisions take place. For this reason it is often called a "rational" model.

Defining the problem in objectifiable (behavioral) terms

For example, in rational terms, hunger and poor nutrition might be defined as resulting from insufficient resources to meet daily needs. The insufficiency of resources may in turn be defined as resulting from inadequate wages, unemployment or low pay, poor education or job preparation, or commitments at home that overtax a family's resources. This orientation to problem definition is consistent with the model's underlying reliance on the basic principles of social science; it seeks to identify a regular, systematic linking of events. This way of defining problems also sets out a series of potentially causal factors that can suggest alternative solutions during later analysis. In the behavioral model, problem definition requires a complete definition, one that looks at all possible elements of a problem and how they may be linked.

Defining the problem in objectifiable (behavioral) terms is thus a critical first step in the behavioral model, and the rest of the analysis succeeds or fails on that basis, depending on how well this first task is done. As discussed in chapter 1, defining the problem presents a complex task for the policy analyst who uses this model, and considerable social science information is needed. The behavioral model makes no allowance for normative orientations toward problem identification. Instead it attempts to integrate all different problem definitions, producing a final definition that may have a number of subparts. This process often establishes a sense of hierarchy within the definition, particularly when complex problems are at issue. The subparts and hierarchical organization yield "alternative sets" of problem definitions.

Creating sets of alternatives

Just as definitions are objectified in this model, so alternatives are stated in behavioral, or measurable, or operationalized terms. To continue with the example above, one set of behavioral alternatives that could address the problem of hunger and poor nutrition would be to provide poor people with money; another set might be to provide poor people with food stamps; yet another would be to provide wages through employment; another would be to provide poor people with surplus food.

These alternatives are called "sets" because each constitutes a distinct grouping of subfactors that must be considered together to build an alternative. For example, providing food stamps might be undertaken in a number of different ways: (1) provide $200 in food stamps per month to poor families with children under age sixteen; (2) provide $75 in food stamps per month to every undernourished person; (3) provide $100 in food stamps to poor mothers who will be willing to purchase them at a 75 percent discount; (4) provide food stamps, up to the value of the poverty line, to all pregnant women. Efforts at problem definition would continue in this fashion to specify all the possible subsets for each alternative, until the list was exhausted.

The process of defining alternatives and their subsets may seem endless, but the usefulness of this model depends upon having every possible alternative spelled out. Identifying all alternatives and all possible subsets for each is another way of defining the problem's conditions in more precise terms, thus eliminating the need to consider normative positions. The more extensively the problem is defined, according to this model, the more likely the right solution to it can be found.

Projecting the likelihood of achieving each alternative set

Projecting the viability of alternatives requires developing something like a hypothesis that can be tested to establish which alternative set is most likely to resolve the problem. The analyst must project, for example, the extent to which hunger might be reduced if families were given $200 a month in food stamps, if undernourished individuals were given $75 in food stamps each, and so on. Proposing which alternatives are most likely to alleviate a problem requires information (data) and a method to examine it (analysis). Information would be necessary, for instance, to determine how much of what kind of food is essential, and how much the food costs; one would also need to know how many individuals or families would be involved, depending on which alternative was chosen.

Because this phase of policy analysis requires a considerable amount of social science data, how much of what kind of data becomes an important consideration. The analyst must become familiar with the "policy sectors" that are relevant to the problem. To determine whether food stamps will assist in reducing hunger, for instance, the analyst must know something about food and nutrition as well as money management.

Without substantive knowledge of the policy sectors involved, the analyst may consult data that are irrelevant and come to a false conclusion about the potential usefulness of the alternative under scrutiny. In 1967, for example, largely at the insistence of Senator Herman Talmadge (D-Ga.), the AFDC program was amended first to permit, then to require that welfare recipients work when they were able. Although the Talmadge Amendment to the Social Security Act was considered by Congress for its marginal value, the analysis of the proposal focused on the impact of the proposed alternative—required work— on reducing the need for welfare. The analysis did not, however, consider relevant information about work. Data about the employability, health, literacy, and work skills of AFDC recipients were not considered. As a result, the Work Incentive Program, as this initiative was called, failed miserably to encourage welfare recipients to work, and failed, as well, to achieve its marginal goal of reducing welfare caseloads. This same scenario was repeated when Congress created its 1988 welfare reform, the JOBS program. The behavioral model was used for policy analysis suggesting that JOBS was not the best way to "reform" welfare, but Congress chose the JOBS alternative anyway.

Examining data appropriate to each alternative set to establish a cost-benefit ratio and calculating the benefit in relation to implementation feasibility

The objective in these two stages of policy analysis is to arrive at some practical ordering of alternatives, from the best to the worst. To achieve this ordering, the costs of each alternative are projected against the benefits the alternative would provide. The first phase in this process requires establishing some cost-benefit ratio. For example, after considerable research the analyst may determine that it costs, on average a certain amount per year to keep a child adequately fed. Other data are then weighed to project the benefits resulting from such an expenditure; the analyst may discover that adequate nutrition has been shown to reduce the risk of several serious health problems, both during childhood and in later life. These benefits might be judged not only worthwhile for the child, but also as a savings in later welfare costs. On these terms a ratio of cost to benefit is established.

Strictly speaking, the lower the cost-benefit ratio, the better. The term implies a ratio with cost as the numerator, benefit the denominator. All other things being equal, it seems clear that a ratio of 1 to 5 would provide benefits more cost efficiently than a ratio of 1 to 2. However, in common parlance this more favorable, smaller proportion is often termed a "high" cost-benefit ratio, probably because "high" suggests maximization, whereas "low" has a connotation of inadequacy. In discussion that follows throughout this book, "high cost-benefit ratio" is used in that common sense, to refer to ratios that (because they are small) are highly cost-efficient.

Once a cost-benefit ratio is established for each alternative, the analyst begins to consider the feasibility of implementation. Providing $200 in food
stamps to every poor family might be calculated to cost $2 billion and result
in improving diets up to the minimum nutritionally acceptable level, as determined by an earlier analysis. Another alternative, providing food stamp supplements up to the poverty level for pregnant women, might be calculated to
cost only $1 billion. The supplement given to pregnant women would reach
only about 10 percent of the people with nutritional needs. Nevertheless, good
nutrition is extremely important for those women, because undernourished
women are likely to have low-birth-weight babies who will be vulnerable to
serious medical problems. Moreover, because of budget restrictions (a common issue in implementation) it may be more feasible to implement this second alternative set than the first, even though from a cost-benefit perspective
the first one is more desirable. (Note that both alternatives represent tacit
agreement on a number of normative issues about the problem.)

Data analysis

By the time the final phase of analysis is completed, all the alternative sets
might be ordered as presented schematically in table 4.2. The model is decep-
tively simple. Once the alternatives are stated and the data are examined to determine which alternative sets best meet the conditions of a problem, a best
alternative is apparent. The table shows alternative sets ranked from A (high
feasibility, high cost-benefit ratio), downward to P (low feasibility, low cost-
benefit). This is a schematic representation; in actual analysis the matrix might
run to many more slots than sixteen, or to many fewer, and cover more or
fewer gradations from High to Low.

**Table 4.2: A ranked ordering of alternative sets A-P as determined by the
behavioral model of policy analysis.**

	Cost-benefit ratio			
Feasibility	High	Medium	Medium	Low
High	A	B	C	D
Medium	E	F	G	H
Medium	I	J	K	L
Low	M	N	O	P

It is in the later phases of analysis that the behavioral model begins to raise perplexing questions. Examining alternatives in terms of their relative costs indirectly introduces values into the analysis. Benefits are often projected in terms of human goods (such as adequate amounts of food), where costs are calculated in dollars. As Simon himself described this dilemma, "The classical theory does not tolerate the incompatibility of apples and oranges."[9] In other words, it is probably impossible to place a dollar value on the benefits of an adequate diet or any other human good, even though it may be possible to add up how much it would cost to provide it. Assessing costs in dollar terms and benefits in some value context does not yield a true cost-benefit ratio. If, for example, poor people do not know the basics of good nutrition and consequently do not use food stamps to buy food appropriately, the real costs of the policy may well be much higher than its estimated dollar cost.

Presenting alternatives to policymakers

The final action in the behavioral model is to see that this amassed information is given to the particular decision makers who have requested it in a form that they will be able to use conveniently and meaningfully. The policy analyst does not make a recommendation, as such, because the model assumes that the best alternative has become evident through the analysis, that clear evidence will have emerged that a single alternative will best resolve the problem. (In table 4.2, this choice would be alternative set A.)

Despite the widespread use of this model of policy analysis, its effectiveness is limited by its highly theoretical orientation. In theory all situations must be identified and explained if one is to be able to discover the best solution. In practice this course is never followed, and even Herbert Simon, the person most closely associated with this model of policy analysis, was obliged to state a major compromise in the model for the sake of applicability.

> In most global models of rational choice, all alternatives are evaluated before a choice is made. In actual human decision-making, alternatives are often examined sequentially . . . when alternatives are examined sequentially, we may regard the first satisfactory alternative that is evaluated as such as the one actually selected.[10]

He further modified the model by contrasting "feasibility" with "optimality":

> In theory and practice . . . the distinction is commonly drawn between computations to determine the feasibility of a program and . . . the optimal program. . . . An optimal program is one of the feasible programs which maximizes a greater pay-off function. If,

instead of requiring that the pay-off be maximized, we require only that the pay-off exceed some given amount, then one can find a policy . . . by methods of feasibility testing. . . . For all practical purposes, this procedure may represent a sufficient approach to optimization, provided the minimum required payoff can be set reasonably.[11]

But if there is no unique "best" alternative in practice, how can one be sure that the best alternative produced by the analysis is really better than other alternatives that may be presented? Simon calls this uncertainty "limited rationality," and given that uncertainty, the model loses much of its authority. Because there may be no such thing as a unique best alternative, the policymaker is free to choose among alternatives and argue that one is the "best" in that it is most feasible, so long as it meets the minimum payoff level. Hence values that were not formally considered in the model may end up determining the best alternative, and the analysis itself may lose some of the authority it purports to add to the decision process.

If the analyst who uses this model lacks strong authority from the strength of the analysis itself to assure the policymaker that the alternative set A (as in table 4.2) is the best alternative, the best policy choice may really be F, G, J, or K. Because the model is designed to be value-neutral, there is no way to consider directly the normative orientation of the problem or the normative issues inherent in the possible alternative solutions. And because there probably is no such thing as a value-neutral problem or solution, if this rational model cannot reveal a clear best solution for the problem presented, the decision maker ultimately will be apt to evaluate the alternatives offered by the model in terms of his or her own values.

Despite these major drawbacks, the behavioral model is an extremely important tool of policy analysis. It generates a considerable amount of factual information, and it orders this information into systematic clusters that permit the analyst and the decision maker to see clearly the outlines of a problem. Moreover, the essential elements of the model, such as data collection and examination, are frequently used in all policy analysis activities; in this way, the behavioral or "rational" model provides a prototype for all policy analysis work. Regardless of the organization in which analysis takes place, elements of this model are likely to be useful, and facility with the model will help the analyst irrespective of the kinds of analytic products that are expected.

The Incremental Model

The incremental model emphasizes the marginal considerations of the policy problem and its alternatives. It represents the opposite end of the policy analysis continuum from the behavioral model, not so much because of the limited way in which it uses social science information, but because it seems to begin with the solution rather than the problem. It is called the incremental model because, in contrast with the behavioral model, it identifies and implements small increments of policy choices until the right combination is found, the problem is satisfied, and the result becomes the policy.

The incremental model is most commonly associated with Charles Lindblom, who has called its process "the science of muddling through."[12] Like a number of policy analysts, Lindblom distinguishes between social science research and policy analysis. In fact, he and his colleague David Cohen have argued that social science research sometimes gets in the way of policy analysis: "Information and analysis provide only one route [to policy-making], because . . . a great deal of the world's problem solving is and ought to be accomplished through various forms of social interaction that substitute action for thought, understanding, or analysis."[13]

The distinction between the positions represented by the behavioral and incremental models is important. Because policy analysis has formed such a close alliance with social science research, many analysts tend to reject the incremental model as not sufficiently scientific to be worthy of serious consideration. Lindblom and Cohen have confronted this criticism with an apt rejoinder:

> Policy-makers attack specific problems in light of a general framework or perspective that controls both explanatory hypotheses and range of solutions that they are willing to consider. . . . [For example] it appears that policy-makers [once] share[d] a framework of . . . academic psychology. They subsequently abandoned it only to take up in its place another that is represented by academic sociology. . . . Hence, even if policy-makers do not turn to [social science knowledge] in many of the ordinarily expected ways—for specific data, evidence, or policy evaluation—they may take the whole organizing framework for their work from the academic social sciences.[14]

Calculating the marginal benefits of choices presently available for dealing with the problem

Investigating choices that are already known may seem to be a contradictory point for beginning a policy analysis. Yet the incremental model deliberately begins with alternatives that appear to be available for resolving the problem at hand and lets comprehensive problem definition rest until these alternatives have been explored. This means that the alternatives under consideration are usually modest and limited, as the full scope of the problem and all its ramifications have not yet been made clear. The incremental model begins this way because of its normative orientation toward problems and their solutions. It assumes that the normative configuration of the problem as a whole is really a representation of a variety of "marginal values" that are difficult to unscramble (a subject discussed in chapter 1). Lindblom argues that, paradoxically, the only practicable way to disclose relevant marginal values, even to oneself, is to describe the policy one chooses to achieve them.

It is important to recognize that marginal values are not unimportant values. For example, in both the WIN and JOBS welfare reform policies mentioned above, getting people off welfare was the central value in each policy. There were other values policymakers expressed, such as "getting tough" with welfare recipients, as well as providing adequate amounts for public assistance and other concerns. These were important values, even though they were not examined in the policy analysis process. These marginal values represent the starting point of the incremental policy analysis process because, the model argues, most people understand "the problem" through their own value lens, rather than in some "objective" way.

Marginality dominates the incremental model, and it is important to understand the idea behind it. As mentioned earlier in this chapter, values are an inherent part of policy-making, and many of the most influential values at work in any policy-making process are not those specifically acknowledged in the policy, but other values, personal and more general, that rise from or become attached to the policy as it develops, as a kind of "fallout." Accommodating these marginal values—absorbing the useful ones and sidestepping the troublesome ones—enables the policy-making process to move forward practically. Table 4.3 is a schematic representation of how an analyst might perceive the incremental process and proceed through it.

Suppose that "the problem" is generally stated as poverty, and suppose that improved nutrition is a policy goal or objective. This total concept is signified at the lower right of the table as the sum of several alternative objectives (here simplified as alternative sets $W + X + Y + Z$; not ranked, unlike alternative sets A-P shown in table 4.2). Each of these alternative sets has marginal values attached to it; what they are, and how important they are in each case, is not yet known. As the incremental process moves forward, these values and their relative importance can be gradually defined. To begin with, however, the analyst may assume a hypothetical weight for the sum of all of them and set it down as a numerical score in the lower right corner, along with the total cumulation of alternatives (in the table this total sum of marginal values has arbitrarily been set as 16). When the four alternative sets are broken down into paired sets ($W + X, Y + Z$; and $W + Y, X + Z$), as shown in the right-hand column and bottom row of the table, these permutations likewise sum to 16, although it is not yet clear exactly how. In other words, in whatever order the alternatives are pursued, the ultimate result will represent the maximized values.

Note that the matrix in which the individual alternative sets $W, X, Y,$ and Z

Table 4.3: Marginality in the incremental model of policy analysis, beginning phase (numerical scores for marginal values as yet indeterminate, but total 16).

	Cost-benefit ratio		Cumulative marginal values
Feasibility	High	Low	
High	W (?)	X (?)	$W + X$ (8? + 10?)
Low	Y (?)	Z (?)	$Y + Z$ (8? + 6?)
Cumulative marginal values	$W + Y$ (8? + 10?)	$X + Z$ (8? + 6?)	$W + X + Y + Z$ (16)

Note: The number 16 represents the desired goal, for example better fed children. The goal is a combination of policy choices (represented by W, X, Y, and Z) that are presently unknown. Because we want to reach a final goal of 16, we need to go through a process of trial and error to see which combinations produce the best results. W + X, for example, may represent strong constituency support (W) to reduce welfare payments (X). W + Y may represent strong constituency support (W) for school breakfasts (Y). In this case school lunches (W + X + Y) may be the best policy even though it may be difficult to obtain.

are laid out resembles that for table 4.2—a scheme for ranking alternatives in terms of cost-benefit ratio and feasibility. (Like the matrix for that model, this matrix too could be expanded to incorporate more alternative sets and more gradations from "High" to "Low," depending on the needs of the analysis.) If the analysis were to proceed according to the behavioral model, as in table 4.2, alternative set W would be the obvious best choice. However, the incremental approach may begin at any point, probably with one alternative set, but perhaps with two or more, and then go on, adding new alternatives, perhaps dropping an alternative that did not work. As experience accrues, the analyst can begin to assign relative weights to the marginal values associated with the alternatives. These can be adjusted to greater or lesser scores as the picture becomes clearer. Emphasis given to the alternatives associated with these values could be adjusted accordingly.

Initiating small changes that affirm the choices that achieve marginal benefits

The analyst thus becomes engaged in efforts to discover a combination of values (or choices) that will achieve the overall goal ($W + X + Y + Z$). More than any other, this phase of the model requires considerable skill on the part of the analyst to keep the analysis from becoming simply a trial-and-error exercise. In order to pinpoint and implement the choices that do clarify what it takes to achieve the policy goal, the analyst must know about (a) values, or normative positions reflected in or by the alternatives, (b) the substantive elements of the policy itself (the subject matter), and (c) information and data relevant to understanding how the small changes might operate.

The values inherent in normative orientations to problems and potential solutions are a focal point of the model. In fact the whole model is concerned with values:

> Suppose an administrator is given responsibility for formulating policy with respect to inflation. He might start by trying to list all related values in order of importance, e.g., full employment, reasonable business profit, protection of savings, preventing a stock market crash. Then all the possible policy outcomes could be rated as more or less efficient in attaining a maximum of these values. This would, of course, require a careful inquiry into values held by members of society and an equally prodigious set of calculations on how much of each value is equal to how much of each other value.[15]

The analyst must be able to identify and account for the values represented by the alternatives, even though it may not be possible to calculate how they relate to each other. This requires facility with the policy sector under consideration. A history of how present policy has developed, including an assessment of which kinds of problems have been important to which people, will shed considerable light on the normative issues involved. For example, the proper treatment of mental illness is a long-standing mental health problem. A history of mental health policy reveals that there has been a consistent tension between two basic solutions to the problem: treating patients in mental hospitals and treating them outside formal institutions in social centers in their own communities, a strategy that originated in Dorothea Dix's work in the 1850s. Drug treatment, mental health clinics, halfway houses, and many other community-based mental health policies that have evolved over the years all reflect values based in deinstitutionalized care. Thus it is safe to assume that any acceptable mental health alternative would have to include some attention to deinstitutionalization in order to gain any public acceptance.

To assist initiation of small, marginal choices, the policy analyst needs substantive knowledge of the policy field. An analyst who uses the behavioral model will probably learn about the policy environment while engaged in problem definition, but the analyst who uses the incremental model begins to operate within a policy field without an explanation of the makeup of the prob-

ithout substantial preliminary knowledge, the analyst would be unable to suggest which choices would or would not maximize benefits, and the whole incremental process would deteriorate into a meaningless trial-and-error process.

Finally, data are essential to the initiation of small steps that affirm the policy choice. The analyst simply must have some knowledge of the status of the people who will be affected by the policy, and of how they will be affected. In particular, the analyst must discover which policy choices would combine values for different groups of people. For example, efforts to release the currently hospitalized mentally ill may place a heavy strain on local community resources for housing and other life management activities; on the other hand, developing mental health services in community-based agencies may not tax federal resources as heavily. Information about the people who are particularly affected by a policy is necessary to understand how small marginal choices might connect and produce an overall policy. For example, if most people in a community's mental hospitals are more than 65 years old and have no family ties, a policy emphasis on deinstitutionalization would yield very different results than if these patients were mostly working-age males with prolonged stress reactions from prior military service.

Accelerating the choices that have produced positive ends and decelerating the negative choices

Lindblom's orientation to policy analysis is instructive here again:

> Making policy is at best a very rough process. Neither social scientists, nor politicians, nor public administrators yet know enough about the social world to avoid repeated errors in predicting the consequences of policy moves. A wise policy-maker consequently expects that his policies will achieve only part of what he hopes and at the same time will [not] produce unintended consequences he would have preferred to avoid. If he proceeds, through a succession of incremental changes, he avoids serious lasting mistakes.[16]

Lindblom calls this approach one of "successive limited comparisons," because a policy is achieved in increments as small elements of it are adopted and modified to fit the circumstances. Here again, policy analysis has a more significant role than might at first appear. This is not a random, trial-and-error effort, where the analyst suggests one option, then another. Rather, successful analysis requires consistent monitoring and evaluation at each step to assess the extent to which the incremental changes do, in fact, achieve the expected results.

The policy analyst may engage in small social research projects during this part of the process to ensure that the positive choices stay on target and the negative choices are eliminated. As this phase progresses, the marginal values become clarified. In table 4.3 which represents the process at the outset, the marginal values are left unspecified. The $W + X$ figure could be, say, 8 or 10; the $Y + Z$ figure could be 8 or 6; $W + Y$ could be 8 or 10; and $X + Z$ could be 8 or 6. Suppose (see table 4.4) that during the adjustment process the marginal value of $W + X$ can be pinpointed as 10. This means that the figure for $Y + Z$ must become 6. In this manner the cumulative marginal values gradually become clarified, and from these it in turn becomes possible to see what weights can be attached to values associated with individual alternative sets $W, X, Y,$ and Z. Notice, too, how the cumulative marginal values determine limits for the weights of the values that can be proposed for the individual sets. In table 4.4 the weight for either W or X cannot be greater than 10 (because $W + X$ has an associated weight of 10), and if the score for X is 10, the values for Y will have to be scored as 0, in which case (now adding downward rather than across) the score for Z would have to be 10 as well. The scores in table 4.4 are midrange numbers filled in to give an impression of how the cumulative choices, once determined, force the choices in the individual cells; they are not absolute numbers that would apply across the board in real applications of the model.

Suppose that the incremental combination of $W + X$, $Y + Z$ seemed to be working in the right direction. Further incremental choices could be made accordingly in terms of the individual alternative sets. In the end, in the hypo-

Table 4.4: Marginality in the incremental model of policy analysis (later phase, with possible arrangement of scores for values).

| | Cost-benefit ratio | | Cumulative marginal values |
	High	Low	
Feasibility High	W (4)	X (6)	W + X (10)
Feasibility Low	Y (2)	Z (4)	Y + Z (6)
Cumulative marginal values	W + Y (6)	X + Z (10)	W + X + Y + Z (16)

thetical case shown in table 4.4, X would turn out to have the greatest weight as a single alternative set, even though it has a less advantageous cost-benefit ratio than W. Hence X would become a main thrust of policy, despite its less than "ideal" configuration in terms of the behavioral model—a not uncommon situation in public policy-making. Under the incremental model, however, the final policy choice becomes a product of finding the right combination of choices that maximizes marginal values.

Combination of choices that produces incremental results consistent with the goal becomes the policy

The policy becomes evident as it is put in place, gradually, piece by piece. Table 4.4 demonstrates that theoretically alternative set X would be the best policy with high feasibility and less than optimal cost-benefit ratio, W might be chosen, even though its value is less, in order to provide both high feasibility and high cost efficiency. Hence it may happen that, as with the behavioral model, ultimate choice in the incremental model may not lie with the alternative that is apparently the "best" in theory. Lindblom explains why this may be true:

> If [direct] agreement on policy as a test for best policy seems a poor substitute for testing the policy against its objectives, it ought to be remembered that objectives themselves have no ultimate validity other than [that] they are agreed upon. Hence, agreement is the best policy in both methods [the behavioral and the incremental]. . . . In an important sense, therefore, it is not irrational for an administrator to defend a policy as good without being able to specify what it is good for.[17]

The policy analyst must carefully monitor the progress of these incremental activities throughout this final stage of the incremental model. The analyst must also be able to present a clear statement of the policy; during the incremental process a number of policy elements will have been attempted, some discarded, some modified, as the final policy takes form. The ultimate policy may represent a large departure from the original position that prompted the first marginal decision. In the end, to recall our ongoing example, it may turn out that providing an adequate diet to people in poverty requires not just food stamps (in whatever way they may be allocated) but a program of education in nutrition.

T HE VIEWS OF THOSE AFFECTED by the problem, the views of those who make policy as well as of those who might carry it out, and the views of various groups that might have connection with the policy are all accommo-

dated by the incremental model. The individual increments of poli
test the strength of values inherent in different normative views of th ,--------
against standards for policy choice such as feasibility and cost-benefit ratios.
Policy choices are made marginally and are based on the strength of the values that operate; these choices are gradually adjusted to approximate an ultimate choice that meets the values and the standards demanded by the policy
sector itself. And because this incremental process ensures agreement among
concerned parties by the time the final policy is realized, the chosen policy by
definition becomes (in Lindblom's view) the best policy. By contrast, in the
behavioral model the best policy is, in theory, the policy objectively determined, even though in practice the best policy may be reached less rationally.
In any event, the culmination of the behavioral model is the designation of
ranked alternatives; the policy choice itself still has to be made and implemented. Policy generated under the incremental model may have superior ap-
peal or utility because it becomes implemented as it is being made.

Consider an example from the Aid to Families with Dependent Children
(AFDC) program. A behavioral policy analysis would probably reveal that
poverty among many AFDC families is due to inadequate child support
payments; the resulting policy would encourage strong efforts to implement
support collections. An incremental model would probably reveal that unemployment among AFDC mothers causes their poverty; work-training and
work-placement policy would be developed from this model. The work-
training program would have high feasibility but low cost efficiency; it
would be implemented as a part of the policy analysis. The child support policy would have high feasibility and high cost efficiency, but upon implementation would conflict with values of various interest groups. Hence the
ultimate policy choice of the behavioral model might, in reality, be relatively
closer to that of the incremental model. This combination of "trade-offs" is
exactly what underlies the drastic welfare policy changes now under way
(see chapter 6).

Policy analysts often compare the incremental model unfavorably with the
behavioral model, preferring the behavioral model for its more systematic approach to analytical tasks. The incremental model also receives negative criticism for its apparent trial-and-error approach and its emphasis on marginality.
On the positive side, the incremental model manages the difficult problem of
addressing values, which in most policy development are likely to be the basis
for choice even when an analysis purports to be "value-neutral." And because
the incremental model approximates the policy-making process, it provides
significant guidance for decision makers, particularly when only small differences exist among alternatives.

For example, in 1985, 1986, and 1987, Congress and President Reagan had difficulty coming to agreement on a budget—a not uncommon situation in federal government. In 1987, however, everyone was in relative agreement about acceptable alternatives, and the choices at hand did not represent major differences. All parties agreed that the deficit should be reduced, that spending should be reduced and taxes raised, and that Social Security benefits should be protected. The disagreements were over the degree of choice, not the choices themselves. Review of additional data may have given greater clarity to the issues, but it was only by small changes, represented by shifts in value positions over how much to control which areas, that enough agreement was reached to achieve a budget.

The Criteria-Based Model

If the behavioral model and incremental models of policy analysis represent opposite ends of a continuum, the criteria-based model marks a midpoint. This model offers the analyst both a full consideration of possible alternatives and, at the same time, engagement with dominant value positions. The model is developed from the methods of policy analysis used by the Congressional Budget Office and refined by the Institute for the Study of Child and Family Policy at the University of North Carolina.

Defining the problem with respect to policy alternatives available for dealing with it

Like the incremental model, but unlike the behavioral model, the criteria-based model begins with a limited range of analysis. The problem definition stage is concerned only with available alternatives for resolving the problem, rather than all alternatives that are theoretically possible. Framing the problem in this way may limit problem definition, but the procedure quickly brings into focus the problem's normative orientation and channels consideration toward those elements of the problem that seem possible to resolve. For example, only about 40 percent of all children living in single-parent, female-headed families receive the mandated amount of child support from their absent fathers. Consequently, many such children are poor. Theoretically, an unrestricted definition of this problem might lead to consideration of such alternatives as limits on procreation, or even infanticide.[18] On the other hand, defining the problem at the outset in terms of tightening enforcement of court orders, improving collection mechanisms, and establishing the paternity of all children limits the way the problem is defined but sets out the major normative themes. The tightened range of alternatives focuses the problem's normative orientation. In this

92

example (see table 4.5) it is well known that high value is placed on an absent parent's responsibility to support his or her children.

Establishing universal and selective criteria for ordering the alternatives
Once the normative positions in the problems are clarified by alternatives, the value positions become apparent. The model engages two types of values— universal and selective—in the process of analysis. These values are called criteria. *Universal criteria* represent value positions that should receive consideration in all problem definition and policy analysis. *Selective criteria* represent value positions with particular relevance for the problem at hand. Thus, for example, to the extent that child support is defined as an issue of collecting support payments from absent parents, parental responsibility becomes one of the selective values in the policy analysis. A full configuration of criteria and possible alternatives is suggested in table 4.5.

Table 4.5: A sample outline of how the criteria-based model might treat the problem of insufficient child support.

	Selected policy alternatives			
Policy criteria	Increase welfare payments	Collect more child support	Establish paternity	Incarcerate nonsupporting fathers
Universal criteria				
Equity				
horizontal	low	high	high	high
vertical	high	high	—	medium
Efficiency criteria	high	medium	low	low
Nonstigmatizing	low	medium	varies	low
Personal preferences	low	varies	varies	low
Selective criteria				
Parental responsibility	low	high	high	high
Adequacy of funds	medium	high	low	low
Ranking (1 = highest)	2	1	4	3

High: alternative maximizes this value
Low: alternative minimizes this value
Medium: alternative neither maximizes nor minimizes this value
Varies: impact varies among population subgroups

93

The analyst's knowledge about the policy environment greatly aids the successful completion of the first two stages in this analytic model. This knowledge helps suggest the alternatives that frame problem definition, and it also determines the selective criteria against which the alternatives will be analyzed. Knowledge of the policy environment also clarifies the meanings that attach to the universal criteria. For example, the universal value of personal preference has a different meaning in child support policies from what it does in mental health policies. In child support policy "personal preference" may refer to how money is obtained; in mental health policy the term may refer to a patient's choice of whether or not to accept treatment. Thus, even though they must be considered in every analysis, universal criteria have specific connotations that must be carefully defined in relation to the particular problem at issue.

Gathering data

Gathering data is necessary to determine the costs, benefits, and feasibility associated with each alternative. This data-gathering proceeds along the lines of the behavioral model. But in contrast to the behavioral model, where all subsets of each alternative are examined, analysis in the criteria-based model examines only the data that are relevant to each criterion. For example, in the first column of table 4.5, the cost of increasing welfare benefits to unsupported children and the feasibility of achieving that increase are examined (first item) to determine whether one proposal would promote one value (criterion) of equal treatment for affected parties—"horizontal equity" in table 4.5. The number of unsupported children might be counted, and the amount of dollars to provide them with at least a poverty level of living would be projected. The resulting information would determine whether the alternative (increased welfare payments) could be expected to maximize the value (equal treatment). A similar set of data would be collected and examined for all the criteria under each of the alternatives.

Weighing costs and benefits of each alternative against the criteria

The cumulative results of this analysis give a comparative view of the extent to which a particular alternative would maximize all or some of the criteria. For example, in table 4.5, data may indicate that increased welfare payments would be a very efficient but not very equitable way of improving child support; in contrast, improving child support collections might enhance parental responsibility but be less efficient in providing funds to unsupported children.

Table 4.5 permits the use of a weighing system that could provide marginal totals for policy decision makers: a high, low, medium, or variable weight is assigned to each criterion under each alternative, as determined by the analysis. Table 4.6, an example of a criteria-based model used by the Congressional Budget Office, weighs criteria against the alternatives by including the costs in each of the cells.

Recommending the alternative that maximizes the criteria

The criteria-based model permits the analyst to point out which alternative maximizes the greatest number of values; it also allows the analyst the option of presenting several alternatives that variously maximize the values that the decision maker favors. For example, in table 4.6 the analyst often notes that if the policymaker wants to apply a particular criterion (that is, maximize a particular value), a particular alternative could be selected. In this way the policymaker can review several possible alternatives in terms of both cost-benefit relationships and value-maximizing positions.

THE CRITERIA-BASED MODEL represents something of a compromise between the behavioral and incremental models, with respect to both problem definition and value management. Using criteria (values) to limit the examination of alternatives is consistent with a normative examination of problems and their consequences. The model also allows decision makers to see clearly the costs, benefits, and feasibility of maximizing particular values. Thus a policymaker has a good picture of the consequences of a particular choice, but the choice itself is not directed by the analysis. This feature circumvents the problem of friction that often develops between analyst and policymaker when the behavioral model is used as an analytic tool, friction that is often resolved in the application of the incremental model by giving very limited authority to the analyst.

The criteria-based model also encourages decision makers to examine their own biases about alternatives and to review a number of alternatives that might more effectively maximize their values. For example, some policymakers might insist that putting parents in jail is the only way to resolve the problem of nonsupport. But table 4.5 shows that this alternative has very weak potential for dealing with the problem. If, however, the policymaker continues to insist that parental responsibility only comes about by incarcerating parents (a value position), the policymaker can still maximize this value (responsibility) and choose an alternative that has better potential for dealing with the problem, such as improving child support mechanisms.

The criteria-based model further makes it possible to focus the analysis, depending upon the intergovernmental framework for policy implementation. As

Table 4.6: An example of the Congressional Budget Office's criteria-based policy analysis model.

Selected characteristics of recipient households in current major housing assistance programs, 1977[1]

Household Characteristics	Section 8 New construction substantial rehab.	Section 8 Existing housing	Public housing	Section 235 Original program	Section 235 Revised program	Section 236	Rent supplements
Average family income[2]	$4,376	$3,506	$3,691	$8,085	$11,532	$6,285	$3,544
Annual family income (as a percent of all households)							
Below $3,000	27.7	37.3	35.4	NA	NA	NA	NA
$3,000 to $4,999	39.0	38.6	32.6	NA	NA	NA	NA
$5,000 to $6,999	21.6	16.0	15.4	NA	NA	NA	NA
$7,000 to $9,999	10.0	7.1	9.6	NA	NA	NA	NA
Above $10,000	1.7	1.0	6.9	NA	NA	NA	NA
Percent of all households with some welfare income	16.2	26.7	42.6	NA	NA	NA	NA
Percent with minority head	27.7	29.8	62.9	NA	23.0	NA	NA
Percent with elderly head	42.9	33.4	35.8	NA	2.1	26.0	31.0
Percent with handicapped member	2.0	2.3	1.2	NA	NA	NA	NA
Household size (as percent of all households)							
Single person	43.1	36.0	33.3	NA	NA	NA	NA
2-4 persons	50.9	53.3	45.2	NA	NA	NA	NA
5-6 persons	5.4	8.4	14.6	NA	NA	NA	NA
7 or more persons	0.6	2.3	6.9	NA	NA	NA	NA

1. Data for Section 8 are as of June 1977; data for public housing, the original Section 235 program, Section 236, and rent supplements are as of September 1977; data for the revised Section 235 program are as of December 1977.

2. Figure reported is the mean family income for the original Section 235 program, Section 236, and rent supplements. Median family income is reported for Section 8, public housing, and the revised Section 235 program.

Source: U.S. Congress, Congressional Budget Office, "Alternate Approaches for Housing the Poor." Washington, D.C., 1978, p. 87.

pointed out in chapter 3, categorical grants and block grants differ considerably with respect to the conditions that influence how they are carried out. Categorical grants are more tightly targeted while block grants provide greater implementation discretion. The criteria model offers the opportunity to consider implementation differences by specifying the extent to which policy will be analyzed with a focus on universal criteria, efficiency criteria, or policy-specific criteria, as policies implemented categorically are more sensitive to effectiveness outcomes. Block grants, on the other hand, suggest a greater emphasis on efficiency criteria, as policies carried out under block-grant authority are more sensitive to efficiency issues, such as getting the job done quickly for the least cost.

Conclusion

The three methods of policy analysis and the methods of social research intersect frequently, but they are different activities used for different purposes. This chapter has given a general overview of social research and shows how it may be applied in three models of policy analysis. These three models—the behavioral, the incremental, and the criteria-based—provide a framework for analysis of policy problems presented in part 2 of this book. Because social research is very important in policy analysis, a general introduction to the kinds of social research most useful in policy analysis follows in chapter 5.

Chapter Five

INFORMATION AND DATA FOR ANALYSIS

Introduction

Chapter 4 considered three models of policy analysis. The *behavioral model* approximates approaches of social science research. It relies upon the process of analysis itself to reveal the best policy choice among a great number of potential alternatives. The *incremental model* best accommodates political decision makers, since it arrives at policy by making incremental choices about marginal issues. It appears to begin with a solution; it concentrates on values. As in the political arena, it emphasizes process and de-emphasizes traditional social science research. The *criteria-based model* blends value management with scrutiny of a narrowed range of possible alternatives. It relies on social science research to suggest the consequences of these alternatives, so that decision makers may choose what seems the best outcome according to various normative orientations to the problem.

Chapters 2 and 3 discussed the range of the policy-making processes and suggested that tasks of analysis differ depending on where information is requested within the process. To the extent that the three models described above provide different kinds of information, the analyst may find it useful to apply different models in different policy-making settings. For example, the incremental model is well suited for policy analysis work in legislatures; the criteria-based model is more useful when administrative agencies are asked to make policy that takes the form of regulations. Table 5.1 shows the relative usefulness of the three models in terms of the various policy-making structures described in chapters 2 and 3. Because the models only represent what might be done in the policy-making process, separate elements of different models may be used in a single analytic effort. Thus table 5.1, like the models them-

Table 5.1: Use of models of policy analysis in different policy decision-making situations.

	Model		
Location of policy process	Behavioral	Incremental	Criteria-based
Administrative	*M*	—	*M*
Executive	*M*	*m*	*M*
Judicial	*M*	—	—
Legislative	*m*	*M*	*M*

M = major usefulness
m = minor usefulness

selves, should not be understood as prescribing the exclusive use of a model in any particular policy-making situation.

This chapter describes appropriate information-gathering processes and how the resulting information might be used in policy analysis. Policy analysis requires the assembly, organization, and dissemination of information in forms appropriate to the policymaker's expectations. It especially requires the systematic use of information. Depending upon the normative views that attach to a problem, the policymaker's needs, and the location of the policy decision, policy analysis may use a variety of information analysis methods familiar to social science research.

Analysis Design

A policy analysis "design" is the plan by which the policy analyst decides what kind of information is necessary for a policy decision and how to obtain that information. The design must include at least three features: (1) some hypothesis about the relationship among the various parts of the problem under consideration, (2) a projection of the kinds of information necessary for understanding this relationship, and (3) a plan for how the information will be examined.

Developing the Hypothesis

To form the framework of a policy analysis design, the analyst determines the factors of the problem to be analyzed, and the relationship that exists among them. Social science research calls this activity "identifying the variables" and "speculating on the association of independent and dependent variables." For example, if poverty is the *subject* ("dependent variable") of an analysis, it becomes necessary to sort out factors associated with poverty and suggest how these factors may be linked together. The associated factors not influenced by poverty and thus independent of it (for example, low wages may exist independently of poverty) are, in social research, "independent variables." The analyst must develop information about the independent and dependent variables in order to understand the relationship between them. Like the social science researcher, the policy analyst tries to establish how independent variables affect the dependent variable. The policy analyst does not want to show a causal relationship, nor is the analyst bound by rules of statistical "significance" that must be followed in the social sciences. But eventually the policy analyst will propose alternatives that are intended to modify the independent variables in such a way that an improved or changed condition can be expected in the dependent variable as well. (Forming some hypothesized relationships between sets of variables is not an exclusive property of social science research, but its usefulness extends to all policy analysis activities.)

A policy analysis design also considers variables and information about them in both a dynamic and a static environment. Unlike social research, policy analysis seeks a change in the dependent variable, accomplished through some modification of the independent variables involved. Changes can take place in the social and political context as it presently is, or in a different context. Static considerations are suggested from the way things presently exist; dynamic considerations are suggested as part of how the present situation might be expected to change. For example, reducing poverty might be considered in the static context of underemployment, or in the dynamic context of a projected shift from a manufacturing-based economy to a technologically based service economy.

Determining the Kind of Information that will be Used

Determining the kind of information that will be used in the analysis becomes clearer as the variables are identified. Sometimes, particularly when an analyst is working with the behavioral model, new information must be developed because existing information about the variables is inadequate. In most cases, however, policy analysis uses existing information. Gathering and using this information is discussed in detail below. Recognition of the appropriate kind of information, and where it can be found, is part of the policy analysis design. Knowledge of the policy area under consideration is critical in choosing the kind of information needed for the analysis.

Policy analysis considers problems and alternatives in the public domain that are addressed by the direction or redirection of public resources. Thus, a policy design must also sketch out, in context of the problem at issue, what does and does not constitute a public interest. Public resources, whether they flow from government or private origins, are not used appropriately for anything other than public purposes, but separating public and private matters is in itself a challenging task in policy analysis. The American political and economic system has developed on principles of private enterprise tempered by contemporary views of capitalism. The policy analyst must sort among contemporary understandings of American democracy to determine the public and private sectors of activity in relation to the problem that needs to be solved.

Planning How the Information will be Examined

The design should also set forth how the information will be examined. Appropriate methods should be set out as part of the analysis design. Here again policy analysis has somewhat different objectives from social research. Policy analysis is concerned with analyzing information only to obtain clarity, not to demonstrate "statistically significant" results. The analyst seldom needs to embark on complex forms of statistical analysis; in fact complex analyses may serve to confuse or delay the decision-making process. The decision maker determines what associations are significant for policy, often on bases entirely different from those social science methods would require. Then the decision maker seeks to examine information that will describe these associations for others. For example, the association between low wages and poverty might need examination only to the point of showing that a large proportion (perhaps 50 percent) of impoverished people are working at or below minimum wage. This might not be a statistically significant finding, but to a decision maker the association of the two factors might be extremely significant in terms of policy. The policy analysis design should thus project not only the methods to be used but also the extent, or level, to which they will be applied.

This principle holds true for both static and dynamic environments. A good example can be seen in the history of Social Security policy. Developing and maintaining an adequate economic base for the Social Security Trust Fund has challenged policy analysts ever since the fund began to grow rapidly in the mid-1940s. Rather than just let funds accumulate until the huge resources would be sufficient to pay social security benefits into the twenty-first century, decision makers agreed to maintain "adequate resources" in place of a fully funded account. At first, policy analysts projected future adequate resources on the basis of static social and economic assumptions—the conditions that existed in 1940. Population growth patterns were assumed to remain constant, as were rates of economic growth. As the nation's economy began to fluctuate in the early 1970s and as the older adult population began to expand as a result of increased longevity, concerns about the financial integrity of the trust fund climaxed. In 1974, the trustees of the fund adopted a dynamic orientation to policy analysis, in which they considered the fund's resources in the context of possible changes in employment, inflation, and economic growth. Policy governing the financial stability of Social Security is now proposed around three or four different pictures of what conditions might be in twenty-five years, rather than on conditions as we know them today. Moreover, the depth of analysis of this information deals with different percentages of change in the three base measures. But though the Social Security Administration is capable of presenting a complex array of statistical information, and often does so for research purposes, the level of information examination for forecasting the fund balances is kept very straightforward.

A Policy Analysis Design Model

A policy analysis design represents a plan by which the entire analysis will proceed. Taking into account the location of the decision-making process, the design is based upon a prior understanding about the parts of the problem and upon assumptions about how those parts fit together. It anticipates a series of policy alternatives that will modify the independent variables as they act on the problem. It identifies the boundaries of appropriate public responsibility. It states the extent to which alternatives will be considered in a present-day context or an anticipated state of affairs. It sets forth the methods and limits of data analysis. Settling these issues of analysis design will probably suggest what approach is most appropriate to the subsequent work of analysis itself. This approach can be determined by considering how the models of policy analysis would apply to the task at hand.

Table 5.2 depicts a sample policy analysis design, with poverty as the subject. In this particular policy analysis five independent variables and five dependent variables are to be considered. The hypothesis suggests that each of the dependent variables may be a product of some or all of the independent variables. The choice of policy domain helps pinpoint which of the dependent and independent variables are the most appropriate for strong public commitment of resources and which may be amendable to shared public and private efforts. All the variables except out-of-wedlock births, single-parent families,

102

Table 5.2: A sample policy analysis design, on the general subject of poverty.

Hypothesis	Domain		Information		Examination	
	Public	Private	Existing	New	Static	Dynamic
Independent variables						
Low wages (a)	X		X		X	X
Racial discrimination (b)	X	X		X	X	
Poor education (a)	X		X	X		X
Children born out of wedlock (c)		X		X	X	X
Single parent families (c)						
Dependent variables						
Poor nutrition (a)	X	X	X		X	X
Lack of money (a)	X		X		X	X
Poor housing (b)	X		X	X	X	
Sickness (a)	X	X	X	X	X	X
High minority birth rates		X	X	X	X	X

a, b, c: Examples of possible associations between variables.

and high minority birthrates have significant elements in the public domain; poor nutrition, racial discrimination, and sickness have interlocking public and private contexts. Adequate information exists to describe some of the variables usefully, but for others, such as poor nutrition and poor education, new information will have to be amassed.

Levels of investigation and analysis and their methods are omitted from the sample design at this point. These are discussed in the last section of this chapter. Most of the variables in table 5.2 have to be examined in both a static and a dynamic environment, though something like poor nutrition might be examined adequately simply in a static state.

As shown in table 5.2, the policy analysis design suggests that low wages and poor education might be examined as combined forces that produce poor nutrition, lack of money, and perhaps sickness, and that information already exists that would permit an analysis in both a static and a dynamic environment. Single-parent families, a private-domain issue, could be examined for impact on the dependent variables relating to the public domain, but new information would be required, and the examination would have to concentrate on the dynamic environment.

Presenting such options in an analysis design facilitates the choice of a policy analysis model, as discussed in chapter 4. For example, if single-parent families are examined and decision making rests with an executive, a behavioral policy analysis model would probably be most useful, and it might open up other alternatives for analysis.

Information Gathering

Once the overall plan for the analysis has been laid in the design, information must be collected that is (1) relevant to the problem, (2) consistent with the design, and (3) appropriate to the analysis process or consistent with the chosen model. Information is needed that justifies the design decisions. In most cases social and demographic data available from existing sources are sufficient to satisfy the design characteristics. Depending upon the design, however, other information may be needed, either data that have not been collected or data that are not available in a useful form or in sufficient detail. In such situations, information must be obtained that uniquely fits the design for the analysis. Some tested methods for gathering information that are used in policy analysis work are set forth below. Sometimes, however, the analyst may have to search for new ways to obtain necessary information.

When Necessary Information Exists

Aggregate data

Aggregate data are one of the richest sources of information but one of the most difficult to use. The best and most familiar aggregate data are those collected by the United States Bureau of the Census. What is now known as the Department of Commerce was one of the original administrative departments in the fledgling American government, and it conducted the first national census in 1790. This and subsequent censuses were required by the United States Constitution as an enumeration of citizens for the purpose of apportioning the seats in the United States House of Representatives according to the states' populations.

The idea of compiling social statistics began with Herbert Spencer (1820–1903). In his highly influential work *Social Statistics* (1850), he envisioned amassing all sources of social knowledge together under a single authority. Influenced by the growing interest in social information, the decennial census enumeration began to collect more elaborate demographic information, and in 1878 the Bureau of the Census published the first *Statistical Abstract of the*

United States. This document is now published at regular intervals, and it provides standard summaries of demographic and statistical data and various forms of social and economic information from several hundred reporting sources.

The censuses, along with a wide range of other sources of aggregate data, offer a vast source of information that is extremely helpful for policy analysis. Somewhat in contrast to survey data, which provide information on particular cases, these aggregate data bring together distinct elements into a general picture in which the individual case can no longer be found. For example, distinct personal characteristics, such as age, race, and gender may be brought together into a whole that describes all persons in poverty, but a single poor individual may be quite different from the picture of impoverished persons represented by this general picture. Thus, although aggregate data by themselves or in coordination with other aggregates may contain extensive information that far exceeds that obtainable by other information-gathering techniques, they may not always define a specific problem accurately, and consequently they are difficult to use.

Because they represent a total picture, built upon a synthesis of numerous distinct elements, aggregate data may not provide sufficient detail for developing adequate policy alternatives. For example, although aggregate data on poverty give a picture that poverty is concentrated among children in single-parent, female-headed households, many poor children live in two-parent families. Many old people are poor, too, and many working adults of both genders are poor. Thus the aggregate picture often has to be broken down into its respective parts, to be "disaggregated," in order to be more useful. Disaggregation may be difficult or impossible because of the way the data were originally collected. The original collection design may not have distinguished, for instance, between working and nonworking families, so that backtracking for that purpose is futile.

Because so many aggregate data exist on so many subjects, several sets of aggregate data can often be used together in a policy analysis. For example, data on poverty and data on employment may be used together to provide more detailed information about children and poverty. Beyond the most elementary comparisons, however, combining data sets may be difficult, because similar elements in the data sets are usually not truly comparable. For example, data on poverty may count persons under age eighteen as children, whereas data on employment may count persons sixteen years and older as adults in the labor force. To use these two sets of data reliably in a close comparison, they would have to be broken down and reconstituted in some way that dealt with the sixteen to eighteen age group consistently. This might not be possible if the data were not originally collected by distinctive (one- or two-year) age groupings that could be retabulated.

The problems involved in using these aggregate data may explain, in part, why these data are infrequently used in policy analysis. Data generated by the Bureau of the Census are used extensively, but secondary analysis of the many other data sets that exist is uncommon. Rather than disaggregating such data, policy analysts and other researchers often prefer instead to develop information that is specific to the problem at hand. They are usually very generous in sharing this new information as it accumulates. The Institute for Research in Social Science at the University of North Carolina, Chapel Hill, like similar centers at most major research universities, has more than five hundred public-use data sets as part of its holdings, and through a consortium of academic institutions it can obtain electronic access to many other such collections. The Bureau of the Census itself lists more than seven hundred sources of aggregate data routinely collected by governmental agencies. Because of the unusual and presently untapped potential that aggregate data have for policy analysis, special attention is given to the use of secondary analysis in a later section of this chapter.

Social indicators

Social indicators provide another form of information useful in policy analysis work. The idea of social indicators was developed during the 1960s as a way of providing social planning information, much as economic indicators, developed by the Council of Economic Advisors, had already been developed to provide economic information as a means of monitoring the nation's economic activity. The idea was drafted into a useful form in 1966 by Mancur Olson, who served as deputy assistant secretary for social indicators in the office of planning and evaluation of the Department of Health, Education, and Welfare. These early social indicators were designed explicitly for policymakers, to lend greater visibility to pressing social problems and to provide insights about the accomplishments of various public programs. The first systematic effort to use social indicators in policy analysis, which appeared in 1969, stated its purpose in part: "Social reporting cannot make the hard choices the nation must make any easier, but ultimately it can help insure that they are not made in ignorance of the nation's needs."[1]

Social indicators were originally proposed as a standardized database of information pertinent to specific policy subjects. For example, social indicators might be developed for national health and include data about births, deaths, illnesses, time lost from work, and personal health practices such as doctor visits. These data could then be examined to reflect the status of the nation's health at a particular point in time, either as a whole or on particular issues. Later the same indicators could be reviewed, and changes in the nation's health status could be determined.

Most early advocates for the use of social indicators argued that such information also could be used to evaluate programs, on the assumption that social programs would and should affect the problem that was first measured by the set of indicators. For example, it was assumed that an expanded Medicare program would influence the health status of older people, with results that could be measured by health indicators over the course of time.

Because social indicators were proposed as a means of monitoring changes in social conditions that were influenced by the existence of various public programs, they became a popular source of information for policy analysis work. Policy analysts of the 1970s suggested that by demonstrating changes already induced by various programs—a form of program evaluation—this type of review could lead to recommendations on policy for further changes or for different kinds of programs. However, social indicators have not been able to continue to provide the kind of information that is generally useful in policy analysis. Although there is certainly a relationship between public programs, public policy, and social conditions, the exact relationship is not clear, and the exact associations may not be the same in all situations.

Deciding which data should be used to establish the indicators is also an imprecise activity. When the normative elements of a particular social condition are recognized, the development of viable social indicators is made more difficult by the necessity of accounting for value positions along with factual data.[2] Hence social indicators may provide useful information for policy analysts, but their development and application may be too complex for direct application in most forms of policy analysis.

Experiments and demonstrations

When used as part of social science research, experiments and demonstrations provide important ways of obtaining very reliable information, often at modest costs. Much information has accrued in recent decades from many small-scale social experiments. To obtain useful information for policy analysis, however, experiments and demonstrations would often have to be conducted on a scale that is impractical to implement. Because policy decisions affect large populations, experiments and demonstrations designed for direct use in policy analysis might require the collection and assimilation of huge amounts of information. Secondary analysis, that is, reanalysis of information obtained by prior experiments and demonstrations—both those conducted for policy analysis and those done for strictly scientific purposes—considerably expands the use of these data for a variety of policy analysis work.

Demonstrations are usually applications of specific research techniques to specific groups or geographic populations, without attempts to control for any exogenous outside factors. They are designed to field-test policy options, to determine how far these options may actually resolve certain problems, with an eye toward showing how something can be done. Because circumstances vary from place to place, demonstrations usually have limited applications. They do, however, generate information that policy analysts may find useful for "fine-tuning" programs after basic policy decisions have been made. They can be very useful aids to the incremental model of policy analysis.

Experiments, on the other hand, test policy applications in controlled environments. They are designed to generate information that can show whether hypotheses or assumptions about causative factors can be verified. Because the innumerable social factors that impinge on policy problems are so difficult to identify completely, much less to control, most social experiments are forced to restrict the scope of their explorative activities. Unrestricted social experiments are extremely costly and time-consuming. For example, a series of guaranteed-income experiments that was initiated in 1963 in two experimental cities in New Jersey and Pennsylvania required additional control groups in two North Carolina counties. Collecting and preparing the information obtained from the experiments in a form that could be useful to policy analysts took nearly five years. Follow-up studies designed to confirm elements of the initial experiments were conducted ten years later (1973) in Seattle and Denver. Even though the policy questions that provoked these experiments have long since been settled, these data provide a source for further study.

Demonstrations and, especially experiments, have had only modest use in policy analysis, and some social researchers believe that this form of information gathering may even inhibit policy choices. It has been observed that "none of the innovative social programs [tested by social experiments between 1968 and 1975] has yet been implemented although at least preliminary results from all these studies have been available for some time."[3] Costs, time factors, and difficulty of translating findings into useful policy may partly explain such reservations about social experiments. Some of the incompatibilities between social research and policy analysis, as discussed in chapter 2, may also explain the limitations of experimental information in policy research.

Nevertheless, more than thirty-six large-scale social experiments were conducted between 1965 and 1985, at an estimated cost of more than $1 billion.[4] These experiments have generated considerable data on important policy issues. With careful secondary analysis, those data could have long-range usefulness to policy analysis, even though their use has been modest to date. (Some of these studies are cited in later chapters of this book.)

When Necessary Information Does Not Exist

Surveys

Surveys are the most frequently used method for gathering additional information. In their most fundamental form, surveys provide a general view of the variables under consideration. For example, a survey of housing in a community may point up the general characteristics of housing and who lives where. Surveys also can be used more selectively to gather detailed information about specific factors of a general subject. For example, more specific information about the general subject of housing conditions might be obtained by surveying certain groups of people, perhaps couples with young children, to determine how housing conditions affect them. In such cases, when surveys are used to elicit discrete information, care must be taken to define the specific focus of the survey. For example, if the survey is to cover couples with young children, the analyst must decide whether all such couples should be surveyed, or only particular kinds of couples, such as families in which both parents are employed.

Thus any survey that moves beyond collection of general information must be concerned with the selection of a smaller population, or a sample, as it is usually impossible to survey the entire population of persons involved. A sample can be thought of as a piece of the whole population, but it is more properly considered as representative of the whole. As such, it may be a general representation or a specific representation. In a general representation, the sample surveyed represents the total population with respect to the information sought; this sample would probably include all types of householders in the community. In a selected representation, the sample surveyed represents a particular part of the whole with respect to the information sought—for instance, leaseholders as opposed to homeowners, or elderly householders as opposed to younger families. Care must be taken to assure that a general representation is composed of randomly selected cases and that a selected sample is carefully controlled, or balanced, so as to include only cases that match the selected characteristics.

Surveys often involve interviewing, or person-to-person exchanges between the surveyor and individuals in the sample. Because interviewers must collect exactly the same information from everyone in the sample, they usually conduct each interview according to a standardized form or questionnaire on which information can be systematically collected for later compilation and analysis. Considerable care must be taken to prepare a questionnaire that will elicit all the necessary information; if something relevant is omitted, the entire survey may be less useful than planned, or even seriously compromised.

Hence questionnaires are often pretested before interviewing officially begins, to assure that they are adequate.

Survey information is most useful when very little is known about the subject under analysis or about some of its parts. Surveys are time consuming, however, and usually expensive. Moreover, it is essential that all contacts be made as planned. Particularly in surveys that require interviewing, response rates must be large enough to ensure that the information generated does reflect reliably the characteristics of the population under examination. Repeated follow-up efforts are often necessary to obtain the information required by the survey.

When a good deal is known about a subject, surveys may not produce enough additional information for analysis, even when narrowly focused on selected populations. Other means of information gathering may be more appropriate. Surveys are more likely to provide useful information in applications of the incremental model, in which general information about the effectiveness of small choices can help guide the policy analysis process and marginal values often are not clear in the initial phases of policy development.

Need assessments

Need assessments are a popular but often abused form of collecting information for policy analysis. They are based on the idea that problems are produced by deficiencies. Something essential is presumed to be lacking. By discovering that deficiency, a need assessment attempts to suggest what might be supplied and how the deficiency might be corrected, thereby eliminating the problem. The abuse of need assessments has arisen from a tendency to assume that the circumstances that define a need are causally related to whatever problem is under study. For example, poverty is often associated with the need for jobs. Clearly there is a need for jobs. But more than half the households in poverty have at least one member employed at least part-time. Thus, although jobs are needed, the lack of jobs does not necessarily cause poverty, and more jobs may not reduce poverty.

Need assessments also suffer from lack of clarity over normative issues. Perceptions of need vary from person to person, even under identical circumstances. In other words, need is a personal impression, and comparisons of need from person to person are difficult. Given this limitation, efforts to define need in aggregate forms useful to policy analysis may be fruitless. Moreover, if preset questions are used that standardize definitions of need—such as questions about whether a person is employed or employable—an additional normative element may be added, and the replies might well be too biased to be useful analytically.

Despite these limitations, need assessments may be useful, particularly when undertaken with surveys, as a way of providing added dimensions to general information collected about a problem or a population. For example, a housing survey might be enriched by extra data about what renters identify as their housing needs, in addition to the general descriptive information amassed.

The delphi technique

The delphi technique was developed out of the Rand Corporation's research into the process of reaching decisions.[5] It is a technique for obtaining information from experts in a field in which information is being sought. The experts are assembled and asked to brainstorm the subject under consideration. The thoughts generated through this process of freely thinking about the subject are then collected in some written form. No thought is rejected, and the experts are encouraged to let down all barriers toward discussion, so that no possible view will be lost.

Once the thoughts are collected in a written form, an effort is made to organize them. As discussion proceeds, general categories become focused around which similar thoughts can be grouped, duplicate ideas are combined, meanings are clarified; specific ideas may be discussed briefly to establish their relation to the overall picture. Once the thoughts are understood better, the assembled group is asked to rank the thoughts with respect to some criterion—usually their relevance to the subject under consideration. Ranking can be done by category or by subject. Then each expert's rankings are summarized and condensed, and out of the process comes a hierarchy of statements about the subject under study. This hierarchy, with its overall ranking, then becomes the foundation of information about the subject.

The delphi technique develops information on a basis that is quite different from the information obtained, for example, by surveys. It provides a refinement of extensive information, integrated and harmonized by the experts themselves. The information thus obtained may be useful at several stages of the policy-making process, not necessarily only at the beginning.

The delphi technique is closely associated with the behavioral or rational model of policy analysis (which also has a strong history in the Rand Corporation), as both the model and the technique seek the widest possible range of views about the subject under consideration. The delphi technique is limited by the knowledge and expertise of the persons assembled. Complete information can be obtained only if that information is available somewhere among them. If those assembled do not represent the complete range of information, the conclusions reached through the delphi technique may actually misrepresent the information the analyst uses.

Although not thought of as a delphi technique, more routine consultation of experts to review a subject and provide information about it is often undertaken during policy analysis. Expert opinions not only help to clarify normative positions—as, for example, when congressional committees hear the testimony of expert witnesses—but also may provide important information about the dimensions of a problem and the likely impact of various policy choices on affected populations. Thus despite the limitations of the delphi technique for obtaining information, every model of policy analysis offers some opportunity where at least a modified version of it would be useful.

Forms of Information Analysis

Social science research has established a great variety of techniques for data analysis that are useful for policy analysis work. The techniques most useful in policy analysis are those that organize the information comparatively and can be used to support the recommendation of one alternative over another. Several warnings are necessary, however.

1. *It is not necessary to demonstrate causal relationships in policy analysis.* Establishing the likelihood that certain alternatives will produce certain results takes precedence over efforts to establish causal relationships. Most policy analysis accepts a "necessary but not sufficient" criterion as the standard for policy recommendations. For example, if policymakers want to improve the quality of high-school education, policy analysis may establish that it is necessary to improve the quality of teachers and teaching. But improving teaching may not be sufficient by itself to improve education, since many other factors, including out-of-school experiences, have an influence on the quality of education. Critics of a particular policy may sometimes want to establish the harsher standard of "necessary *and* sufficient." But even though that standard may be appropriate to some conditions of social science research, it has little usefulness in policy analysis, because it would be almost impossible to achieve.

2. *Deciding what information to include in the analysis may be difficult.* Although the vast array of available sources might seem to suggest that mountains of information are readily at hand, the analyst must make careful choices of what information will be most useful. Often the best procedure is to work backward—to try to reason what analysis would be most convincing to support one or more of the possible alternatives. For example, on a complex issue it might become obvious that policymakers would understand alternative solutions better if they were summarized in the form of ratios that could be com-

pared; the analyst could then seek information from which such ratios could be developed.

3. *Comparable units of analysis must be used.* Mixing units of analysis leads to confusion when recommendations are made. For example, at the outset of an analysis, student-teacher ratios may be used as an expression of the problem of poor education—a perfectly sound measure. But suppose the outcome is measured on different terms, such as higher test scores, also a perfectly good measure. Student-teacher ratios and test scores measure different elements of the educational process, and in different ways. The student-teacher ratio gauges the interaction between teachers and students. Test scores, on the other hand, produce a scale that shows the relative position of students with respect to each other. This confusion may be similar to saying that a basket of fruit can be had by filling the basket with oranges. Certainly, if the measure "a basket" is a general one, the basket is full of fruit. But if the basket is measured specifically, it is not filled with fruit; it is filled with oranges. And in either case, to echo the adage, one cannot reliably introduce apples into the reckoning.

THERE ARE TWO TASKS, therefore, that a policy analyst must accomplish in the actual analysis of information: (1) The analysis must examine data comparatively, usually by employing statistical analysis, to arrive at conclusions about the facts; (2) The analysis must present a picture that communicates these factual conclusions, along with the alternatives they suggest. The types of statistical analysis employed therefore often depend upon the ultimate use of the policy analysis. If in final form the facts or their related alternatives are obscure, then no matter how good the treatment of information may be, the policy analysis suffers. The analyst must take into account who is likely to use the analysis and whether the user can understand how the information has been digested and the facts obtained. The analyst must also resist the temptation to overanalyze information. Today's computer technology permits complicated statistical analysis of large amounts of information. The essential differences of purpose and method between policy research and social science must be kept in mind.

Methods of Analysis

In general, information analysis for policy-making purposes should rely on simple, generally understood methods that present clear pictures and remain within the framework of appropriate policy use. Usually, the policy analyst will restrict information analysis to (1) descriptive statistics for categorical and continuous variables and (2) simple bivariant analyses such as correlations and occasional multiple regressions.[6]

Descriptive Statistical Analysis

Descriptive statistical analysis is most frequently used in policy analysis because it provides the policymaker with easily grasped information. For example, one might have a population for which age and weight are known. This population could be described by how both variables are distributed, or by locating and describing the variability of the distribution itself, and its shape.[7] The mean (the arithmetical average of all values), mode (maximum concentration of values), and median (the midpoint value) most often provide the best descriptions of how the population is distributed.

Descriptive measures of variability of the population include the range (difference between the highest and lowest value), the variance (the extent to which all the values are close to a central value like the mean), and the standard deviation (the extent to which the variation in the distribution follows a "normal" pattern). Figure 5.1 portrays a normal "frequency distribution" (distribution of individual values) within a particular population. Note that one standard deviation includes slightly more than two-thirds of all the frequencies, two standard deviations include about 95 percent of the frequencies, and three standard deviations include almost all the frequencies. The standard deviation is helpful in describing the distribution of frequencies, as, for example, when more or fewer of the frequencies than "normal" are included within one standard deviation, or when more or fewer frequencies lie on one or another side of the central measure (see figure 5.2).

For the policy analyst this "shape" of the distribution may be of critical interest, particularly when coming to grips with issues such as possible unintended consequences from policy choices (see chapter 4).

For example, suppose figure 5.2 represents the number of poor single parents who have children in the home. In the normal distribution, the number of poor parents is evenly distributed on each side of the mean number of children per family. It would be safe to direct any policy for such a group of people at the "average case." But when the distribution is skewed to the right or the left, a policy directed at the "average case" would be less effective. If the situation were represented by the distribution skewed left (long tail to the left, hump of the curve to the right), the best policy would take into consideration poor single parents who had more than the average number of children—perhaps those with four and five children.

Distributions may not fall within a single curve; frequencies may clump at

Figure 5.1: Normal distribution of frequencies around a mean and standard deviations (dotted lines).

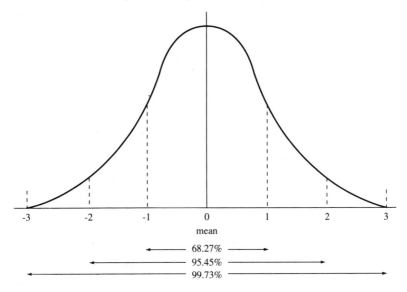

Figure 5.2: Shape of different distributions.

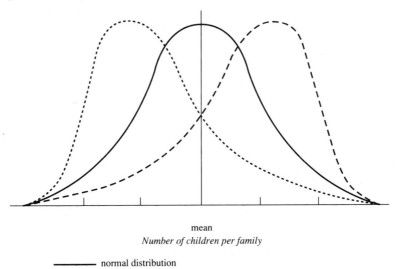

mean
Number of children per family

⎯⎯⎯⎯⎯ normal distribution
⎯ ⎯ ⎯ ⎯ skewed left (positive)
.... skewed right (negative)

more than one spot, each at a varying distance from the centerpoint. Table 5.3, for example, gives figures for an unequal distribution that would make a graph similar to a bimodal skewed distribution (a two-humped curve, with emphasis off-center), but with more detail as to exactly where the curve deviates (see figure 5.3). This extra detail has been achieved because the distribution has been divided into ten percentiles. Percentiles are often used to describe the shape of population variability. For example, if table 5.3 referred to the distribution of age of all persons in a sample population, one could say that 5 percent of people in the sample are in the first age percentile, 5 percent in the second percentile, 10 percent in the third, and so forth.

Bivariant Analysis

There are many situations in policy analysis where the effect of a single variable will suffice as the subject of study; for instance, when an analyst may need a clearer picture of poor, single parents. Much policy analysis, however, deals with the effect of two or more variables on a subject. For example, the policy analyst might be interested in both the job status of poor, single parents and the number of children they have, rather than only in the number of their children. Analysis would then have to be designed to show how the two variables interact with poverty. Social science research has devised a wide range of statistical procedures for bivariant analysis, but most tasks useful for policy analysis can be accomplished by using a few of the most common of these techniques.

One of the most powerful analytic tools for policy analysis is the *ratio*. A ratio states a proportional relationship between two factors that have something in common. A ratio states the share of something with respect to something else. For example, the numerical relationship between teachers and students can be stated as a ratio, as long as they share something in common—a classroom, for instance. A different ratio of teachers to students would exist if they were perceived as sharing something else in common, perhaps the school as a whole.

Ratios are most frequently expressed in percentages, as, for example, in statements such as, "Poverty increased from 12 percent in 1979 to 18 percent in 1985, indicating that nearly one in every five persons in this country is poor." This statement uses total population as a denominator. Even though it does not tell very much about where poverty may be most severe—among single-parent families or among blacks, for example—because the information must use a common base, the statement does provide a simple and useful picture of how poverty has changed in six years.

Table 5.3: Equal and unequal percentile distributions of 100 persons.

Percentile	Distribution	
	Equal	Unequal
1st	10 persons	5 persons
2nd	10	5
3rd	10	10
4th	10	10
5th	10	5
6th	10	5
7th	10	40
8th	10	10
9th	10	5
10th	10	5
Total	100 persons	100 persons

Figure 5.3: Graph of values shown in table 5.3.

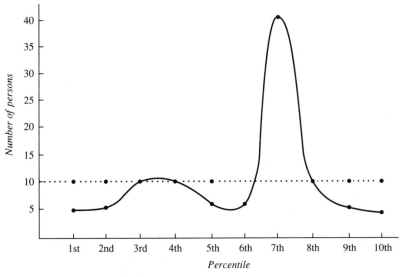

- value for each percentile
- —— unequal distribution
- ···· equal distribution

117

To be usefully compared, ratios must be based on the same denominator. A very common type of ratio in policy research uses increments of population as a denominator—for example, the number of births or deaths per 1,000 persons, frequently called the "birth rate" and "death rate." Simple ratios of this kind can be very informative, as comparisons of sets of them can present a composite portrait of a particular condition. For example, using 1,000 persons as a uniform, or common denominator, the rate of births, deaths, accidents, severe illnesses, visits to doctors, and number of days spent in hospitals can be considered together to learn something about the quality of health in the nation.

This picture may be too imprecise, however, because it deals with a general population. The analyst might need to know more about the quality of health among special populations, for example, the poor. To do so, new common denominators would have to be found in the data, perhaps based on all persons below a certain income, or all persons who received welfare assistance. Unfortunately, for reasons inherent in aggregate databases, creating these more precise ratios may prove difficult, because it is difficult to identify an appropriate common denominator. And of course, ratios with different denominators should never be compared, for that creates a false impression.

Ratios constructed from the outset with denominators other than the general population may be more useful in policy analysis work. For example, ratios of poor children (numerator) per single-parent family (denominator), or poor children per school district, and so forth, could present fairly specific pictures of children in poverty.

Ratios are often compared in policy analysis when they should not be. They should not be presented so as to imply that two variables consistently affect a third when that consistency may in fact not exist. For example, suppose that time spent in the hospital is greatest among older people, and that high percentages of older people leave the hospital with improved conditions; nevertheless, comparing the ratios of hospital days per person for groups under and over age sixty-five as a way of describing the overall quality of health among older people may have very little meaning and may even distort the picture. On that basis it might seem that hospitalization is the best way to provide the best health care for older people. Common sense should guide the choice of ratios to be compared.

Also widely used in policy analysis work are *correlations*, which show how two or more variables are associated, without implying that they are causally related. An analyst often needs some idea of how closely factors such as work and poverty, for example, are associated, or correlated, and whether they correlate negatively or positively. Figure 5.4 portrays a simple representation of a positive correlation between weekly income and number of hours worked: for

Figure 5.4: Sample correlation of weekly pay and hours worked per week.

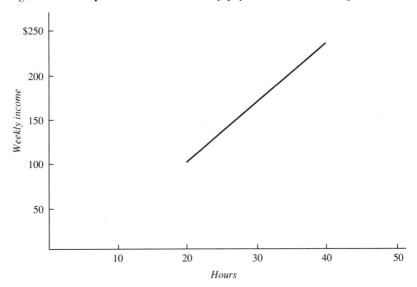

each increment of increased work there is a corresponding incremental increase in wages. A typical negative correlation would show one variable increasing as the other decreases.

The strength of a correlation may be gauged by determining its "correlation
coefficient," r. An r value of 1.0 would characterize a perfect positive correlation; that is, for each unit of movement in one variable there would be a similar and steady movement in the other variable(s). An r value of zero would
indicate that there is no correlation between variables, that is, that they do not
interact. The positive correlation between work and wages shown in figure 5.4
seems to be strong, but it is not perfect.

The coefficient r is derived on the basis of the individual numerical values
in the data. If these values are plotted out on a graph, they probably will not
make a straight line but will instead form a cluster that suggests a line; the
statistician "fits" the line to the cluster by calculating r. Less scattered clusters
will yield an r closer to 1.0 (see figure 5.5). On this basis it is possible to suggest the extent to which a change in one variable is related to a change in the
other(s). The square of the correlation coefficient, r^2, indicates the degree to
which variation in one variable is explained by variation in the other(s). If
work and wages have a correlation of $r = .8$ (as in figure 5.5 sample B), then
64 percent ($.8 \times .8 = .64$) of the variability in wages would be explained by the

Figure 5.5: Comparative strengths of two sample correlations.

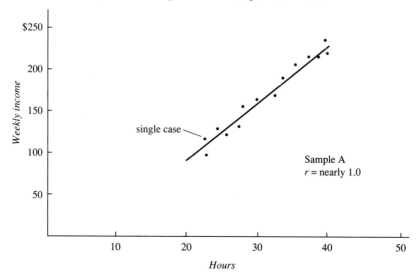

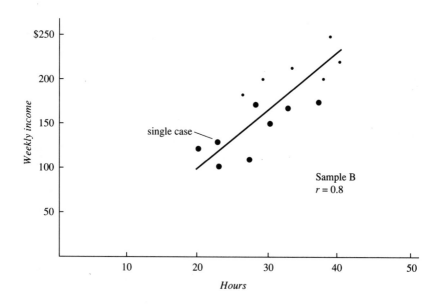

number of hours worked. In other words, although the overall pattern in figure 5.5B suggests that, on the whole, for every hour worked, hourly wages increased, this was not exactly true in every case.

In all cases the analyst must remember that correlation statistics do not imply causal relationships among variables. Common sense should also govern the choice of variables to be compared. After all, "spurious" or "nonsense" correlations are entirely possible. For example, through the same statistical techniques shown in the examples given here, a strong correlation might be demonstrated between the rising cost of concert tickets and the increasing number of people in poverty.

Much as correlations reveal the associations between two or more variables, *regression analysis* seeks to project values for one variable on the basis of known values for other associated variables. Regression analysis is particularly useful for examining more than one independent variable in terms of what influence each might have over different dependent variables. *Multiple regression analysis* should not be undertaken with more than four variables at a time.

Conclusion

Much more could be said about data analysis, but these few basic techniques should be understood by analysts so that the results of data analysis can be presented clearly. Even if not personally responsible for the statistical analysis of the data, the analyst must understand the results. Data analysis is only one step in the policy analysis process. The process begins by clarifying the variables to be studied and determining the type of information that will be useful for understanding how the variables operate. It continues by subjecting the information to a statistical analysis in order to produce information about the problem and the variables that interact in it.

The choice of a policy analysis model plays an important part in shaping the policy analysis design. The behavioral model, for example, may call for information from experiments or demonstrations, whereas the incremental model may require surveys. Similarly, analysis of information produced under the behavioral model may require complex statistical analysis, whereas information acquired by examining secondary data sources may lend itself to more descriptive methods.

A policy analysis must clarify the normative issues of a problem, isolate the important variables for study, develop the information necessary to understand how the variables operate with respect to the problem, and, finally, examine this information in such a way as to suggest meaningful policy alternatives.

The entire process cannot be prescribed in advance. The numerous ambiguities, drawbacks, and dilemmas in policy analysis and decision making mentioned in these first five chapters should reinforce awareness that policy analysis is as much an art as a science.

The framework of these five chapters has been intended as a guide to the background and general processes of policy analysis. The chapters that follow examine major policy subjects by discussing each in terms of the elements of the policy-making process as they have been described thus far.

PART II

Policy Analysis
Applied

Technical ability alone is not enough to conduct a useful policy analysis. Part I notes that understanding the particular policy sector that is the subject of the analysis is an essential part of the analysis. The chapters in part II are designed to provide the student of public policy analysis with background information in five sectors of social welfare policy: income maintenance, health, housing, children, and older adults.

These five areas have been selected for several reasons. First, each has a national policy significance that stimulates policy making across the full spectrum of policy decision making. For example, housing policy has a comprehensive national policy framework, as contrasted with education policy, which has a very small national policy framework that touches only selective parts of education policy because most education policy is local policy developed within the states' educational expectations. Second, the policy areas selected for review in part II exercise at least some policy authority over almost all social welfare policy in the nation. Depending upon what is included, policies in these five sectors govern almost 90 percent of all public domestic spending and almost 60 percent of public spending at state and local levels. Thus the reach of these five policy sectors is extremely wide. Third, these five policy sectors were selected because there is considerable definition, or agreement, about their scope. Each has been the subject of public attention for many years, and consequently their general scope has been established.

The selection of any policy area for discrete study immediately raises questions of boundaries: where does this area end, and another begin? As discussion proceeds in part II, questions may arise as to why, for instance, policies that seem to deal with children are treated under the topic of income maintenance policies, or policies directed at older people and housing seem to overlap. Some of the answers to these questions are simply matters of judgment—deciding which policies fit best with which policy sectors.

But on closer examination it is possible to talk about two major streams of social welfare policy in America. One stream deals with specific populations. The other deals with special issues. Table II.1 gives a general scheme showing how these streams overlap. Policy for the aged crosses income maintenance policy, health policy, housing policy, and other special-issue policy sectors; income maintenance policy crosses policies that are developed for special populations. The main focus of

Table II.1: Intersecting policy sectors, horizontal and vertical.

	Policy by populations					
	Aged	Children	Sick	Poor	Middle class	Rich
Income maintenance	▓	▓	▓	▓		
Health	▓	▓	▓	▓		
Housing	▓	▓	▓	▓		
Other						

▓ = Major social welfare policy areas for study.

124

analysis in part II is the social policy sectors that deal with vulnerable populations—the shaded areas of the table.

Part II begins with an examination of income maintenance policy (chapter 6), then moves to health policy (chapter 7) and housing policy (chapter 8). Chapters 9 and 10 review policy for two special groups: children and older adults. Curiously enough, no clear policy sectors exist specifically for the "poor." Policies directed at this group are highlighted repeatedly in discussion of all five policy sectors.

Chapter Six

INCOME MAINTENANCE

Introduction

In the broadest sense public policy for income maintenance covers all efforts to protect and ensure a steady flow of income for all Americans. From this perspective, earned income (usually wages) and unearned income (usually rents, dividends, and gains on capital) are subjects for income-maintenance policy, as are government-sponsored income transfer programs. Income-maintenance policy consequently overlaps with tax policy, employment policy, and wage policy, among other sectors of public policy.

The whole idea of income-maintenance policy has been emerging slowly in America. Until 1935, only about sixty years ago, there was nothing that could be called "income-maintenance policy." Instead each state, and often each locality, had specific programs that provided varied amounts of money to needy persons, under widely varied circumstances. Programs to provide money to the aged, the unemployed, the dependent child, the blind, and the sick were fragmentary activities, changing frequently, and the benefits that were provided were highly dependent on the whims of those who provided them.

The Great Depression, a period between 1929 and 1935 when as many as one-third of the labor force was unemployed, signaled the need for a change. Local agencies had no funds to distribute to the destitute, and states themselves were facing bankruptcy. Only the federal government had the capacity to intervene effectively to reverse the flow of the depression, and correspondingly, provide financial support to the millions caught up in it. The architecture of today's income-maintenance policy, found in the Social Security Act of 1935, emerged from the environment of the Great Depression (see figure 6.1).

But even the early income-maintenance policies created by the Social Security Act fell short of any comprehensive income-maintenance policy. Indeed the Social Security Act resembled a patchwork of different programs: some for children, some for the aged, some for the unemployed, and so forth, all stitched together by a single piece of legislation to resemble an income-maintenance tapestry.

Over the past sixty years this tapestry has been reworked into a more coherent whole, and the creation of an income-maintenance block grant has given even more definition to American income-maintenance policy. But even after sixty years of refinements, America's income-maintenance policy retains its two most significant original characteristics: it is a piecemeal system, and the pieces are constantly being reassembled. This chapter examines the income-maintenance pieces and in so doing provides a context for an income-maintenance policy analysis.

Figure 6.1: The architecture of American social welfare.

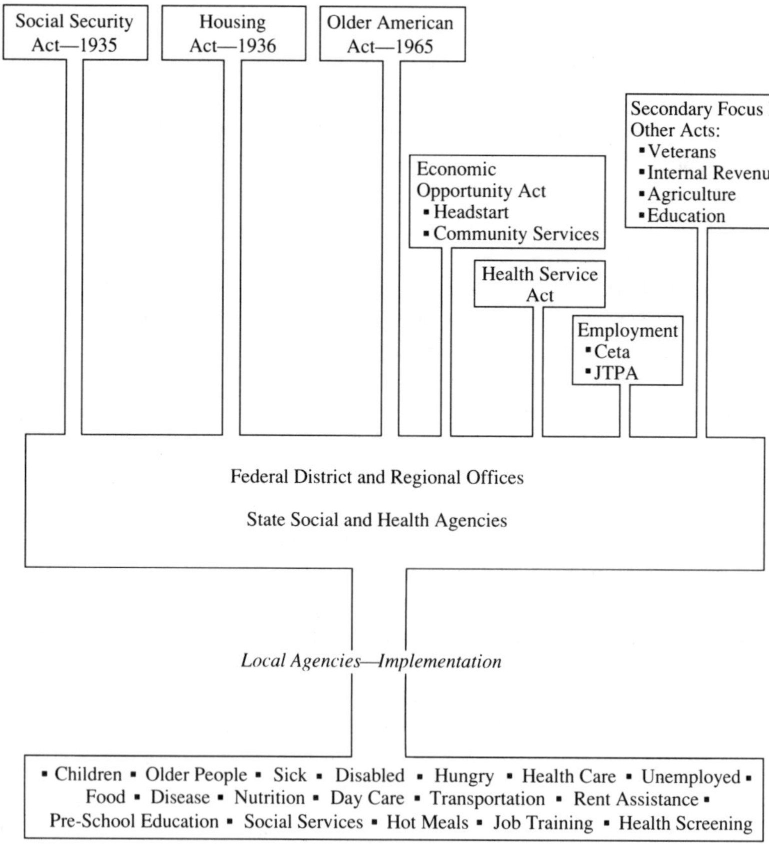

Social Security Act—1935	Housing Act—1936	Older American Act—1965

Secondary Focus In Other Acts:
- Veterans
- Internal Revenue
- Agriculture
- Education

Economic Opportunity Act
- Headstart
- Community Services

Health Service Act

Employment
- Ceta
- JTPA

Federal District and Regional Offices

State Social and Health Agencies

Local Agencies—Implementation

- Children ▪ Older People ▪ Sick ▪ Disabled ▪ Hungry ▪ Health Care ▪ Unemployed ▪ Food ▪ Disease ▪ Nutrition ▪ Day Care ▪ Transportation ▪ Rent Assistance ▪ Pre-School Education ▪ Social Services ▪ Hot Meals ▪ Job Training ▪ Health Screening

128

Though it is difficult to separate one part of income-maintenance policy from the whole for special policy focus, this chapter explores the part of income-maintenance policy that deals with the problems of the poor, the near poor, and those who would probably be poor if not protected by existing income-maintenance policy. This limited treatment seems justified in the American political and economic climate, which places a high value on economic freedom, individual self-reliance, and a market economy. The history of American (relatively) free enterprise suggests that although markets do operate effectively most of the time, for most of the people, sometimes they fail for everybody, and frequently for some portions of the population.

Because market failure wreaks havoc in individuals' lives, there have been many public attempts over the years to remedy the effects of market failure. This body of policy, often referred to as income transfers, or income redistribution, has been an enduring focus of federal policy since the Great Depression, and the passage of the Social Security Act (1935). The legitimacy of this policy is challenged constantly by changing public attitudes about the appropriate political balance between government activity and the American economic system. Over time, and in different sectors, government interaction with established economic institutions has enjoyed varying degrees of public support; the result has been a seesaw effect on the whole subject of income-maintenance policy.

Normative Issues: The Uneven Terrain of Income Maintenance

Income maintenance carries with it so many normative concerns that if agreement can be reached on a subject, relatively little additional policy analysis may be necessary. Discussion about the definition of poverty, the relationship of work to welfare, and the changing roles of women as household heads often dominates contemporary debates over income maintenance. Yet beneath these and other normative questions a protracted debate smolders over equitable and equal formulations for income allocations. *Equality* refers to evenly proportioned shares of income or other benefits, based on some measure like the amount of income or the form of the shares; it concerns like treatment of like persons in like circumstances. *Equity,* on the other hand, aims at fairness; for example, the fair value of property is its total value beyond that which is owed on it. Equity may promote equality, but it often calls for an unequal treatment of persons. Since the time of Aristotle, equity has been considered a central measure of justice.

In America, income is not distributed equally, nor would one necessarily expect it to be. An equal distribution of income would mean that income would be evenly divided: everybody, or every group, would receive the same amount. In table 6.1, which shows actual distribution of income in the United States over twelve years, it is obvious that each 20 percent of the population does not receive 20 percent of the total national income.[1]

This information leads to several observations. First, though unequal distribution of income might be accepted as inevitable, one in which the highest fifth of the population receives ten times more than the lowest fifth does not seem equitable. Second, the relative shares of income have not changed much over a twelve year period. However, the changes that have occurred shift more income from the poorest to the richest, while the middle remains about the same. This does not seem fair either.

Any income-maintenance policy of any significance will have the overall effect of shifting the distribution of income. That is why equity and equality are such strong features of debate in income-maintenance policy. To be equitable requires greater equality; and greater equality will require a redistributed income profile in America.

On the surface at least, equality in the matter of income maintenance is measurable, that is, amenable to statistical monitoring. Equal income maintenance would mean providing the same amounts to people in the same circumstances. However, measuring equality of income is complicated by the different units of "income" that can be used in the measurements. One common measure is the flow of income, as in monthly earnings or in income from investments. But subsidized medical care, gifts, disability allowances, fringe benefits, reduced taxes, and similar goods can excite extensive debate among policymakers about the type of income that should be counted—the *numerator* of income measurements. Defining the *denominator,* equality in income

Table 6.1: Distribution of money income among American families.

	Percentage of total national income			
Portion of population	**1980**	**1985**	**1990**	**1992**
Lowest fifth	5.3	4.6	4.6	4.4
Second fifth	11.6	10.9	10.8	10.5
Third fifth	17.5	16.9	16.6	16.5
Fourth fifth	24.1	24.2	23.8	24.0
Highest fifth	41.6	43.5	44.3	44.6

Source: Statistical Abstract of the United States (1987), Table 733; (1992), Table 704; (1994), Table 716.

maintenance, can have similarly far-reaching implications. Individuals, couples, households, and families may all serve as units of measure. Determining equality of income statistically thus requires many choices, not only about the monetary units that reasonably may be applied but also about the units of population to which they might apply.

In discussions of income-maintenance policy, equity often seems opposed to equality. To be fair to those in poverty, for example, often means redistributing income to them, and those who pay for this redistribution often complain that they are treated unequally by tax laws. In the case of poverty, equity may be valued over equality. But in other matters of income policy, like taxes, equality may be valued over equity. Thus many fundamental normative issues have been raised as a means of harmonizing tensions over issues of equity. Though very important, these normative concerns are not always visible as open issues in debates on income-maintenance policy. For example, interest in equity becomes less visible when the issue is poverty versus work, even though it lies just beneath the surface of debate. If a person does not work, the fairness of income maintenance becomes confused with feelings about the fact that the person does not work. Wage earners often ask, "Why should I support them if they do not work to help themselves?" This question ignores the problem of fairness to people who, though willing to work, cannot find jobs or must consent to take work that pays too little to be worthwhile.

Although equality and equity constitute the broad normative framework for deliberations on income-maintenance policy, several more specific normative dimensions find expression in policy analysis. These more specific normative issues eventually provide operational clarity to equality and equity. They answer questions about how equality and equity can be achieved through a variety of policy options that can be examined through policy analysis. In the American system, for instance, capitalist ideology drives most of the normative debates over income-maintenance policy. Capitalism values hard work as the means to economic independence. The work ethic is valued highly in America, and this ethic often suggests that poverty is the result of not working or not working hard enough. This is why it is difficult to analyze income-maintenance policy in the normative context of equality and equity without a specific focus on the interrelationships of poverty and work. This is why, "Why should I support them if they do not work to help themselves?" remains such a vexing question to many Americans.

The following are the most significant normative issues raised by income maintenance for people in poverty:

1. *Measurement of the poverty level.* Should a mathematical measure be established, or should poverty be defined in relation to individual conditions?

2. *Elements of the poverty measure.* Should in-kind benefits and non-wage income (for example, Social Security) be included in the measurement, or should only earned income be included?

3. *The form of income maintenance.* Should both cash and in-kind benefits be distributed, and, if so, in what proportion to each other?

4. *The unit of distribution.* Should income maintenance be made available to the family, or to the individual? How should a family be defined?

5. *The distribution of the income-maintenance burden.* Should it come from general revenue taxes, or from other contributions (such as Social Security), and, if both, in what proportion?

The following are key normative issues raised by income maintenance and work:

1. *Work and welfare.* Should welfare be given to people who work but do not earn enough by working?

2. *Work in place of welfare.* Should welfare be used to enforce work and discourage dependency?

3. *Work incentives.* Should incentives, such as child care, be given to support some kinds of workers? All workers? Should these work incentives be counted as welfare?

4. *Ability to work.* Who is capable of working, and who determines this? For example, should teenagers be expected to work?

5. *Availability of work.* Should people be required to work at low-paying, dead-end jobs that have little social usefulness?

6. *Work and other values.* Should rewards be given to those who do work, such as retirement benefits, paid vacations, free medical care?

Many of these normative issues that direct the development of income-maintenance policy emerge from the political economy of American capitalism, and they have become institutionalized in American economic activities. Inheritance taxes and progressive income taxes, for example, institutionalize efforts to achieve equity over equality, whereas laissez-faire capitalism and the market system institutionalize efforts to achieve equality based on individual effort. It is impossible to propose income-maintenance policy that does not account in some measure for the range of normative issues that have become enmeshed in the present political economy.

Examining Normative Issues
Measuring Income

Measuring income is complicated by several issues: "earned" versus "unearned" income, the value of in-kind benefits, and the establishment of standards to judge income adequacy. Usually income from wages, or "earned" income, provides the base for these measurements. Income from investments and annuities, including Social Security and retirement income, government transfers (welfare), and gifts and savings as liquid and nonliquid assets (wealth), constitutes "unearned" income. Unearned income is extremely important to some groups of people, particularly older adults, even though it is not usually part of the way income is measured. However, an important paradox emerges when these forms of "unearned" income, such as dividends and private insurance premiums are used to calculate eligibility for public programs, such as Supplemental Security Income. Obviously, any income measurement such as a poverty index must take into account what is measured. Because earned income is more likely to be used in income measures, groups that rely more on unearned income may seem less well off financially than they actually are. On the other hand, some forms of unearned income are not available for everyday living purposes; in that sense people with a lot of unearned income may be, practically speaking, worse off than those who have little.

A second complication is the difficulty of assigning value to in-kind, or nonmonetary, products. What is the value of housing, medical care, or day care? And, because these products substitute for income, should they be considered as income for purposes of income-maintenance policy? Older people who own their homes may be considered to have a form of income substitute. Similarly, workers who are given health care benefits by employers conserve personal funds they otherwise might spend for these purposes.

In-kind benefits are distributed very unevenly throughout the population. For example, total federal government spending for all social programs, including cash and in-kind programs, when added together is more than enough to raise the poor above the present poverty index. In 1993 the Congressional Research Service compiled information regarding cash and in-kind income-maintenance programs using information from the U.S. Census Bureau, the Budget of the United States, and various sources of agency expenditure reports, from both federal and state government. In this report only 23.9 percent of all income-maintenance benefits were provided in cash for the FY 1992 reporting period. The remaining 76.1 percent of need tested income-maintenance spending was through various in-kind programs, with medical expenditures leading the list with 456.2 percent of all means tested welfare expenditures.

The share of cash expenditures as a portion of all income-maintenance expenditures has been decreasing over the past 25 years, while the share of in-kind benefits has been increasing.[2] Table 6.2 shows these trends.

About 93 percent of all poverty families receive some form of income tested income maintenance support in both cash and in-kind benefits. The Earned Income Tax Credit (EITC) has become the greatest source of cash benefit for both male and female-headed poverty families, but the value of this cash benefit varies for both family types. The various forms of income-maintenance cash and in-kind benefits provided to male and female-headed poverty families by type of program clearly indicate the value of in-kind income-maintenance assistance (see figure 6.2).

Income adequacy is a third problem that makes measuring income difficult. What may be adequate for one person in one place is not necessarily adequate in another context. In general, determining adequacy of income represents an effort to apply standards to fiscal measures. These standards may vary greatly depending upon who is asked to apply them. Standards for adequate income as applied by the social worker, the businessman, and the welfare recipient would probably vary considerably—an apt illustration of the saying, "reasonable people may reasonably disagree."

Adequacy is an important consideration in formulating income measurements themselves. Income measured as "family" income may appear adequate

Table 6.2: Composition of need-tested benefits.

	Percentage share of total aid					
Form of aid	FY68	FY73	FY78	FY83	FY88	FY92
Medical aid	29.8%	29.3%	29.0%	33.2%	38.4%	46.2%
Cash	46.7	37.6	29.1	26.8	26.6	23.9
Food benefits	5.5	10.4	11.1	14.8	12.4	11.8
Housing	4.9	9.1	8.7	9.8	8.6	7.1
Education aid	5.3	4.9	5.1	6.0	6.8	5.5
Jobs/training	4.7	2.7	11.6	3.6	2.2	1.9
Services/other	3.1	6.0	5.1	4.2	3.8	2.9
Energy aid	0	0	0.3	1.6	1.2	0.6
Total	100.0%	100.0	100.0	100.0	100.0	100.0

Source: Vee Burke, "Cash and Non-Cash Benefits for Persons with Limited Incomes: Eligibility Rules, Recipient and Expenditure Data." (Washington, D.C.: Congressional Research Service), September 1993.

Figure 6.2: Cash and noncash* welfare benefits received by poor** families with children, 1991

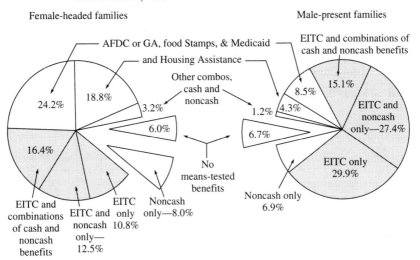

* Cash welfre benefits shown are: Aid to Families with dependent Children (AFDC) and General Assistance (GA). Noncash benefis shown are: Food Stamps, Medicaid, and Housing Assistance.
**Poor before receiving cash welfare

▨ Receives Earned Income Tax Credit

Source: Vee Burke, "Cash and Non-Cash Benefits for Persons with Limited Incomes: Eligibility Rules, Recipient and Expenditure Data," (Washington, D.C.: Congressional Research Service), September 1993.

even when individuals' income in that family is inadequate. Income measured over the course of a year may fail to show inadequacies during layoffs or seasonal periods of unemployment. Income measured over a lifetime will probably fail entirely to show a true picture of adequacy. The way income is measured may change the policymaker's view of income adequacy. Income-maintenance policy may change while the resources any given individual may possess remain constant.

Work and Income-Maintenance Policy

Work is a primary measure of personal value in American society. "What do you do?" is often the first question asked of a new acquaintance, and the answer may determine the future course of the friendship. Work also establishes a dividing line in income-maintenance programs. *In the United States, six of the eleven most costly welfare programs are available to people who do, or have, worked. The other five are available to people who do not, or have not, worked.*[3] Furthermore, considerable effort has been devoted to finding answers to questions of whether welfare discourages people from working and whether work eliminates the need for welfare. Empirical evidence from one of the most comprehensive social experiments ever undertaken shows that adequate income maintenance does not significantly discourage people from working.[4] But even though this and other evidence is clear, the contrary normative view prevails. Most people still believe that income maintenance erodes the recipient's willingness to work.[5]

Income-maintenance policy is often criticized by those who think that welfare payments replace work. Yet the vast majority of those in poverty are much too young, too old, or too sick to work. Depending upon how poverty is measured, about 70 percent of all persons in poverty are unable to work. Even so, half of those in poverty have at least one family member working at least part time, and two-thirds of these are working full time.[6] Thus there is no strong empirical evidence that income maintenance comes at the expense of work initiative.

There are several important permutations of these issues. The appropriateness and type of work, the value of work incentives, and the treatment of women are important work-related questions that affect income-maintenance policy.

Appropriate work

Those who do not work are faced with constant pressure to seek work whether it is appropriate work or not. Inappropriate work often includes jobs for which people are poorly educated, jobs that are not economically feasible, and jobs that have no future. People in poverty who are not working usually have limited skills and poor motivation, whereas most of the jobs that are available usually require some skill and strong motivation. Hence most of the jobs that are available are not appropriate for most welfare recipients. Job creation and job training for low-income people can be expensive undertakings. Capital investment of $10,000 to $15,000 to develop a single position may take as long as five years to begin to show profit. Training for the job can cost another $5,000 to $10,000 over a five-year period. Jobs that do exist for low-income people are often dead-end jobs: seasonal work, part-time jobs, or "spot" employment opportunities. Moreover, taking or keeping many of these jobs may be too expensive for a poor person. Lacking in medical and fringe benefits, requiring transportation to and from worksites, and usually devoid of arrangements or subsidies for child care, these jobs may not pay enough to make them worthwhile.

Putting a poor person to work requires difficult and costly supporting policies—perhaps more costly than providing income maintenance. Before income-maintenance policy could incorporate a work policy, considerable development in employment policy would be necessary. The Family Support Act (welfare reform in 1988) which created the Job Opportunities and Basic Skills (JOBS) training program proposes to put welfare recipients into jobs that require millions of dollars up front for basic education, for example, before job searching can even begin. Establishing a livable minimum wage, ensuring fair-employment opportunities for all, creating and maintaining public-sector jobs, protecting the authority of organized labor, and reforming the tax laws to protect the wages of the low-income worker would be necessary before a synthesis between work and income maintenance could be achieved. For example, a working mother with two children would have to earn approximately $6.16 per hour at a full-time job to stay out of poverty. These earnings would not cover work-related expenses such as child care and transportation. Present minimum wage is $4.25 per hour.

Work incentives

Although the major incentive for working is its immediate financial reward, nonmonetary rewards can provide powerful work incentives. Nonmonetary rewards help to define higher quality work. Medical and child care benefits, paid vacations, employer-sponsored recreation opportunities, attractive working environments, employer-subsidized travel (business trips), company cars, and club memberships may equal or even surpass money income as considerations for accepting a particular job. The most powerful work incentive may be income protection in retirement through employer-subsidized pension plans, personal savings, and Social Security (employers are required by law to pay half their employees' Social Security taxes). These forms of work incentives are completely consistent with institutionalized capitalism, and for the most part they reflect an American compromise between equity and equality. But work *dis*incentives are more likely to enter discussions of income-maintenance policy. Punishments, in the form of reduced benefits, seem to prevail when public income-maintenance policies are proposed, in contrast with the positive work incentives created in the private sector.

Treatment of women

Treatment of women has greatly complicated the relationship between work and income-maintenance policy. In both single-parent and two-parent families, mothers are expected to provide primary care for children, but in low-income families and particularly in single-parent families, women are also expected to provide primary financial support for their children as well. To such women work presents a serious ideological conflict. On the one hand, Americans generally believe that work should be an option for women with children; but for a large number of women, and for all poor women, work outside the home for wages is a necessity. In all these cases, child care must be arranged if the mother is to work, but child care resources are scarce, costly, and unappealing, often making work outside the home seem even more unattractive. As with work incentives, income-maintenance programs that are directed at working women, such as the Aid to Families with Dependent Children (AFDC) program, seem to criticize mothers for not working and penalize them with low financial payments—even though others in upper-middle-class families are often praised for staying home with their young children.

Single parent families

Single parent families, particularly when headed by a woman, are highly vulnerable to poverty and consequently likely to need income maintenance. Table 6.3 shows the percentage of families with children by family type and poverty status. The District of Columbia leads the list of states by far, with over 53 percent of all families with children headed by a single parent; 47 percent of these families are headed by a single female. Also high on the list are Mississippi (28 percent), New York (26 percent), Michigan (26 percent), Florida (25 percent), and New Mexico (25 percent).

Eight out of ten (81.19 percent) of all single parent-headed families with children are likely to be poor in New Hampshire, followed by 78.78 percent in North Carolina, and 78.59 percent in Maine. Unquestionably, single parent

Table 6.3: Percent of poverty rate by family type and state.

State	Male head	Female head	Both	Both in poverty
Alabama	3.14	20.06	23.20	73.31
Alaska	5.80	16.01	21.81	57.04
Arizona	5.47	18.78	24.26	59.15
Arkansas	3.41	17.99	21.40	75.10
California	5.55	18.30	23.85	54.60
Colorado	4.32	17.98	22.30	65.68
Connecticut	3.12	18.30	21.42	72.72
Delaware	4.12	17.79	21.91	74.70
District of Columbia	6.01	47.03	53.03	68.53
Florida	4.81	20.24	25.05	75.38

Table 6.3: Percent of poverty rate by family type and state. *(continued)*

State	Male head	Female head	Both	Both in poverty
Georgia	3.58	21.28	24.87	69.77
Hawaii	4.45	13.30	17.75	60.30
Idaho	4.17	13.44	17.61	63.49
Illinois	3.68	19.03	22.71	65.06
Indiana	3.89	17.08	20.97	70.36
Iowa	3.34	14.55	17.89	75.81
Kansas	3.58	15.29	18.87	70.19
Kentucky	3.28	17.15	20.43	72.83
Louisiana	3.91	23.81	27.72	66.02
Maine	4.22	16.25	20.47	78.59
Maryland	4.16	20.19	24.36	70.61
Massachusetts	2.95	19.66	22.61	73.24
Michigan	3.89	21.74	25.63	69.05
Minnesota	3.61	14.97	18.58	73.42
Mississippi	3.72	24.05	27.77	68.14
Missouri	3.59	18.14	21.73	72.48
Montana	4.47	16.22	20.69	66.74
Nebraska	3.28	14.93	18.21	69.75
Nevada	6.44	19.04	25.47	74.30
New Hampshire	3.92	13.19	17.11	81.19
New Jersey	3.58	16.81	20.39	70.91
New Mexico	6.50	18.59	25.09	57.45
New York	3.93	22.32	26.25	65.80
North Carolina	3.73	19.35	23.08	78.78
North Dakota	3.06	13.07	16.12	70.99
Ohio	3.65	19.22	22.87	67.55
Oklahoma	3.74	17.55	21.29	70.85
Oregon	5.43	17.45	22.88	72.23
Pennsylvania	3.70	17.01	20.71	70.36
Rhode Island	3.58	19.03	22.61	72.97
South Carolina	3.60	20.72	24.31	69.41
South Dakota	3.67	14.27	17.94	65.99
Tennessee	3.46	19.49	22.95	75.78
Texas	3.85	17.64	21.49	55.43
Utah	2.85	12.89	15.74	54.20
Vermont	4.92	16.36	21.28	74.76
Virginia	3.56	16.93	20.49	73.74
Washington	4.86	17.57	22.44	69.16
West Virginia	3.60	15.49	19.09	65.46
Wisconsin	3.62	16.77	20.39	66.49
Wyoming	4.42	14.78	19.20	69.45

Source: U.S. Bureau of the Census, *Statistical Abstract of the United States* (1990).

families are likely to be poor families, giving rise to the great concern for the relationship between family composition and poverty status in contemporary income-maintenance debates.

Income-Maintenance Policy and Issues of Implementation

Normative issues raise a number of important questions about the implementation of income-maintenance policy. Who should receive what kinds of benefits? Should these benefits be provided directly, in the form of cash payments, or indirectly, via in-kind benefits or special tax treatments? Cash benefits are praised for their flexibility and the autonomy they allow recipients. In-kind programs target the use of resources and often contribute to the national stock of the benefit being used; for example, providing housing as a means of maintaining income requires that housing exist or be created so that it can be provided. Special tax treatments likewise have a targeting influence on public benefits. The tax law that permits homeowners to deduct mortgage interest from their federal tax liability was designed to stimulate private home ownership; exempting older adult homeowners from property taxes encourages them to maintain an independent (noninstitutionalized) life-style.

Issues of implementation also arise when it becomes useful or necessary to assign a cash value to in-kind benefits. In 1993 the Congressional Research Service estimated that 6.2 million families with children had pre-tax cash income (including income from AFDC and General Assistance and Supplemental Security Income) but still remained below the poverty line, for a poverty rate of 21.1 percent families in poverty. If the value of food stamps, free and reduced school lunches, rent subsidies, and medicaid were counted as cash, the poverty rate would drop 5 percentage points to 16.1 percent. Of the approximately 35.7 million poor persons in 1991, 73 percent lived in households that received some form of income-maintenance cash or in-kind benefit. Accordingly the value of all benefits for all persons would reduce the overall poverty rate for all persons to 9.2 percent.[7]

But cash distributions and in-kind distributions are difficult to equate in income-maintenance policy analysis. They represent separate distributional choices; some people are benefited by one, others by another. Most in-kind programs are restricted to specific groups of people. Public housing, for example, is reserved for the poor who need housing, but not for the homeless. The food stamp program is available to households, not necessarily to families. At first low-income households were required to purchase stamps with cash, at which time they were given "bonus stamps." But very poor large families frequently did not have sufficient cash to make the purchase, and consequently they tended to avoid using the stamps. This selectivity of in-kind programs limits their usefulness as alternatives to income maintenance. Spurred by the 1995 welfare reform debates, food stamps are moving toward becoming a direct cash supplement.

Questions about implementation also arise in debates over who the distributing agent should be: the states and localities, or the federal government, or some combination of public and private agencies? Chapter 3 discussed the structural, political, and economic complexities inherent in America's vertical policy framework. Because of the limited federal authority for public spending, income-maintenance policy is particularly sensitive to vertical distributional bottlenecks. To develop its income-maintenance policy, the federal government has been confined to social insurance programs and a grant-in-aid mechanism. The social insurance programs receive their authority from the federal government's constitutional right to tax citizens for the special, precise purpose of creating a government-backed insurance program. These revenues constitute a special fund and must be used for the purpose of benefits for unemployment, retirement, and permanent disability. They cannot be used for other purposes; the complete elimination of these programs would not help reduce the national debt or assist federal support to other programs because if these insurance programs were discontinued, so would the special taxes that fund them.

Issues of equality and equity are enmeshed in distributional questions. To the extent that the federal government is the distributor, and to a lesser extent as the states are, equality becomes the norm, and equity is more difficult to achieve. The social insurances are a good example of the application of the principle of equality. Workers are taxed the same, and their benefits are determined by the same standards. A form of equity is achieved in Social Security because benefits are determined on the basis of individual earnings. But equality challenges equity in the broader sense, for the very richest retiree still collects Social Security and at a very high rate even though the benefits may be taxed.

Equity is more easily obtained when choices about distribution are closest to the users. It is easier to decide what is fair when considering a particular person, in a particular situation, at a particular time. Nevertheless efforts to achieve equity in this manner have often caused mischief, as some particular situations have been decided not so much on the basis of what was fair, but in terms of achieving compliance with ideologically based behavioral norms. The history of income-maintenance policy development so clearly illustrates the problems inherent in obtaining equity that equality—and consequently federal standards—has most commonly become the basis for distributional decisions.

Income-maintenance policy then is layered with overlapping normative issues that stem from inherent conflicts between equity and equality. The range and complexity of these many normative issues greatly complicate the task of policy analysis, since policy decisions are often made on the basis of normative issues that cannot be easily analyzed. For example, the question of whether mothers should work or stay home and care for children would be difficult to answer in terms of empirical information, and more likely would be decided on the basis of attitudes about mothers. Normative decisions about what is considered income, or what levels of existence constitute poverty, similarly must often be made without empirical guidelines.

Because so many value choices must be made about income-maintenance policy, policy analysis in that field must account for a wide range of marginal decisions that may direct which course the analysis takes, as well as that of subsequent decision making. Because these normative questions require complex political choices, the incremental model may offer the best framework for analyzing income-maintenance policy. The major normative questions would become the criteria against which different alternatives could be examined. This analytic framework is represented in table 6.4.

The Background of Income-Maintenance Policy

Since about the middle of the nineteenth century, debates over the normative issues relating to income maintenance have fixed with some certainty the public responsibility for income-maintenance policy. Presently "poverty" is officially defined or bounded by a poverty index based on income, most likely from wages. Public responsibility for the portion of the population that is not eligible to work—namely, children, older people, and the sick—begins at the level of the poverty index (the "poverty line") and moves down the scale, in most situations, to bring the recipient up to that level. At present, income-maintenance policy generally treats in-kind benefits as a separate question, although in some cases their cash value is taken into account, thus blurring the distinction. Income-maintenance policy also equates work with rising out of poverty. When this equation does not work well in particular cases—as with working mothers—a variable definition of poverty often emerges.

The poverty index is one measure of income used in income-maintenance policy discussions. This measure counts cash income from earnings, interests, and rents, and by calculating what a family needs to live on, establishes a line that says if a family has less than this amount, it is a poor family. Table 6.5 provides information about the poverty index for the previous six years. Each year the poverty index is adjusted for increases in costs of living. From this information it is possible to see that even in applying such modest income levels to determine who is poor, about 17 percent of all Americans have incomes below those set forth in table 6.5 and are therefore considered to be living in poverty.

Most income-maintenance policy has generally become the responsibility of the federal government, and most is authorized by the Social Security Act, first legislated in 1935. The broad federal income-maintenance authority granted in

Table 6.4: Normative issues and possible alternatives in income-maintenance policy.

	Income type		*Work*			*Distribution*	
Normative issue	Cash	In kind	Required	Incentives	Training	Federal	State/local
Income-maintenance policy							
Management issues							
Elements of measurement							
Form of income maintenance	X						
Units of distribution							X
Distribution of the burden						X	X
Income-maintenance and work							
Work and welfare				X			
Work instead of welfare			X				
Work incentives							X
Ability to work					X		X
Availability of work							X
Work and other values						X	

Note: Using one criteria-based policy analysis framework set forth in chapter 4, the matrix would be filled in by the policy analyst. X reflects policy choices inherent in 1995 welfare reforms.

Table 6.5: Poverty Guidelines. [1]

Number of persons in family	Annual amount index	Monthly
1	$ 7,360.00	$ 613.33
2	9,840.00	820.00
3	12,320.00	1,095.00
4	14,800.00	1,233.33
5	17,280.00	1,440.00
6	19,760.00	1,646.66
7	22,240.00	1,853.33
8	24,720.00	2,060.00
Over 8, add each person	3,720.00	310.00

Income for a family of four [2]	
Year	Annual
1993	$14,350.00
1992	13,950.00
1990	12,650.00
1989	12,100.00—Census Year

1. U.S. Bureau of the Census and Department of Health and Human Services, January 1, 1995.
2. Family size usually used in poverty discussions.

1935 presented a sharp contrast to earlier public attitudes, stated eloquently by President Pierce as early as 1854, which held that all income-maintenance and other social policy was the exclusive responsibility of the states.

The Social Security Act recognized the difference between those who could work and those who could not. Somewhat in contrast with today, in 1935 there was good reason to believe that once someone found a job, the job would generate enough income to keep the worker out of poverty. This presumption gained greater support as the original Social Security Act was changed during the next fifty years and as the income-maintenance program authorized under the act matured. Specifically, Social Security and unemployment insurance, legislated in 1935, and medical insurance for the aged (Medicare), legislated in 1965, were designed to reward employment by establishing universal, government-administered programs to protect participants in the labor force against involuntary loss of wages. Income-maintenance programs for those unable to work were authorized in 1935 through Aid to Dependent Children (later AFDC), Aid to the Aged, and Aid to the Blind, and, in 1950, through Aid to the Disabled. These latter three programs were merged as Supplemental Security Income (SSI) in 1972.

In addition to the Social Security Act, significant income-maintenance policy has been established under income tax laws that provide special tax treatment for low-income families with children and families with elderly or disabled people in the home. The earned income tax credit has become an important form of income maintenance for family members who are employed at below minimum wages.

Income tax laws also provide a large tax deduction to people who own their homes (weighted toward the early years, when income is likely to be lower); but these are usually middle-income working people well above the poverty level. Thus implementation of income-maintenance policy through tax laws may more generally help people who live above the poverty line than those who live below it.

Another important issue of income maintenance arises from the Social Security Act's division of program responsibility between the federal government and the states. States are given great flexibility in administering income-maintenance programs for nonworking populations.

Under federal authority, income-maintenance programs that were funded by the categorical grant-in-aid "entitled" everyone to receive financial aid (such as Aid to Families with Dependent Children) if they met the eligibility criteria. By creating an income-maintenance block grant, nonworking populations will be more vulnerable to uncoordinated changes in eligibility criteria from state to state, and will no longer be "entitled" to support when the pool of block grant funds is spent.

The major income-maintenance programs under the Social Security Act are presented in summary form in table 6.6. Although income-maintenance policies and programs have changed considerably over the years, the normative issues that have shaped them remain. Many of the work and nonwork income-maintenance policies have been modified to bring their implementation into closer alignment with present-day understandings of those original normative issues, but few policy changes have been made to address new normative issues. For example, income-maintenance programs today continue to take form in terms of a distinction between poverty and work. They fail to take adequately into account the large number of working poor.

Table 6.6: Existing income-maintenance programs operating under the Social Security Act.

Program (title, date)	Function	Population served	Administrative authority
Social Security (Title II, 1935)	insurance	workers	federal
Unemployment compensation (Title III, 1935)	insurance	workers	federal/states
Aid to Families with Dependent Children (Title IV, 1935):			
• Assistance (Income and maintenance block grant)	assistance	nonworkers	states
• Work incentives	services	workers and nonworkers	
• Child welfare (Child welfare block grant)	services	nonworkers	states
• Permanent planning (Child welfare block grant)	services	nonworkers	states
• Child support (Title IV-D, 1974)	services	workers and nonworkers	states/federal
Supplemental Security Income (Title XVI, 1972)	assistance	nonworkers	states/federal

The Programs

Social Security

Title II of the Social Security Act is its largest and most comprehensive income-maintenance program. In fiscal year 1992 Social Security paid out $286 billion in monthly benefits to more than 41.5 million beneficiary units. Only 62 percent of these units (with 63 percent of the payments) were retired workers. Social Security also provides benefits to disabled workers, wives and husbands of retired workers, and children, widows and widowers, and parents of workers (see table 6.7). Between 1983 and 1992 both the number of beneficiaries and the payments increased for widows and widowers, reflecting a demographic shift in the characteristics of the older adult population. Social Security truly is a comprehensive income-maintenance program for workers and their families.

There has been much criticism of the Social Security Trust Fund and the wisdom of transferring large sums of money from present workers (young people) to retired workers (older people). However, the program is dynamic enough to be adjusted as these concerns become more compelling. Social Security taxes are paid into a fund that can be used only for Social Security insurance purposes. Congress decided as early as the 1940s that the Social Security Trust Fund need not hold the full contribution of each worker to his or her retirement account: in fact such a strategy would have created a socio-economic disaster because if the trust fund were to grow to full maturity, the government rather than the private sector would hold massive and disrupting amounts of capital. Thus the Social Security program became a pay-as-you-go program and an intergenerational transfer program many years ago. In other words, younger people pay the retirement costs for older people and have done so throughout the entire life of the program. However, although the ratio of persons sixty-five years old and over to persons eighteen to sixty-four years old had remained relatively constant since the 1940s, it is now beginning to change. In 1960, there were 17 older people for every 100 younger people of working age. By 1995 this had risen to 29 per 100; the relative burden across generations has increased, though not unreasonably. This ratio will become critical as the "baby boom" generation ages. Estimates range as high as 35 or more retirees for every 100 working-age younger people by the year 2000.

The Social Security program is effective. It distributes 68 percent of all income-maintenance funds of the federal government (excluding veterans' benefits). The trust fund is maintained by mandatory contributions (taxes) adjusted each year to keep the fund solvent. The tax rate itself is compared with that of other countries. The present tax rate, equally shared by employee

Table 6.7: 1992 Social Security benefits.

	Beneficiaries		*Monthly benefits*	
	Thousands	*Percent*	*Billions of dollars*	*Percent*
Retired workers	25,758	62.1	$179.4	62.7
Disabled workers	3,468	8.4	27.9	9.8
Wives and husbands	3,382	8.1	16.4	5.7
Children	3,391	8.2	13.6	4.8
Widows and widowers	5,205	12.5	47.1	16.5
Others	303	.7	1.6	.5
Total	41,507	100.0	$286.0	100.0

Source: Statistical Abstract of the United States (1994), Table 582.

and employer, is approximately 16 percent higher, rising from 10.4 percent in 1972 and 14 percent in 1985. In 1992 about 97 percent of households with an aged householder collected Social Security payments. From 1983 to 1993 approximately 23 percent of all families received some Social Security, including 31.8 percent of white and 21.4 percent of black female-headed families. Benefits are distributed via monthly checks mailed to the recipient. Social Security operates to some extent on a basis of equity, since benefits are calculated in part on the basis of previous earnings. Social Security is also efficient. Administrative costs as a portion of total program costs have remained constant at about 1.2 percent per year since the early to mid-1940s.

At present Social Security is considered to be income. It is now taxed. It is also computed as income for determining eligibility for means-tested programs such as SSI and for a variety of in-kind benefits, particularly Medicaid. All these in-kind programs are extremely important for Social Security recipients. For example, if the value of in-kind benefits is not counted as part of their resources, one-quarter of all people over age sixty-five live below 12.5 percent of the poverty level. When in-kind public support such as food, housing, and medical benefits is taken into account, this rate drops to as low as 7.7 percent, depending on how the benefits are valued. (Medical benefits for Social Security recipients are also considered separately in chapter 7.)

The adequacy of Social Security benefits is frequently questioned. Because these benefits vary with work history and are not based on need, many people who live on Social Security are also forced to rely on other forms of income maintenance. The average monthly benefit payment for 1993 was $589. The average benefit for retired workers was $653, for wives or husbands of retired workers it was $337. The average benefit of $589 per month calculates to $6,078 or $892 less than the $6,970 poverty threshold for a 65-year-old person in 1993. By contrast the average Social Security payment in 1983 amounted to $517 a year more than the poverty threshold for a 65-year-old person.

However, Social Security may seem more adequate when the Social Security benefit is compared with preretirement earnings. In general, Social Security was originally expected to replace about two-thirds of preretirement income. The other third was expected to come from the worker's savings. Social Security provides a greater share of preretirement income for low-income people than for high-income people, but still, by itself, without in-kind benefits, particularly medical benefits, Social Security is inadequate for most recipients. Social Security never was intended to carry the full income-maintenance load for retired people, and its adequacy must be evaluated against its original intention.

Work incentives play an important role in Social Security benefits. Benefits are determined by a complicated formula that is based upon average wages and the amount of time the worker was employed during which Social Security contributions (taxes) were paid. Hence both in theory and practice, stronger attachment to the labor force provides greater benefits. And Social Security benefits are paid only *after* a person is no longer working. Recipients may continue to work for wages, but in these circumstances the benefits are reduced drastically. Practically speaking, therefore, Social Security recipients do not work. Full Social Security benefits are paid at age sixty-five, and partial benefits can be received at age sixty-two. If a person chooses to continue to work past these ages, no benefits are provided until he or she decides to retire.

The adequacy and equity of Social Security are especially problematic for women. A person becomes eligible for Social Security in two ways—on the basis of his or her own work record, or as the spouse of an eligible person. In the latter capacity a recipient is entitled to benefits equal to 50 percent of the spouse's benefits. This may seem reasonably equitable, but it may not be adequate as financial support. On the other hand, because women's wages in employment covered by Social Security have traditionally been about 50 percent of men's wages, a woman's benefits, if established on the basis of her own work, are usually considerably less than a man's—which raises questions about both adequacy and equity. Moreover, women are likely to have sporadic work histories, having taken time off to remain at home rearing children; this also results in lower benefits. Several proposals (discussed later in this chapter) have been made for correcting these problems.[8] Current modes of distribution have also raised some protest; if a wife accepts 50 percent of her husband's benefit as her rate of benefit, the combined monthly benefits for the couple are disbursed in a single check, made payable to the husband.

Unemployment Insurance and Workers' Compensation

Unemployment insurance and workers' compensation were also original programs of the Social Security Act. Like Social Security, these programs were developed for those who were working to ensure an income during periods of unemployment. Unemployment insurance provides benefits when a worker in employment covered by the program becomes unemployed through no fault of his or her own. Workers' compensation provides benefits for workers who become injured or disabled on their jobs. Both programs operate under federal laws, but they are administered by the states. To fund unemployment insurance, the federal government collects taxes from employers on the basis of the amount of employment they report, and keeps these funds in accounts ear-marked for each state. States then determine the exact benefit payment when someone becomes unemployed. Benefits are distributed directly, through weekly checks.

Unemployment insurance raises several issues of equity. Most significantly, it is available to less than half of the unemployed population. In 1993, for example, when unemployment officially stood at 7.2 percent of the labor force, only 2.8 percent was receiving unemployment benefits. The explanation for this limited coverage can be traced to eligibility rules and differences in the states' administration of the program. Only workers in "covered" employment are eligible for benefits, and many jobs in which low-income people are likely to work are excluded from program coverage, for example, part-time jobs, jobs with few employees, and most types of agricultural work. Moreover, because the states have administrative responsibility for the program, different state policies govern when benefits begin, duration of the benefit payment period, and status of the recipient during that period.

Because unemployment experiences vary from place to place, benefits paid to workers can differ considerably. In 1992, for example, the average weekly unemployment payment in the United States ranged from a high of $226 per week in Massachusetts to a low of $132 per week in Mississippi. In general about 55 percent of the unemployed received some unemployment benefits in 1992.[9] This lack of equity is a serious problem, as a different real value is attached to unemployment insurance depending upon the state in which one resides. The program itself, however, is highly efficient. Administrative costs are higher than for Social Security because the program also offers employment counseling services to its beneficiaries. The cost of unemployment insurance is quite reasonable, averaging about a 2.5 percent tax per year on wages, levied on employers.

Only earnings from work are calculated in determining eligibility for unemployment benefits. A person could become unemployed, receive income from interests and rents, receive some in-kind benefits, and still receive unemployment benefits. Considering that unemployment benefits amount on average to less than 40 percent of average weekly wages, it is no surprise that in-kind benefits are very important to the unemployed. Because unemployment benefits are so inadequate when compared with regular earnings, food stamps and medical benefits under Medicaid can be especially important resources.

Work incentives are an integral part of unemployment insurance. To be eligible for benefits, an unemployed person must have worked in covered employment and must be willing to go back to work if a suitable job becomes available. Moreover, that person must have worked in covered employment for a certain number of weeks, not just for a short while, and the unemployment must have resulted from circumstances other than the person's performance on the job—such as a plant closing, or layoffs. Under such conditions, women are at a great disadvantage. They are often employed in uncovered positions, especially part-time work, and hence ineligible for benefits. If they do qualify, their weekly benefit payments will probably be quite low, since they also typically make lower wages than men.

Aiding Families with Financially Dependent Children

For many persons "welfare" means Aid to Families with Dependent Children (AFDC). As one of the programs that originated with the Social Security Act, AFDC has undergone many changes in the past sixty years. It has been one of the most controversial programs, for in one way or another, it has touched on almost all the normative issues that underlie income-maintenance policy. AFDC originated from the idea that financial assistance had to be made available to children when there were no wage earners available to support them. At that time, the strong prevailing assumption was that women were responsible for caring for children at home, and men were responsible for supporting the home and family financially. In 1935 and immediately thereafter, and particularly during World War II, it was not uncommon for men to die while still quite young, leaving their wives and small children with no easy means of support. It was presumed that in most cases employed men would be covered under Social Security and that if they died while their children were still in their maturing years, these children would receive Social Security benefits. Thus AFDC was planned as a small and temporary income-maintenance program.

But America has changed considerably since 1935. Traditional family patterns changed in the postwar era. Women were no longer expected to remain at home, but were seen as wage earners as well. Divorce became more frequent, and out-of-wedlock births increased. Blacks migrated to urban areas, leaving the protection of small communities and local farms, and urbanization required formal programs of income maintenance to replace informal and often inadequate systems of financial aid. And in the 1960s the massive movement toward equal civil rights for all minorities swelled these welfare programs, particularly AFDC, with blacks.

One stunning consequence of these changes was the increased numbers of dependent children who had living fathers who were not supporting them financially. Instead of representing a solution to the problems of poverty, AFDC came to be seen as a cause of poverty. Critics argued that the program encouraged loose sexual behavior and work irresponsibility—thus placing the issue of work versus welfare at the center of the debate.

Of all income-maintenance policies, those that supported AFDC have been the most unequal and inequitable. AFDC has operated as a state-administered, state- and federally-funded, means tested, "entitlement" program that paid a monthly benefit to dependent children and their adult caretaker(s), usually their mothers. Benefit levels have been determined according to a standard of need established by the state in which the child resided. In no state has this standard of need been based on the federal poverty index, and no state provided a benefit that matched or exceeded the poverty index. Hence from the standpoint of equality, not only were children and adults treated differently from state to state, but, also, within each state AFDC recipients were treated differently with respect to the definition of their needs. The standard of need set by each state ranged from $1,513 per month for a one parent family of three in 1993 to a low of $312 for the same kind of family in Missouri. Again, using 1993 as the comparison year, the maximum monthly AFDC grant ranged from $120 in Mississippi (constituting an amount equal to 13 percent of the poverty threshold) to $923 in Alaska (constituting an amount equal to 79 percent of the poverty threshold). In 1993 42 states' AFDC payments were less than 50 percent of the poverty threshold and when adding the value of food stamps to AFDC, Alabama and Mississippi's combined payments were still less than 50 percent of the poverty threshold.[10]

Over the years AFDC had been changed to strengthen the relationship between work incentives and provision of benefits. In 1967 women who did not have preschool children at home were encouraged to work, and in 1969 they were required to work before they would be granted benefits. The 1988 welfare reform legislation (JOBS) required all able-bodied adults who are included in an AFDC household work or receive job training and/or education. By 1993 only about 39 percent of the AFDC families were mandated to participate in this program, and only about 20 percent of this group actually did participate.

The experience with work incentives in the AFDC program demonstrates how difficult it is to resolve normative issues about work incentives in general. Most data suggest that work programs have been ineffective at getting people off welfare and making them more attractive employees. Appropriate jobs for poorly educated and poorly trained people are very difficult to sustain at rates of pay that will offer sufficient incentive to chose work over welfare. They pay poorly, usually have no fringe benefits, tend to be harsh forms of work, and more than likely are temporary. To obtain such work a woman must find child care and carry out other household duties, in addition to working. The rewards are seldom greater than the costs of going to work. Moreover, social science research suggests that mandatory work training programs may have a negative effect in helping people get work. By contrast, when well-paying jobs are accessible, people are eager to work.[11]

Confusion over women's roles is at the heart of many work-incentive issues. After World War II, social values strongly supported women as wives and mothers who created and maintained a home for their husbands and children. These values protected the option that mothers with dependent children could choose to remain at home or to seek employment. But a gradual alteration in the value of women as homemakers, the increase in single-parent, female-headed ("nontraditional") families, and an increase in out-of-wedlock births combined to change attitudes toward women in general and led to punitive treatment of low-income and black women in particular. As various work-enforced programs were appended to the AFDC program under Title IV of the Social Security Act, poor women were no longer given an option to stay at home and care for their children. Growing evidence suggests that few women have role options anymore, and poor women in particular are forced to play the dual roles of homemaker and breadwinner. The Congressional Research Service predicts that by the year 2000 the number of children with two parents and a mother in the labor force will decrease to about 30 percent.[12]

The pending welfare reform does away with many of the older program criteria established for the AFDC program. States would receive a block grant of federal money for income maintenance to spend in ways the states may determine on support for those without income. Only modest federal restrictions would apply to the use of these federal funds, including limitations on how long an individual may continue to receive financial support, and restrictions on the use of these funds in situations where children are born out of wedlock to adolescent mothers. Most significantly, there are proposed relaxed "maintenance of efforts" required of the states in the way these funds would be used, meaning states would be free to reduce the matching state and local funding required under the previous AFDC program if they choose to do so. Since state and local AFDC matching spending usually amounted to about one-half of total AFDC spending, without state income-maintenance contributions, income-maintenance grants to individual families would either have to be further reduced, or the number of families provided income maintenance would have to be cut drastically. Only after some years of experience will it be clear how this major policy change would modify income-maintenance policy.

Child Support Enforcement (CSE) Program

CSE was created by Congress in 1974 because of growing concern over the large number of parents who were not supporting their children financially. Complete discussion of this program is reserved for chapter 8, which is devoted to child-welfare policy. But because this program has important income-maintenance functions and because it is part of Title IV, an income-maintenance section of the Social Security Act, the program also deserves attention here.

CSE is available, through the parent under whose care they live, to children who are not receiving child support, whether they receive AFDC or not. Because almost two-thirds of all single-parent households live in poverty and many more live close to the poverty line, better child support from absent parents could dramatically lift their income status. In 1991 there were 10,110,000 single parent families and 16,624,000 children under age 18 living in these families. Only 75.2 percent of those entitled to child support actually received any, and the average amount of child support per year was only $2,995. About $26 billion in child support was owed by noncustodial parents in 1984, and only $4 billion was collected.[13] By 1992 collections had reached $13.3 billion. Obviously, optimal use of the program would have significant consequences for government income-maintenance efforts. CSE maximizes equity, is efficient, and could provide adequate income maintenance for many families.

Supplemental Security Income (SSI)

SSI was created in 1972 under Title XVI of the Social Security Act by lumping together the original programs of Aid for the Aged (formerly Title I), Aid for the Blind (formerly Title X) and Aid for the Disabled (created in 1950 as Title XIV). These three public aid programs were means-tested programs for the aged, blind, and disabled, and, like AFDC, were administered by the states. SSI continued the tradition of income-tested programs for the same groups of people, but it shifted program administration to the federal government, which now "guarantees" a basic monthly benefit to every aged and disabled person who meets federal criteria of eligibility. Because the federal benefit level is so low, states may decide to supplement this benefit if they choose. Even though there is a maximum allowable SSI benefit, actual SSI benefit payments may not always reach this level due to the ways states supplement SSI, and due to financial resources that may be counted in determining the SSI payment. For example, in 1992 the maximum allowable SSI payment for an individual was $423 per month and $625 per couple. But actually the average SSI payments were $196 per individual and $449 per couple per month. Overall SSI provides income support at about 75 percent of the poverty level, and 79 percent of the poverty level when a Social Security payment is included.

SSI raises many questions about equity because it overlaps with Social Security. Both Social Security and SSI provide benefits to adults who are unable to work because of age or disability. In the case of Social Security, however, the benefits are paid because the recipient "earned" the right to benefits by working. SSI becomes available when an individual's financial resources are not sufficient to raise him or her above the SSI eligibility level. Because Social Security benefits are considered as income for determining eligibility for SSI, many Social Security beneficiaries find that their Social Security benefit disappears when they begin to receive SSI.

Table 6.8 displays how SSI creates a problem of equity for Social Security beneficiaries who have low benefit levels. The older person in this example essentially loses the value of private retirement income and the value of Social Security, with the exception of $20 per month that the Social Security Administration "passes through" (does not count as income). Ironically, the SSI recipient ends up still on the edge of poverty. Certainly the $440 total approaches the average Social Security payment mentioned earlier in this chapter. But 89 percent of all SSI recipients are also receiving Social Security; in these terms, their years in the labor force have no value when compared with other beneficiaries who are receiving SSI independently of eligibility for Social Security. In a perverse way, the work-earned benefits of Social Security are used under this policy to pay for the unearned benefits of SSI. SSI also has many of the same problems with equality that AFDC does, since states still set standards for total benefit payments by choosing how they will supplement

Table 6.8: Financial overlap between Social Security and SSI: An example for a retired person over age 65.

Income source	Monthly income
Private insurance policy	$ 25.00
Social security	275.00
Total income	$300.00
SSI benefit level	$420.00
Less income	-300.00
Subtotal	$120.00
Social Security pass-through payment	20.00
Total SSI monthly check	$140.00
Summary	
Social Security check and insurance income	$300.00
SSI check	140.00
Total income for individual	$440.00

SSI; despite some standardization, SSI benefit payments vary considerably from state to state.

There are no work incentives associated with the SSI program. Whoever meets its financial eligibility standards receives assistance. Largely for this reason, the program raises few questions of equity and equality in treatment of women.

Earned Income Tax Credit (EITC), Homeowner Mortgage Benefits, and State "Homestead" Exemptions

Tax credits are not usually thought of as income-maintenance programs, but they must be considered in this context for purposes of policy analysis.[14] Tax credit programs differ from those previously discussed because they provide a subsidy indirectly, through the tax codes. EITC works like a negative income tax: families with children whose family incomes fall below $23,755 are entitled to a tax "refund," even though they may have paid no tax to begin with. For example, a family with an income of $11,000 and two children may receive $2,528. This amount may also be distributed prospectively, equaling a nice supplement to monthly earnings. The 1995 Congressional Budget reductions have cut expenditures for earned income tax credit in half.

Mortgage credits and "homestead" exemptions are based on policy for housing and for aging, and hence might seem unrelated to the present discussion. However, like CSE, they have some significance as income-maintenance mechanisms that should be mentioned here. Homeowner mortgage credits were established in the 1930s deliberately to stimulate private-sector housing development by permitting a tax credit against owners' taxes on the basis of the interest paid on the mortgage in owner-occupied homes. In 1993 the value of these tax and mortgage benefits totaled $41.7 billion on average. The value of home mortgage benefits for a family earning between $50,000 and $75,000 per year amounted to $1,179 on average for each family. Over 85 percent of one estimated mortgage deduction is received by approximately 25 percent of taxpayers with incomes over $50,000. Hence such benefits most commonly accrue to upper-income people, usually in amounts greater than the average stated above. Conversely, low-income people are not likely to own their own homes, and those who do may not have generated enough related expenses to be able to use these credits against their taxes.

Though other tax incentives that serve income-maintenance functions for all taxpayers similarly offer minimal benefits to low-income people, deductions or exemptions for maintaining dependent children or older adults in the taxpayer's home do provide credits that may be critically important to some families. Mortgage benefits and dependent allowances can also have important income-maintenance consequences for independent older people, many of whom have borderline financial stability.

A number of states add to these tax credits through a series of property-tax exemptions specifically for older people. Sometimes referred to as "homestead" exemptions, they relieve older people of all or mostly all of the state tax liability on their homes. These state policies represent considerable savings for many older people and consequently are meaningful income-maintenance policies. The exemptions permit many older people to continue to live in their own homes and communities when increased taxes might otherwise force them to sell and move away to cheaper and less amenable quarters.

Focusing the Analysis

The development of income-maintenance policy provides a classic example of incremental policy building. Even though many of the individual programs seem to conflict with one another, the policies that exist offer a general normative consistency. Because these policies have been shaped over about half a century (since 1935), normative issues have been addressed by creating new programs to overlay the old; in this way, complex value-related questions have been resolved, but at the expense of a coherent set of programs. Income-maintenance policy continues to develop marginally in order to resolve constantly changing value conflicts. For example, developing income-maintenance work incentives in the face of the continued overall ineffectiveness of the AFDC program represents successful efforts to realize contemporary values through the program despite the fact that the program, by objective criteria, fails to satisfy income maintenance. These new values contrast with historical values around which AFDC policy was originally developed, namely equal access to adequate income support for all economically deprived children.

Income-maintenance policy analysis, therefore, must identify and organize normative positions and suggest which values might be maximized by adjustments to the formidable array of policies and programs that already exist. The incremental model of policy analysis offers the best guidance to policy analysis in this sector. In order to frame the policy analysis, it is important to review, in summary fashion, the major normative (value) issues and the costs and benefits of the major income-maintenance alternatives that presently exist (step 1 in the model described in chapter 4).

To condense discussion, it might be stated that the major existing normative issues surrounding income-maintenance policy are:

1. Work (labor force attachment) is highly valued.
2. Adequate benefits are valued.
3. Reasonable, straightforward program administration (i.e., efficiency) is valued.
4. In-kind benefits are important to target resources, but not valued as income-maintenance policies.
5. Equitable treatment for women that provides viable options for them is valued, if not yet well implemented.
6. Direct payments are valued, rather than forms of tax credits.

Relative costs and benefits can be assigned to the array of marginal values, as those values have potential for realization through the existing programs (step 2). A general idea of the costs and benefits of the marginal values, and how they might be realized through individual programs, has been conveyed through discussion in previous sections of this chapter. A sample scheme for reviewing costs and benefits together with programs is presented in table 6.9; a complete policy analysis would provide a more detailed expression of normative costs and benefits.

Assuming that policymakers would want to choose policies that would reduce costs and increase benefits, the costs, benefits, and programs could be reorganized as the marginal values take on greater clarity (step 3 in the

Table 6.9: Costs and benefits of marginal issues in income-maintenance policy.

Program	Costs	Benefits
Social Security	• Very expensive • Unequal treatment of women • Not means-tested	• Comprehensive coverage • Related to work initiative • Not means-tested • Fits nicely with tax schedules
Unemployment insurance	• Equality issues • Federal money, but state administration	• Related to work initiative • Adequate benefits
Temporary assistance	• Very poor benefits • Poor interface with other programs	• Partially related to work • State administration for equity • Necessary for dependent children given today's family structure
SSI	• Poor benefits • Unequal treatment of recipients	• Universal administration • Guarantees an income floor
Tax credits	• Not targeted on poor • Expensive	• Improves work initiative

incremental model). Table 6.10, which shows a partial sample incremental framework, suggests what incremental adjustments might be made, taking as baseline policy the five major income-maintenance policies and programs that presently operate. (Child Support Enforcement has been omitted here; but see special considerations of the topic in chapters 4 and 9.) Efforts to reform each of these programs would be designed to move each closer to desirable marginal value positions. Because each program has its own limitations and unique circumstances, policy modification would be modest in some cases. However, by adjusting all five policies toward the cumulative value positions, a better integrated and more consistent income-maintenance policy should become possible (step 4).

Once again, a complete policy analysis would show more detail than presented in table 6.10. The total marginal values (a–f) are those described in step 1. The cumulative marginal values represent a summary and refinement of the materials presented in table 6.9. The policy choices are matched against the marginal values. To complete the policy analysis, efforts similar to those reflected in table 6.10 would have to be undertaken for all sets of marginal values with assigned costs and benefits.

Table 6.10: An incremental scheme for income-maintenance policy analysis.

Feasibility		*Cost-benefit ratio*		*Cumulative marginal values*
		High	Low	
	High	(1) Social Security	(5) Tax credits	Equitable for income benefit distribution
	Low	(1) Social Security or (2) Unemployment	(3) Temporary assistance (4) SSI	Reasonable economic costs
	Cumulative marginal values	Relationship to work Adequate benefits	Inadequate Inequitable	(a) Related to work (b) Adequate (c) Reasonable administration (d) Connects with in-kind benefits (e) Equitable for women (f) Direct payments

Recommendations

On the basis of the data presented earlier in this chapter about the present operation of income-maintenance programs, the normative issues, and the model represented in table 6.10, it is possible to offer some recommendations for modifying income-maintenance policy.

Social Security could be expanded in its coverage and made more equitable in its allocation of benefits. Social Security is already positioned to come closest to the overall values sought. The fact that about half the poor are working at least part time, but without benefits such as Social Security or unemployment insurance, minimizes job attachment for this group of people and suggests that job attachment alone will not provide them with sufficient income protection to prevent them from dipping in and out of poverty. Expanding Social Security for the marginally employed would enhance all marginal values. Efforts to bring other groups into coverage, such as federal employees, suggest the need to expand Social Security even further.

Expanding Social Security coverage to employees who work less than full-time would also help minimize some of the inequitable treatment of women. Approximately 30 percent of all employment in the country is work that is less than thirty-five hours per week, and most of these jobs are held by women. Consequently, women are less likely to establish adequate Social Security benefits on their own; perhaps they may establish no independent benefits at all. Better coverage for women would diminish the dramatic inequities in benefit distribution.

Unemployment insurance could be expanded for the same reasons. The percentage of unemployed who are unable to collect unemployment insurance would strongly indicate that those at the lower end of the work force, who may need assistance the most, are apt to find it inaccessible. In this sense adequacy, equity, and labor force attachment are undermined by restrictions in the program. Expanding both insurance programs—Social Security and unemployment insurance—would also guarantee a base of income to the most vulnerable workers without a serious increase in tax rates, and general program adequacy could be maintained without serious tax adjustment.

Aid to Families with Dependent Children has been viewed as an income-maintenance program failure for many years, and gradually it will be phased out. Nearly 7.3 million children will continue to need financial support, however. Modifying programs that provide specifically for children (see chapter 8) may have sufficiently greater advantage than modifying income-maintenance programs in general. From a programmatic standpoint, eliminating the federal role in the income-maintenance AFDC program turns present amounts of federal funding over to the states, which are permitted to administer this element of income-maintenance policy outright. This option might improve program efficiency, but the history of AFDC suggests that such a step might make other marginal values—such as adequate benefits—even more unreachable.

Supplemental Security Income, like AFDC, has become inequitable and inadequate as a base of income-maintenance policy development. Yet the number of persons served by this program is much smaller than that reached by AFDC, and the total continues to decline significantly. At present there are about 4 million SSI recipients, 89 percent of whom are also collecting Social Security. If Social Security were improved, the SSI program could be reduced even further. Almost two-thirds of all SSI recipients are disabled workers who have achieved at least some coverage status under Social Security. Conceivably, by expanding Social Security and reducing the income-maintenance responsibility of AFDC and SSI, a federal block grant for financial assistance could be large enough for the states to provide general assistance to people not covered by the federal income-maintenance programs. If these alternatives could be harmonized with improved programs directed specifically at children (see chapter 9), considerable policy reform could be achieved.

Tax credits provide some income maintenance, but mostly for people who are working and generating sufficient income to make such credits a meaningful form of income support. Housing mortgage credits, in particular, are not very well directed at income-maintenance issues, and however necessary they may be to achieve other social goals (such as the creation of additional housing), they do not speak to income-maintenance issues very clearly. If these credits were standardized and consequently reduced in the aggregate, the savings might be diverted to more effective income-maintenance programs.

Summary

Income-maintenance policy has been focused less on the subject of income than on a series of substantial normative issues that are at the heart of American policy debates in general. Issues such as work, the treatment of women, what counts as income, and which groups should benefit from policy, all come to rest around what may be the most highly valued product of American society: money. Hence consideration of policy that protects income is crisscrossed with a great variety of issues that are expressed in money-related terms.

It is the restructuring of Title IV-A (AFDC) of the Social Security Act from the categorical form (as it was originally created) to an income-maintenance block grant that illustrates quite dramatically the relationship between policy development and normative problem definition as discussed in chapter 4. In 1935, financially dependent children were understood to result from fathers being absent from the home, usually due to the father's early death. Mothers were expected to be at home rearing children. By the 1950s, the requirement that fathers provide financial support was believed to cause them to be absent from the home, thereby resulting in financially dependent children. Thus Title IV-A was changed to make it possible for children to receive income maintenance without the absence of the father. Mothers were also encouraged, but not universally required, to work.

But the absence of (usually) fathers from the home continued, and to counter this new perspective on income for dependent children, Title IV-D was added to the basic income-maintenance program. The 1995 welfare reforms strengthen the child support enforcement program requirements considerably. However, the numbers of dependent children persisted, causing escalations every year in AFDC's "entitlement" provisions. Welfare reform in 1988 required education, work training, and work placement as Title IV-F was added to the Social Security Act. But few mothers gained employment, and most of those who did remained employed for less than a year. Under increasing presure from the states for more flexibility, combined with a changed normative view as reflected in the 1994 elections, particularly in the U.S. House of Representatives and in most states, the 1995 income-maintenance block grant reflects yet another change in the normative perspective. Instead of prescriptive federally initiated programs, income-maintenance policy now seems to be telling states and localities to do whatever they think best to reduce income dependency—a form of income-maintenance "policy" curiously devoid of policy.

The role of the states with respect to the federal government has been a particularly thorny one. The federal government has the capacity, which the states lack, to fund income-maintenance programs. But the federal government has severe constitutional limitations on how it can spend those funds. The whole history of income-maintenance policy development and implementation has thus given to state political structures a great influence over the development and administration of income-maintenance programs. This latitude accounts for a great variation in program implementation from state to state, which has inevitably led to inequality. There are advantages to state administration, but these are more obvious in policy areas other than income maintenance. To this extent expansion of Social Security, and of federal insurance programs in general, would also help to shrink state generated inequality in income maintenance.

Finally, the difficulty of connecting income-maintenance policy with policy created to assist the three most economically vulnerable populations—the aged, children, and the sick—has become an important issue in itself. Income-maintenance policy must not be thought of simply as a broad, horizontal policy directed at the poor, but as relevant for all groups, and intersecting with vertically arranged policies that deal with specific populations.

Consistent with the picture of policy intersections suggested by the table in the introduction to part II, the following chapters discuss health and housing policy as horizontal policy issues, and the aged and children as vertical policy issues. Some comments about the intersections of these policy sectors are offered in the concluding chapter.

Chapter Seven

HEALTH

Introduction

By 1991 Americans were spending more than $751.7 billion a year for health care—13.2 percent of the gross national product (GNP) almost doubling expenditures over the previous five-year period. Consumer health and health care have become a national preoccupation, from those whose medicine chests are bulging with prescriptions and over-the-counter medications, to those whose pantry shelves are equally jammed with health foods and "natural" products, reflecting a different approach but equal concern. In spite of the high level of expenditure and heightened public interest, the nation's health has not shown dynamic improvement. The death rate has remained relatively unchanged since the early 1960s, and the infant death rate has slowed its decline and even shows signs of a slight increase.

Health policy is as laden with normative issues as any sector of public policy, and in many respects health policy is intertwined with all social welfare policy. Thus health policy is enmeshed in a complex web of public issues and policies that shape both public perceptions of health and health policy itself. For example, the relationship between high health risks and current environmental conditions is well known, yet health policy continues to develop as a reaction to environmental effects rather than as a solution to them. This and other ambiguities in health policy raise questions about whether a relationship exists at all between the amount of money spent on health care and the factors most frequently associated with good health.

Normative Issues

Defining Health

A number of general normative issues cloud efforts to analyze health policy, and current definitions of health top the list. "Absence of illness" is a necessary but not sufficient definition of health for contemporary policymakers. The ingredients of a full definition of health today range from good medical care to genetic engineering, from adequate health insurance to adequate means to afford basic health care. The variety of normative issues covered by contemporary definitions of health cannot be accommodated within the scope of any single policy analysis. Understanding the underlying problems of defining health is essential background knowledge for all health policy analysis.

David Mechanic, a well-known medical sociologist, sets a definition of health in a broad context.

> In all ideas of health and disease—whether specific or more general—is some concept of normal fitness and behavior. But concepts of health, fitness, and acceptable behavior, as well as those of disease and disability, depend on the state of health institutions and health science on the one hand, and the social and cultural context within which human problems are defined on the other.

In this sense diseases are easily recognized because they do not align with assumptions that people make about the state of good health, which "has been seen as a condition of equilibrium."[1] This idea of equilibrium, so important in the early days of medical theory and practice, remains a crucial element in present-day efforts to understand health as a balance, not merely as the absence of disease.

It is therefore almost impossible to define health from a normative position without thorough examination of the entire social structure in which people interact with their environments. The most straightforward approach for policy analysis would be to assume that health policy is a composite effort to maintain or to restore equilibrium, so as to prevent or remedy disequilibrium, usually understood as disease. Thus, invariably, most definitions of *health* deal in one way or another with the idea of *disease*.

This focus on disease as a key element in the definition of health is compounded by normative approaches toward dealing with disease itself. For example, most definitions of health care emphasize *treatment* rather than *prevention* of disease. Accordingly, public efforts to restore sick people to a state of healthy equilibrium have far outweighed efforts to prevent disequilibrium from occurring in the first place. Preventing disease, however, is much more effective and much more cost-effective than treating it. Medical history of the past two centuries, especially of more recent decades, offers many dramatic examples. Most severe childhood diseases have been eradicated; smallpox, cholera, and yellow fever are almost unknown in the United States and have greatly diminished worldwide; emerging technological knowledge may permit biological alterations that would in time eradicate the more common genetically linked diseases, such as sickle-cell anemia.

Efforts to prevent disease are based on a different set of values from those that underlie efforts to treat disease. Prevention requires a commitment to the future over the present, a willingness to adjust and change certain patterns of behavior, and a dedication to improved living standards at public expense. These values may require a restructuring of individual freedoms. The values that support treatment of diseases, on the other hand, reflect more personal concerns. Treatment is more individually focused, and more consistent with values based in America's traditional ideals of individualism and self-sufficiency. Though the public may financially support the research necessary to determine appropriate preventive measures, it is often unwilling to accept the constraints on individual behavior that would implement such policy. For example, mass immunization programs remain voluntary, rather than mandatory, and even though the use of seat belts, public education about them, and the decrease in injury from wearing them during automobile accidents is well documented, the public fails to support seat belt laws on the basis that individual choice should determine whether they are worn.

The preference for treatment over prevention has led to an emphasis on *cure* rather than *care*. The normative definition of health as the absence of disease encourages medical emphasis on repair and restoration to a state as close as possible to the patient's condition before the illness occurred. Determining this prior condition is often an important measure for establishing a treatment goal and gauging its success. "Baseline" medical data generate a framework that is necessary and helpful for later medical intervention. "This is normal for you," or "This is normal for a person with your age and history," are phrases that provide guidance to treatment, starting points to look back to, and, if possible, to return to.

The idea of care, on the other hand, makes no claim for repair or restoration. The focus of care is continued maintenance at the present functional level with as much support and comfort as possible. While not in opposition to cure, care tends to emphasize adjustment to current circumstances. Care may be just as individualized as cure; in many circumstances it is more appropriate than cure. But the emphasis on cure has persisted to the point that in current usage the term "health care" usually means a series of efforts to effect a cure.

Although these normative positions on basic definitions of health and health care remain latent in policy debates, the American approach to health policy takes a fairly consistent stance. Specifically, American health policy (1) defines health as an absence of disease, though permitting considerable latitude in the definition of disease, and (2) enhances both prevention and treatment of disease, with the greater emphasis on treatment. Too often prevention carries with it restrictions on individual freedom, a price too high for most Americans to be willing to pay. Health policy oriented toward treatment supports much greater emphasis on cures than on care (see table 7.1).

Health-Care Products

Although considerable agreement exists on normative definitions of health *care,* the provision of that care can still raise difficult issues of equity, equality, and freedom of personal choice. Throughout the remainder of this chapter the usual term "health care" is used to refer to health care *and* cure as stated above.

Equity is often debated in terms of the quality of medical care received. For example, do the poor get the same quality of care as the wealthy, and should they? *Equality* is especially troublesome when considering access to health services. For example, the poor, who often do not have private physicians, may be obliged to accept emergency rooms as a primary source of care.

The various forms of public and private health insurance have evolved in an effort to deal with issues of both equity and equality by placing a third party

Table 7.1: Paradigm of health-care policy context.

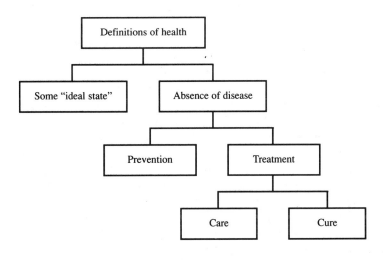

between the patient and the health system. Under this scheme, the patient deals directly with the health care provider for the service, and the provider and the patient deal with the third party to pay the cost. This separation of the individual patient from direct responsibility to the provider for the cost of services rendered has been blamed for the escalation of medical costs in recent years (a topic considered in greater depth below), but it has helped to enhance both equality of access and equity of medical care for Americans.

Preference satisfaction is a pervasive issue in health care. At one level health-care providers' preferences may underlie their reluctance to move toward more efficient approaches to health care. The private, general practitioner and the doctor-patient relationship remain the central focus of America's health-care system, even though in many situations other medical professionals may be more appropriate providers and supervisors of primary and secondary health care. For example, most medical workups for routine physical examinations are done by the nursing staff, physician assistants, and laboratory technicians. Pharmacists know more about dispensing drugs than the average general practitioner. And medical engineers are often more qualified than doctors to administer complex diagnostic and treatment procedures, maintain the complex equipment used for these procedures, and monitor and interpret the results.

From the patient's point of view, the choice of a physician to manage the requested or required care clearly maximizes personal preference. Moreover, personal choice also dictates what kind of medical interventions are necessary and desirable. Preference satisfaction becomes expensive, however, when the choice of services is removed from direct responsibility for paying for them— as is the case with health insurance. In other words, if people can choose whatever health care they want, without much concern for what they may have to pay, they may choose services that are not medically justified. Such choices accelerate the use of existing services, create demands for new services, and quickly contribute to rising costs in health care.

Preference satisfaction may be market sensitive: if more people want certain products, those products become scarcer and their prices rise to a level that balances demand with resources. Policy pressures toward equality—that is, aimed at equal access—have created an insurance system that has kept the relative costs of health care (as measured by what it costs the user) exceptionally low. On average, the individual user pays only about 9 percent of the full cost of services received; public and private insurance covers the rest. In this environment, market forces can exacerbate inflationary pressures on medical care: "The patient and his agent, the physician . . . can elect the most expensive (and presumably the best) services available—more expensive than they might elect if third party payments did not exist."[2]

Unrealistically low consumer costs for health care have been complicated by public efforts to increase the supply of health care products so that cost alone does not prevent equal access or yield inferior services. Important public policy milestones have made public funds available for constructing local hospitals and educating doctors, and publicly supported reimbursement systems (Medicare and Medicaid) have kept high-quality care within the reach of the whole population, regardless of the individual's ability to pay. Such policies both stimulate supply *and* increase demand, in an environment of third-party contracts that preserves personal preference by keeping prices to the consumer artificially low. This combination of normative choices, made in health policy over the decades since 1940, lies at the center of today's concerns over health policy and provides the basis for current policy analysis.

The Boundaries of Public Responsibility for Health Care

A clear delineation between public responsibility and private choice is an important normative issue in all policy sectors, but it has particular importance for the analysis of health-care policy. The government supports private enterprise in health care to the extent that public responsibility for health care is necessary for certain groups in the population if all citizens are to reap the benefits of a healthy society. At the same time, however, public responsibility is always compromised by private choice. Some people can always afford to do things differently. Table 7.2 summarizes the division between public and private responsibility for expenditures for certain types of health services in 1991.[3]

In that year 56 percent of total national health-care expenditures was paid by the private sector (a 3 percent reduction over 1986 expenditures), but total out-of-pocket expenditures were only 19 percent (compared to 25 percent in 1986). The remainder, almost 44 percent of national health-care costs, was paid by public funds. Most funds come from two federal programs, Medicare and Medicaid, both of which showed significant percentage increases in the past five years. This picture affirms the strong presence of government, mostly the federal government, in the provision of health-care services and financial support for health care, all of which is provided in the private sector. Government coverage and private-sector insurance payments together came to about 73 percent of total expenditures.

Table 7.2 also offers confirming evidence that health policy is inclined sharply toward treatment rather than prevention, toward cure and restoration rather than care. Excluding medical research, less than 5 percent of all health cost expenditures in 1991 were directed toward prevention. Table 7.3, which

Table 7.2: National health-care expenditures by type.

Type	1985		1991	
	millions	percent	millions	percent
Private sector				
Out-of-pocket[1]	$105,638	24.9	$144,260	19.2
Insurance premiums	133,256	31.4	244,367	32.5
Other	5,434	1.3	24,081	3.2
Medical research	377	0.1	910	0.1
Construction of medical facilities	5,489	1.2	8,193	1.1
Subtotal	$250,194	58.9	$421,811	56.1
Public sector				
Medicare[2]	$ 72,292	17.0	$122,803	16.3
Medicaid and other public assistance	43,685	10.3	104,941	14.0
Workers' compensation	8,169	1.9	17,793	2.4
Defense department	8,395	2.0	12,809	1.7
Temporary disability insurance	56	a	64	a
Maternal and child care	1,191	0.5	1,999	0.3
Public health activities	11,894	2.8	24,533	3.3
Veterans' hospital care	8,733	2.0	12,185	1.6
Medical vocational rehabilitation	264	0.1	593	0.1
State and local hospitals	7,340	1.7	12,697	1.7
Mental health, alcohol-related, and similar	3,171	0.7	5,503	0.7
Medical research	6,996	1.5	11,674	1.5
Construction of medical facilities	2,571	0.5	2,365	0.3
Subtotal	$174,757	41.1	$329,960	43.9
Total	$424,953	100.0	$751,771	100.0

1. Stated as "direct patient payments" in previous tables.
2. Medicare and Medicaid showed the largest increases from 1985 dollar-wise, from $115,977mm (27.3 percent) to $227,744mm (30.3 percent).
a. 0.008%

Source: Statistical Abstract of the United States (1994), Table 148 and (1987), Table 126.

examines health expenditures by object, shows that almost 96 percent of all expenditures in 1991 were for personal health services and supplies. More specifically, 87 percent went toward personal health care, in large proportion to hospital and physician services. Health expenditures other than services and supplies constituted only 4 percent of the total. Expenditure shares have remained constant over the last five years.

Public responsibility for intervention in private-sector activities is usually justified when markets are not efficient, as when the full price of a product is not reflected in the market price (economists attribute the differential to "externalities"). When the poor cannot get needed medical services in private markets, government intervention is justified, either through direct service programs or by providing funds so that services can be purchased. In that sense, social externalities would define situations in which the marginal costs of services must be paid by the general public for private-sector health prod-

Table 7.3: National health-care expenditures by object.

Expenditures	1985	1991
Health services and supplies		
1. Personal health-care expenses		
a. Hospital care	39.2%	38.4%
b. Physicians' services	19.5	18.9
c. Dentists' services	6.4	4.9
d. Other professional services	3.0	4.8
e. Home health care	6.7	1.3
f. Drugs	1.8	8.1
g. Eyeglasses and appliances	8.3	1.6
h. Nursing home care	2.6	8.0
i. Other health services	—	1.9
Cumulative total	87.4%	87.9%
2. Insurance administration	6.3	5.8
3. Government public health	2.6	3.2
Cumulative total	95.7	96.9
Medical research	1.7	1.7
Construction of facilities	2.6	1.4
Total	$409.5 billion 100.0%	$751.8 billion 100.0%

Source: Statistical Abstract of the United States (1994), Table 149 and (1987), Table 127.

ucts (services and materials) when it would be difficult and unwise to deny them to anyone. For example, it would be difficult and unwise to deny anyone police and fire protection and waste disposal, just as it would be unwise or impossible to deprive a portion of the population of a clean and toxin-free physical environment. In similar terms, victims of some rare or newly recognized diseases may agitate for government relief for costs of specific medicines, which are exceptionally expensive because recently developed or salable only to relatively small populations; arguments vary over whether the government should cover the loss to the manufacturer, or should subsidize individuals' payments for such medications.

Because health care is clearly a private market activity in America, public activity focuses on efforts to help those who are unable to purchase adequate medical care. Medicare and Medicaid constitute about 30 percent of all health spending. Both programs are designed to allot money to citizens to allow them to buy essentially privately determined health products. Some would argue that public responsibility should be taken a step further—that health care should be, overall, a public rather than a private responsibility. This normative position is justified to the extent that it would eliminate "externalities" as described above. However, under such conditions the public interest would be more inclined to support preventive activities, since it would cost less to supplement the private market with private funds, as is presently the case (see tables 7.2 and 7.3). On the other hand, to assert that financial support for health services should be an entirely public responsibility, despite the private nature of the current health-care market, fails to take into account the limitations that should be placed on the use of public funds. For example, should someone have the same right to public funding for cosmetic surgery as access to emergency services after an accidental injury? Except in unusual cases involving fiscal accountability or political liability—such as publicly funded abortions— the dividing line between public and private responsibility for providing health care has not been clarified in public policy.

The lack of clarity about the public role in health care has become more pronounced as government efforts have stimulated the supply of resources. For example, to answer increased demand after World War II, the Hospital Construction Act of 1946 (the Hill-Burton Act) provided federal funds to construct community hospitals. These hospitals were required to serve low-income people. Although most hospitals constructed under the act to budget some funds consistently toward services to low-income patients, no exact formulas were established, and similar policies were not included in related government efforts, such as federal funding for the education of doctors and other health professionals. Thus, without a clear policy on public responsibility for health care, the increase in supply of medical resources, combined with increased demand for the resources and stimulated by public funding, has not only caused continuing cycles of rising costs but also left public health-care policy to drift toward accommodating whatever individual preferences seemed to emerge. In a curious twist of capitalism, individual choice is no longer controlled by the market, but nurtured by apparently unlimited public support. This drift might be compared with a public policy to provide cash supplements for individual recreation, which, though intended to promote better physical conditioning, would also permit people to buy tickets to football games if they preferred.

The recent effort on the part of the Clinton administration to reform America's health-care system unexpectedly confronted a number of these discussed ambiguities. No initial thought seems to have been given to the dividing line between public and private responsibility for health care. Recognizing that health care was primarily a private market activity, President Clinton's health-care reforms at first sought to regulate this private market activity as government regulates other sectors of private enterprise. But unlike other private-sector activity, government has a legitimate role in providing, or ensuring, the provision of health services, just as government has responsibility to see to the provision of other public utilities such as highways and airports. The failure to clarify exactly what constitutes a legitimate public responsibility, immunizations, for example, distinct from private responsibility for health care led to unprecedented confusion and eventful erosion of any support for health-care reform.

Methods of Implementation

Health-care policy directed toward treatment has been implemented primarily through insurance programs that reduce the risk of large financial expenditures for individuals by spreading the costs among participating groups and over long periods of time. Other kinds of insurance—for example, accident, fire, or life—pay out benefits to the user; under health insurance, however, control of benefits rests not with the user, but with the insurance company and the health-care provider. In other words, as a way of protecting individuals against high medical costs, health insurance has created a health-care system in which the provider treats the patient but collects from the insurer. The user no longer controls either the cost or the product.

Health insurance is thus essentially a funding mechanism, and as such it presents several limitations to health policymakers. The central issue at stake is cost control. Because insurance so dominates health policy, it is important that the analyst have a clear understanding of its basic operations.

Two insurance systems operate in America—private and public—and health-care policy is extremely difficult to control through either. Of a total population of more than 239 million Americans, some 190 million (about 81 percent) are covered under some type of health insurance. The other 19 percent, according to most studies, are people in a borderline state of poverty— not eligible for income-maintenance programs and related public health insurance, yet not well enough employed to be eligible for employer-sponsored private coverage, which generally is offered only to full-time workers. These uninsured people can receive health care at free public health agencies that have outpaient clinics, or at hospital emergency rooms. Many receive no health care at all. The Reagan administration sought to restrict public Medicaid funding, and as eligibility for income-maintenance programs has also been tightened, the number of people without adequate health care has increased sharply in the 1980s. The Clinton administration sought to set controls on the insurance industry, only to have the providers, consumers, insurance companies—in short, everyone, raise objections.

The Private Insurance System

The private health insurance system is usually characterized by an employer-sponsored health-care plan in which employee, employer, and (where applicable) union participate in financing the plan and determining the benefits. Approximately 136 million people are covered under such plans. For many years the major private health insurance carrier was Blue Cross/Blue Shield (BCBS), but in recent years a vast array of competitors has entered the business.

The prototype for the Blue Cross system was founded in 1929 by Justin Kimball at Baylor University, for schoolteachers in Dallas, Texas.[4] The idea arose because so many of the teachers had unpaid hospital bills. Under Kimball's original plan a premium of 50 cents would cover expenses for twenty-one days of hospital care in a semiprivate room. Ten years later, after Blue Cross had become an established hospital insurance plan, the California Medical Association established a similar insurance scheme to cover payment of doctors' bills. This system gained much acceptance among physicians and was added to the Blue Cross programs as Blue Shield. By the mid-1970s there were about seventy BCBS plans in the United States, with a total enrollment of nearly 85 million "subscriber units."

The seeds of present policy dilemmas, particularly those faced by the public insurance programs of Medicare and Medicaid, were sown in these early phases. Three important founding principles still affect the operations of

174

health insurance today. Reforms that do not account for these early problems, which have become locked into the structure of American health insurance, will fail to satisfy present-day policy. Similarly, the use of health insurance as a primary tool in the development and reform of health-care policy is severely limited by the continuing existence of these principles.

First of all, it must be recognized that health insurance does not provide cash benefits (indemnities) in the sense that accident, or fire, or life insurance does; it provides service benefits instead. Certainly the subscriber still receives a pro forma statement of costs absorbed by the insurer; but in effect what the subscriber has gained is not an indemnity, but the service itself, such as emergency treatment or a hospital stay. For these benefits, as with other forms of insurance, the subscriber pays an advance subscription, or premium, at regular intervals. Premiums for other kinds of insurance are calculated on the basis of actuarial tables that can project fair prices against future payoffs with considerable accuracy. Estimating the need for future service benefits is a more difficult task. This difficulty is compounded when public policy continues to stimulate the development of new health products (both services and materials).

Second, Blue Cross began as an aid to payment of hospital bills—in fact it functioned more as an insurance program for hospitals than for patients. In the early days, hospitals accepted the Blue Cross payment even if it did not cover the full cost of care. If Blue Cross did pay the full cost of covered hospital services, that cost was often discounted by hospitals in exchange for the certainty of receiving payment for services rendered. Blue Shield began with the same objective—a method for guaranteeing payment of doctors' bills—and it also offered service in place of indemnity. Unlike Blue Cross, however, Blue Shield's service benefit concept was more difficult to establish, since the price for services was often based on negotiations between doctor and patient. Efforts to standardize rates for physicians' fees were essential to the fiscal integrity of the program. "Usual, customary, and reasonable" (UCR) rates were determined, but these could only be implemented if physicians agreed. Thus control of Blue Cross rested with hospital administrators, and control of Blue Shield rested with the doctors.

Third, because BCBS provided more protection to providers than to health-care consumers, participation was at first limited, usually to people with modest incomes. Blue Cross costs and benefits were developed specifically for hourly wage earners, on the assumption that salaried employees would be able to afford better care without needing insurance. Blue Shield plans at first were limited to employed people who earned less than $3,000 per year. The per-unit-of-service reimbursement to physicians on the basis of UCR standards was acceptable to doctors who were expected to give care to low-income people anyway. The individual physician usually covered those costs by charging the wealthy more to balance the difference.

To make matters worse, advances in medical technology soon began to undermine the fiscal integrity of BCBS plans. Medical subspecializations proliferated as new technologies developed, producing a shift in the location of service providers. Because most new technology could not be purchased by the individual physician, hospital-based services took on a new dimension. Services of hospital-based physicians in specialized disciplines such as radiology and anesthesiology could now be included in costs covered under Blue Cross. This form of reimbursement made the hospital into an umbrella organization that established its own service systems—which in turn placed additional burdens on BCBS funding. Hospital services now ranged far beyond bed care, and hospitals were forced to invest in expensive equipment that could only be paid for as the costs were written off against Blue Cross. For example, new equipment costs were built into comprehensive costs of hospital care, whether or not the individual patient/subscriber had actually used the new equipment. These higher hospital and physician costs put financial pressure not only on the insurer but also on uninsured patients.

In 1947 the Supreme Court ruled that employee benefits, including health insurance, had a legitimate place in bargaining between labor and management. This ruling opened the door for enrollment of salaried workers as well as others who had hitherto been restricted from joining BCBS. These new subscribers pressured for more and expanded health insurance coverage, placing greater fiscal strain on the insurance system. By the time Medicare and Medicaid were developed in 1965, BCBS had developed elaborate methods for absorbing the increased financial pressures. Limitations on service benefits surfaced between BCBS and physicians and hospital administrators. The age-old fear that nonmedical people—in this case, hospital administrators and insurance companies—would be telling physicians what to do, emerged in full force.

In 1978 Blue Cross and Blue Shield merged, reflecting nationwide pressures from states and the federal government toward standardization of benefits and reimbursements. The merger marked the end, for practical purposes, of the surrogate role BCBS had played for hospitals and doctors, and put the corporation in the position of a true third party in the triangle of medical care—a party with legitimate rights to negotiate both costs and benefits. However, the surrogate attachment remained latent in the concept of service benefits, which, in the climate of rapid technological advancement in medical care and universal availability of insurance, contributed significantly to increased costs. In this environment Medicaid was bound to add inflationary pressure by making more funding available for services. Efforts to contain costs by restructuring benefits proved generally ineffective as long as benefits remained in the form of services, and as long as reimbursements for them were protected by the providers.

The Public Insurance System

The public insurance system consists of two elements: Medicare and Medicaid.

Medicare

Medicare is a government-financed system of health insurance for Social Security beneficiaries. Because Social Security extends to survivors of covered persons and to the disabled as well as the elderly, it is available to a wide variety of subscribers. About 31 million people are covered by Medicare. Eighty-nine percent are over sixty-five years old; 10 percent are working age; 1 percent are children under thirteen years old.

Medicare is insurance, and it operates almost exactly the same as BCBS and similarly to other private insurance programs. By paying a monthly Medicare premium the subscriber receives basic benefit coverage for hospital care and major medical and surgical expenses. Like private sector plans, Medicare includes deductibles and copayments. Medicare, part A, is hospital insurance that pays for in-patient hospital care, nursing-home care, home health care, and hospice care, less a yearly deductible. It is provided as part of the Social Security benefit package, financed by the Social Security payroll tax, a small monthly premium, and a monthly assessment. Nursing home care is limited and requires a copayment for each of the first days of care per year.

Medicare, part B, covers medical costs associated with illness, such as Blue Shield does. It is funded by a monthly premium of (about 25 percent of the cost) and by federal funds from general tax revenues (the remaining 75 percent). For the premium, 80 percent of service costs are then paid by Medicare. The other 20 percent, and any medical expenditures that Medicare will not cover, must be paid by the individual. Most participants buy other insurance, such as BCBS, to cover the deductible and uncovered expenses, causing increased complexity in efforts to clearly distinguish between private and public responsibility for health care. The costs and covered benefits change frequently from year to year.

Because Medicare is insurance, it is faced with problems that are inherited from private-sector programs: service benefits, with fees set by providers; inability to control costs; and a third-party status, but with inadequate authority to direct policy. Hence, like private-sector programs, it is biased in favor of the service providers. Under part A, for example, Medicare emphasizes in-hospital care, which is expensive. Current (mid-1990s) average hospital room charges per day have risen to more than $525, not including the costs of medical services required by the illness itself. Less expensive, nursing home costs average nearly $1200 per claim. Care at home, by contrast, costs less than 30 percent of nursing home care, and less than 1 percent of an average hospital stay. Since the great majority of Medicare subscribers are older people, the age group that has the highest rates of hospital use, this emphasis on hospital coverage is essential. But it has meant that expenses for long-term routine care of patients outside hospitals—for instance, convalescents, invalids, and some of the terminally ill—are virtually unrecoverable. Part B has similar provider biases in its basic package: 77 percent of its expenditures go to physicians, and less than 1 percent to care in the home.

Medicaid

Medicaid is not an insurance program, but it operates like one. The program disburses federal funds to states, which use the money along with their own funds to pay for health care for poor people. States operate Medicaid programs by administering them directly or by contracting with private insurance agencies for administrative services. States set the conditions of eligibility and establish the benefit package consistent with federal regulations. States must provide medical care for people who are recipients of aid in federally supported, means-tested income-maintenance programs. They may also provide medical care to other low-income people who have such large medical expenses that they would qualify for income-maintenance programs if those expenses were paid from personal funds—a form of relief often called a medical "spend-down."

As with private insurance and Medicare, Medicaid recipients choose their own health-care provider(s) and negotiate their own health care accordingly. The services rendered are paid for by Medicaid as if covered by insurance.

About 19 million people are covered by Medicaid. Medicaid expenditures amount to more than 10 percent of all health care and 25 percent of federal health-care expenditures. Current costs are about $105 billion annually, of which 60 percent is funded by the federal government, and the remainder by state and local governments. Because Medicaid is available to income-maintenance recipients and other low-income people who cannot meet their own medical expenses, it acts as a supplement to Medicare for older people who need skilled nursing or intermediate care. In fact, about 17 percent of all Medicaid recipients are older people whose Medicare benefits have been exhausted. Half of Medicaid beneficiaries, however, are under age 21. Still large segments of the population in poverty—childless couples, marginal employees, and the unemployed under age 65—receive no public medical insurance because they are not eligible for income-maintenance programs. In short, only about 40 percent of people who live below the poverty line receive Medicaid.

Like Medicare, Medicaid is driven by service providers' demands. Table 7.4 shows the proportions of Medicaid spent on various forms of services. Hospitals, nursing and intermediate care homes, and physicians' fees absorb more than 80 percent of Medicaid expenditures. Indeed, expenditures for Medicaid are quite similar to those for Medicare, suggesting that both programs function to subsidize a medical care industry that is dominated by expensive hospital-related costs, with very little support for health care outside the existing medical structure. Hence as prices rise, public funding must increase, contributing to another rise in prices in a spiral of inflated medical costs. Notice the large increase in family planning expenditures in spite of the ban on the use of Medicaid funding for abortions.

Table 7.4: Medicaid expenditures for different types of services.

	1986	1992
Inpatient hospital	31.4%	29.8%
Nursing facility services	16.5	27.1
Intermediate care facility	25.8	9.9
Physicians' services	8.0	7.1
Dentists' and other medical professionals' services	2.9	1.6
Hospital outpatient services	5.4	6.1
Clinic	.9	3.2
Laboratory	1.3	1.2
Home health-care services	5.9	5.6
Prescription drugs	.5	7.8
Family planning	1.4	.6
Total	100.0%	100.0%

Source: Statistical Abstract of the United States (1994), Table 162 and (1988), Table 611.

Current Health Policy Options

Cost-Containment Delivery Systems

A number of efforts have been made to contain the costs of medical care. The first sought to reduce the growth in public spending through the Medicare and Medicaid programs. Proponents have reasoned that if costs could be contained and even reduced in these public insurance programs, the containment policies could be spread to private insurance programs. The Health Care Financing Administration (HCFA), which administers the Medicare and Medicaid programs, first attempted to contain hospital costs by initiating a system of peer review for hospital care, to verify whether hospital stays and medical services were appropriate. This system monitored medical services by examining patients' records to ensure that hospitals would not keep patients beyond a period absolutely necessary, merely to generate revenue for the hospital. Experience with this system during the late 1970s suggested that for the most part hospital and other medical services were appropriately handled. The peer review system itself was costly, however, and often excessively intrusive.

As a result of that experience, HCFA decided to modify its payment system from one that reimbursed for care already received (retrospective payments) to one based upon established rates for specific services that might be needed (prospective payments); this was to be accomplished by creating a system of diagnostic related groups (DRGs). Under this prospective payment scheme providers are paid a set amount for a particular problem that they have agreed to treat. If treatment turns out to cost less, the provider keeps the difference; if it costs more, the provider absorbs the additional costs. This alternative policy has not yet been completely implemented. There is no evidence that it will result in substantial reductions in public spending for medical care, and some critics fear that the DRG system will discourage providers from treating "unprofitable" medical problems.

Health Maintenance Organizations (HMOs)

A different effort to reduce public spending for health care, particularly medical care, has come through the increased use of health maintenance organizations (HMOs) as alternatives to prepaid insurance programs that emphasize medical care and treatment. To understand how HMOs operate requires another brief glance at the recent history of medical practice and health insurance.

At the time when BCBS plans were expanding, new structures of medical practice were also emerging that differed from the discrete units of doctor, patient, and hospital. By the late 1960s five clear patterns for providing medical care had become standard:

1. In the traditional manner, the patient went to a physician, who organized a plan of medical care for the patient and provided services directly or through constituents.

2. The patient organized his or her own care, often with the result that the patient had several doctors, depending on the problems involved. This was partly a response to the rapid increase in physicians' specialization after World War II.

3. As hospitals increased in technological capacities and began to expand clinical services to outpatients, many people began to use out-patient clinics to receive medical care without dependence on any specific doctor or medical practitioner.

4. Because many low-income people had little access to ordinary medical care, they waited until medical problems became acute and then resorted to emergency rooms, which usually treat people first, assuming an emergency, and ask questions about payment later.

5. In a variation on the traditional doctor-patient pattern, and as a way of providing costly new technologies through private practice, physicians began to practice in groups.[5]

Physicians quickly recognized the advantages of group practice. Patients could be offered a variety of specialized services at the doctors' offices; operating costs could be shared; many supportive services, such as routine laboratory work, could be done at less cost to the patient and greater convenience to the doctors. Moreover, the patient could be seen in a more comprehensive environment, often including all family members; this encouraged provisional health maintenance services as well as more traditional treatment services. In many instances, however, it proved difficult to obtain insurance reimbursement for services provided by group practices. Splitting the fee in order to satisfy insurers' fee-for-service criteria was troublesome and sometimes impossible. Setbacks of this nature seriously limited the expansion of group practice.

Shortly after World War II, Henry H. Kaiser the automobile manufacturer, launched a new and creative program for providing medical benefits to his employees. For the same amount as the usual insurance charge, the subscriber could receive comprehensive medical care in a group practice that he organized. All forms of care were made available to members, but the practice was designed to promote preventive medicine (health maintenance) in preference to treatment, on the assumption that it cost less to keep people well than to treat them when they became ill. The Kaiser plan quickly began to spread as a group practice option, setting the stage for the development of HMOs generally, and the Health Maintenance Organization Act of 1973.

The Kaiser-Permanente model of medical care was an important development in the funding and organization of health care. First, it emphasized prevention and education to maintain a state of health. Second, each program was designed to integrate hospital and physician services by controlling both resources in a single program. To accomplish this, Kaiser-Permanente programs usually constructed their own inpatient facilities, thus controlling overall health-care costs within each organization. Third, and no less important, the Kaiser-Permanente plans substituted a "capitation" payment system for the fee-for-service system. Under capitation the cost and reimbursement rates are based on the number of people served, not the services provided. By freeing group practices from the usual fee structures, Kaiser-Permanente programs had greater flexibility to offer whatever services were appropriate—for example, health education—rather than only services that were reimbursable. It also made HMOs an attractive alternative for public funding of health care, and finally led to federal funding of HMOs and the encouragement of their widespread use.

At present there are about 230 officially recognized HMOs across the nation, serving about 12.5 million people. An HMO must meet certain criteria to obtain official recognition:

1. It must have an organized system of health care in a geographic area in which it assumes responsibility for providing that care.

2. It must have a defined and agreed-upon set of basic and supplemental health maintenance and treatment services.

3. Its subscribers must be voluntarily enrolled.

4. It must have certification as a group HMO or as an individual practice association (IPA). (Under the latter arrangement, physicians contract to see HMO patients on a capitation basis, but may also see their own patients on a fee-for-service basis.)

An approved (officially recognized) HMO is eligible to receive Medicaid and Medicare reimbursement on a person-by-person (capitation) basis as an exception to established Medicaid and Medicare regulations, and some private insurance companies similarly approve and reimburse insurance claims for services received through HMOs. The advantages of an HMO are the generally lower overall costs for total health services provided, even though individual cases may incur higher costs than normal. HMOs avoid the fiscal limits on health services that are created by insurance-based reimbursement systems. They therefore provide more comprehensive and health-oriented (rather than treatment-oriented) services. Capitation also makes it easier for HMOs to fund services for low-income people, and federal reimbursement for HMO services has enabled the expansion of "well-health" services into many traditionally lower-income urban centers.

Efforts to control the public costs of medical care have been difficult when insurance pays for services. The development of HMOs offers hope both for redirection of health-care policy and for containment of service costs. Nevertheless the present organization of medical care still leaves most health-care decisions in the hands of individual patients and their doctors. This suggests that redirected public funding alone will not be enough to produce comprehensive changes in health policy.

The unsuccessful attempt to reform health care by the Clinton administration resulted in an increase in HMO-type health service plans. Under the threat of a "single payer system," both hospitals and insurance companies began efforts to restructure their health-care products. Although no legislation ever materialized, the single payer system anticipated a single provider for all the health-care needs of each individual covered under a specific program. This would have meant that hospitals, for example, would not be reimbursed for services to John Doe unless John Doe received all his medical care from the same hospital. Thus hospitals began to acquire individual and group medical practices to expand the patient base of their services to include routine, non-hospital forms of health care so they could become a "single payee."

In like manner insurance companies began organizing individual and group practices into health maintenance organizations (HMOs), whereby physicians could function as an HMO by meeting HMO standards, even while continuing their status as individual practitioners. Thus the 1994 health-care debates brought about some subtle shifts in the provision of health-care products, even without legislation. There is great doubt, however, that these changes will do very much to reform health care, as they seem to give traditional providers of traditional services a level of protection in the highly volatile world of health-care policy.

Noninsured Health Care

Public support for health care provided without insurance reimbursement amounts to less than 10 percent of all health expenditures (see table 7.2). The most important of such programs are (1) the Maternal and Child Health programs, (2) spending for local public health programs, (3) the United States

Public Health Service, (4) special programs under the Health Services Block Grant, and (5) programs supporting medical research. There are also other programs that implement health policy even though their expenditures are not budgeted as health-related: environmental programs, for example, and the Special Supplemental Food Program for Women, Infants and Children (WIC), usually considered an income-maintenance program.

Maternal and child health (MCH)

MCH began as an original part of the Social Security Act of 1935. The program transfers federal money to the states for the provision of pre- and postnatal health care to mothers and infants. This care centers on examination and screening for medical problems, monitoring pregnancy, well-baby checkups after birth, and considerable health education. In most cases MCH funds are channeled through local health departments, which generally provide a wide range of health maintenance services to a wide spectrum of the local population. Hence it is difficult to say exactly how many mothers and children benefit directly from the public funds spent specifically for the purposes of MCH. The MCH budget includes special funds for the provision of care and health services to handicapped children, which have been an extremely important source of fiscal encouragement for state and local health maintenance programs for such children. Many experts believe that the long range steady decline in infant mortality rates and the decline in the number of low-birth-weight (premature) babies can be attributed to pre- and postnatal care provided by MCH and WIC.

Special supplemental food program for women, infants and children (WIC)

WIC originated in 1975 as a program to identify women likely to bear children who would be vulnerable to medical problems. These women, who are also likely to be poor, are given a medical examination, monitoring during pregnancy, and special food supplements to ensure that they have an adequate diet throughout pregnancy and as long as they continue to breastfeed their newborn children. The program began with about 500,000 participants, but quickly expanded; it now covers about 2.8 million "high-risk" mothers. Along with MCH, WIC is highly valued for reducing the incidence of low-birth-weight babies, but it has also become an extremely important source of supplemental income for many low-income mothers.

Taken together, MCH and WIC implement one of the few publicly funded preventive health-care policies. This provides an unusual opportunity for comparing the relative costs for prevention and treatment. Children who weigh less than 2,500 grams (5 pounds, 8 ounces) at birth run a great risk of needing costly health care. The average cost of care during a child-bearing period is about $3,000, of which $750 is the average cost of prenatal care. Neonatal intensive care in hospitals averages $10,000 to $15,000 for each occurrence. Infants with low birth weight are highly susceptible to early childhood diseases and are also prone to develop severe respiratory problems during their first year of life. Nearly 250,000 such infants are born each year. Suppose that 20 percent of them would need $10,000 worth of intensive care in a neonatal hospital unit apiece—a conservative estimate (no precise figures exist). Suppose too that 25 percent of the total 250,000 would develop birth-related problems sometime during childhood (the first five years of life), at a cost of $5,000 per child—another conservative estimate. On these terms total treatment costs for low-birth-weight infants would come to about $5.3 billion per year. C. Arden Miller estimates that for every dollar spent on prenatal care, $5.36 will be saved in medical costs in the twelve months following delivery.[6] Total preventive expenses through MCH and WIC together in 1991, however, were only $3.5 billion.

United States public health service (PHS)

A variety of important programs are funded through and/or administered by PHS. The Public Health Service Act created the agency in 1944, and it has been recreated and modified many times since, as new health programs are launched and moved around in the federal bureaucracy. At present PHS includes the Center for Disease Control (CDC), the Food and Drug Administration (FDA), the National Institutes of Health (NIH), the Health Resources and Services Administration (HRSA), and the Alcohol, Drug Abuse, and Mental Health Administration. Through research and regulation in their fields of activity, CDC, FDA, and NIH provide a broad range of public health maintenance and protection services. NIH has done considerable research in health maintenance and disease prevention through eleven research institutes and in a variety of public spending areas ranging from children to the elderly.

HRSA administers professional training programs, funds for health planning, and funds for a few federally financed direct service programs. These programs include outpatient mental health programs, alcohol and drug abuse prevention and treatment programs, general funding for local public health services, and funding for service programs for special groups such as hemophiliacs. In 1981, under the Omnibus Budget Reconciliation Act, these programs were placed under the Health Services Block Grant, and their funds were given to states to spend as they see fit in these general program areas.

In summary, the public noninsurance programs are focused toward health maintenance, but they represent only a small proportion of expenditures for public and private health care. Some of these programs provide services directly to individuals; others are directed toward larger community issues of public health and protection from disease, through long-range research and regulation. The services provided through these programs are likely to be closely associated with local public health agencies. Consequently they have come to play an important part in health care for low-income people across the nation.

Policy Analysis

Some analyses of health policy consider public and private health-care issues together, on the assumption that public spending for health has increased both demand and supply, forcing costs inevitably upward. This line of analysis seeks public, mostly federal, regulatory alternatives that will limit hospital and physicians' costs—the crucial factors in cost containment, as discussed above. A recent analysis by the American Enterprise Institute takes a fairly typical stance along these lines:

> The central issue is not whether a system of government price and entry controls can succeed in decreasing [health care] costs, although success has so far proved elusive. The key question is what the health care delivery system will look like ten or twenty years from now if we squeeze providers through policies that do "work" in the sense of creating a slowdown of spending, but without changing the basic inequity in our health care financing system.[7]

This combined approach, however, does not address some of the crucial normative issues identified at the beginning of this chapter, particularly the entrenched bias toward treatment and cure in current conceptions of health and health policy.

Other analyses try to separate public from private health policy and focus on the high cost of federal spending, which is primarily directed at reimbursement for services performed in the private sector. Because this focus restricts the analyst to public-sector funding, assuming that the private sector is a world unto itself, it narrows considerably the range and scope of alternatives that may be presented to policymakers. For example, a recent study by the Congressional Budget Office states:

> Major ways in which the federal government could bring market forces to bear upon medical costs include: altering the tax treatment of employment-based health insur-

ance; offering Medicare beneficiaries a voucher to purchase a private health plan; and other adjustments in the Medicare reimbursement and benefit structures.[8]

In contrast with these approaches, the analysis suggested here attempts to examine the full range of normative orientations within a context of alternatives reflected by contemporary health programs. The criteria-based model in slightly modified form offers the best strategy for such a broad-scale analysis, precisely because the range of normative views is so wide, the normative issues cut across public and private health activities. A set of clear alternatives offers the opportunity for evaluating recommendations against normative criteria.

A summary paradigm of this analysis is presented in table 7.5. The universal criteria and policy-specific criteria have been discussed as normative issues at the beginning of this chapter. The alternatives have also been mentioned in discussion above, and little needs to be said about them at this point, with the exception of "regulation against risks," which refers to policies (such as laws requiring the use of seatbelts and motorcyclists' helmets, or bans on smoking) that are intended to protect against health hazards. Policies of this nature apply equally to all concerned, and they are cost-effective, but they are difficult to implement because they restrict personal choices so severely. Relative values (high, medium, low) in table 7.5 have been derived from preceding discussion of the criteria and the alternatives.

The paradigm presents no surprises. Insurance reimbursement plans rank highest in personal choice, preference satisfaction, and treatment, and low in cost containment and areas of prevention and care. The health services rank highest in universality, cost constraint, prevention, and public commitment, and low in personal choice, treatment, and preference satisfaction. Among insurance and reimbursement schemes the most appealing alternatives are Medicare and HMOs; public health clinics and mental health and drug treatment agencies look appealing among the service programs. The analysis affirms what seems to be the present status quo in health policy.

However, because relatively good, health-related information exists, it is possible to draw a "health profile" from health indicators and in this way expand discussion about normative views of health. For example, it is possible to specify the mortality rate and then question whether that rate modifies our impression of, say, equity, or of one of the other criteria. The vital statistics of American society present the following health profile.

The live birthrate has shown a slight increase since 1978. It now stands at about 16.1 live births per 1,000 population. The live birthrate is 1.48 times higher for blacks than for whites, and black babies are 2.2 times more likely to be born with low birth weights. Low birth weight is the single most impor-

Table 7.5: Paradigm of health policy analysis, criteria-based model.

ALTERNATIVES

	Insurance/reimbursements				Health services				
Normative orientations	Public health insurance	Medicare	Medicaid	HMOs	MCH	WIC	Public health clinics	Mental health, drug/alcohol	Regulation against risk
Universal criteria									
Equality (access)	Lo	Med	Hi	Med	Hi	Hi	Hi	Hi	Hi
Equity (quality of care)	Med	Med	Med	Med	—	—	Med	Med	—
Efficiency (cost containment)	Lo	Med	Med	Med	Hi	Hi	Hi	Med	Hi
Preference satisfaction	Hi	Med	Med	Med	Lo	Lo	Med	Med	Lo
Universality	Lo	Med	Hi	Med	Hi	Hi	Hi	Med	Hi
Policy-specific criteria									
Maintain equilibrium (care)	Med	Med	Med	Hi	Lo	Lo	Hi	Hi	—
Restore equilibrium (treatment, cure)	Hi	Hi	Hi	Hi	Lo	Lo	Med	Lo	—
Prevention	Lo	Lo	Lo	Med	Hi	Hi	Med	Lo	Hi
Personal choice	Hi	Hi	Hi	Hi	Lo	Lo	Lo	Lo	Lo
Public commitment	Hi	Hi	Hi	Med	Hi	Hi	Hi	Hi	Hi
	Hi = 3	Hi = 3	Hi = 5	Hi = 4	Hi = 5	Hi = 5	Hi = 5	Hi = 3	Hi = 5
	Med = 2	Med = 6	Med = 4	Med = 6	Med = 0	Med = 0	Med = 4	Med = 4	Med = 0
	Lo = 5	Lo = 1	Lo = 1	Lo = 0	Lo = 4	Lo = 4	Lo = 1	Lo = 3	Lo = 2

tant factor in changes in the live birth rate. Among unmarried women—a population group most likely to experience poverty and depend on Medicare and Medicaid for medical expenses—birthrates are 18.2 per 1,000 for white women and 81.4 per 1,000 for black women.

According to the latest Census Bureau report, infant mortality rate in 1990 stood at 9.2 deaths per 1,000 live births. The infant mortality rate for blacks was 18, more than two times as high as that for whites (7.6 per 1,000). Although progress has been made, United States still has one of the highest rates of infant mortality of any industrialized nation—higher than 19 other nations including Japan, Hong Kong, and Spain. When only the white infant mortality rate is considered only twelve countries have lower infant mortality rates.

Longevity has been increasing. A person born in 1980 could expect to live 73.7 years while someone born in 1990 could expect to live 75.4 years. Someone who turned 65 in 1980 could expect to live another 16.4 years, while someone who reached age 65 in 1990 could expect to live for another 17.3 years.

Table 7.6 summarizes the top ten death rates by cause. Diseases associated with aging lead the list. The major causes of death involve organ failure, an area that in recent years has received much attention in terms of medical research and technological advances in treatment. Perinatal deaths and accidents are not leading causes of death in the population as a whole, but perinatal conditions may exist for years before becoming evident. Accidents are the most likely cause of death among people 25 to 44 years old; automobile accidents lead the list. Like perinatal conditions and some major diseases, accidents often require costly care preceding death.

Activity-limiting conditions affect 14.4 percent of the population (up from 11.7 percent in the 1970s), and limitations of major activities of daily living affect 10.9 percent (up from 9.1 percent). For these individuals this disability translates into an annual average of 19 days per year of restricted activity, 6.9 days in bed, and 5.1 days lost from work. Activity-limiting conditions are associated with income and age. In 1991 people with less than $11,000 income per year were more than twice as likely as those with greater incomes to have activity-limiting conditions, and almost three times as likely to be limited in their major areas of activity.

Use of medical care is difficult to determine accurately in terms of income and class. However, some surveys show evidence that the poor are less healthy and get less care than the wealthy. Between 1964 and 1974 there was a change in this general trend, as a result of Medicaid and other efforts to bring the poor into the health-care system. For example, the poor at least began to see doctors as often as the nonpoor; poor women began to receive pap smears and breast examinations almost as commonly as other women; and poor women who saw a physician during early pregnancy increased from 58 to 71 percent.[9]

Table 7.6: Death rates by cause per 100,000 deaths.

	1986	*1992*
Heart disease	328.7	272.5
Cancer	184.0	204.3
Strokes	71.3	56.3
Accidents	43.9	33.8
Pulmonary disease	25.7	35.8
Diabetes	15.1	19.8
Liver disease	12.8	9.7
Atherosclerosis	12.2	6.3
Suicide	12.0	11.7
Perinatal conditions	9.4	6.2

Source: Statistical Abstract of the United States (1994), Table 125, and (1988), Table 112.

Although other data sources could provide a more thorough illustrative context for health policy analysis, the profile sketched here offers some clear summary points. The mortality rate is creeping up, although the trend was reversed for a brief while during the 1970s. Black people and poor people, and particularly black children at birth, are at greater risk for health problems. The major causes of death are now conditions generally associated with aging. (At the turn of the present century, by contrast, major causes of death were childhood illnesses and industrial accidents.) This, along with rising life-expectancy estimates, provides a good measure of progress in health. Among several contributing factors is modern technology, which has made it possible to preserve life in ways that were undreamed of fifty years ago.

The Medicaid program has brought medical care to the poor toward a greater parity with the care enjoyed by those who have direct access to private-sector medical services. Unfortunately, however, some large groups—such as black infants and children—remain at risk despite these expansions in health-care policy; they need better preventive health programs. Greater amounts of health maintenance, or care, services are similarly needed for another large segment of the population, the elderly.

Recommendations

When the alternatives are balanced against the criteria in the context of present-day experiences with health policy and the health profile of the nation, it becomes apparent that revision of some values might modify the weight given to certain alternatives. For example, health services seem to be at least as important as insurance programs in plotting a future health policy. Considering the health profile outlined above, a strong normative argument could be made that the effectiveness of present spending patterns for health care will have little long-term effect on health if a corresponding buildup of health services does not take place, particularly in the area of preventive services. The proportion of public spending devoted to such services does not suggest an even-handed development.

In general the public insurance programs have brought low-income people closer to the mainstream of medical care, but at very great expense. Experience with private insurance systems suggests that it is impossible to control the escalation of costs that is almost certain to take place under such circumstances; consequently it is difficult to argue in favor of some form of nationalized health insurance program at this time. Cost containment and alternatives to medical care that are effective and cost-efficient (such as HMOs) must come from the providers.

The health services emphasize the very criteria that health insurance fails to deal with very well: maintenance and care. However, health services do not satisfy personal preference criteria in a way that public support for insurance does. In particular, public health efforts have a high degree of equity, but they rate comparatively low in terms of personal satisfaction, feasibility, and treatment. In practical terms, because individuality plays such an important part in health policy, efforts to achieve public health services, especially preventive health services, are apt to be extremely limited. Thus the feasibility of developing such services may remain low for years to come.

Chapter Eight

HOUSING

Introduction

Although finding a place to live is a trying experience for most Americans, the difficulties usually are limited to finding the kind of housing that suits personal tastes, rather than actually finding shelter. People may have to struggle to find the right style of housing in the right neighborhood at the right price, but in most cases they do find housing that satisfies their wants and needs. In other words, for most people, in most circumstances, housing policy in America is effective. For some, however, an adequate place to live seems almost unattainable; this need poses serious problems that erode the whole foundation of American housing policy. Thus housing policy, like health and income-maintenance policy, must be specific enough to deal with problem cases but broad enough to satisfy the expectations of all.

Normative Issues

Three general issues shape current housing policy: (1) standards, (2) developing the housing supply, and (3) housing subsidies and their distribution.

Housing Standards

Housing standards set the context for considering other normative issues. America does not tolerate "zero-standard" housing; squatter cities, tent towns, or cardboard communities would violate housing codes in every part of the nation. The vast slum housing that does exist in America is considered inadequate because it only barely meets, or fails to meet, local housing standards.

Several types of standards contribute to these norms. Land-use standards are usually applied by local governments, beginning with zoning laws that say what kinds of housing can be developed on what kind of land. Single- or multifamily housing, lot size, specialized land uses, and master land use plans all set standards for housing development before building even begins. Construction standards center on building codes, which require that electrical wiring, plumbing, foundations, roofs, walls, windows, doors, and virtually every element of construction be undertaken in conformity with specific rules. Building codes usually reflect standards developed by national groups—often the federal government itself—but actual construction requirements may vary considerably from place to place. Moreover, zoning ordinances and building codes both interlock with standards set by insurance companies and lending institutions. For example, specific grades of roofing materials are required by fire insurance underwriters, and banks will not lend money toward the purchase of uninsured housing. Finally, trade unions may set work standards that affect how housing is developed. Different skilled tradespeople must be hired for different tasks—plumbers for plumbing, electricians for wiring, and so on—all of whom must abide by legal standards and may also have agreed-upon standard procedures among themselves.

These formal standards, often expressed as requirements, contribute greatly to initial costs of housing, but they do ensure a certain quality of housing. Well-built housing lasts longer, which means longer replacement cycles and consequently lower overall housing costs. But questions are often raised as to which standards are necessary for quality and which exist for extraneous reasons. For example, are restricted lot sizes necessary for quality, or are they really forms of economic and racial segregation? Are some electrical and plumbing standards necessary for quality and safety, or are they appeasements to unions? Federal government regulations for housing developed using federal funds impose additional standards. For instance, grant proposals for funds under the Community Development Block Grant (part of the Housing Act) must consider and plan for historical property, flood plain management, wetland protection, noise, manmade hazards, air and water quality, transportation, sewage disposal, and solid waste disposal.[1] These requirements raise housing costs, but can it be argued that they contribute to the overall value of housing as well?

Informal standards also contribute to housing costs. For example, land sold in certain neighborhoods may be bound by covenants that require development of housing within a special (usually high) price range, or within certain criteria for size and appearance. Personal preferences also set informal standards. Even though the deplorable practice of housing segregation has been made illegal through fair housing laws at various levels of government, many whites still refuse to live in neighborhoods that have blacks or other minorities in residence. Neighborhood amenities—schools, shops, public transportation, recreation, and cultural opportunities—all contribute indirectly to housing standards and cost.

Substandard housing is defined as the opposite of good-quality housing, again through the application of standards. Formal definitions of substandard housing are determined on the basis of violations of local building codes, such as incomplete plumbing, but housing may be substandard even when it is in conformity with formal standards. Much of the housing in inner-city slums meets formal criteria for standard housing, but most people, including many who live in it, consider it substandard. This creates a frustrating cycle. A particular building, for instance, may simply need one or two repairs, but because the community is considered generally substandard there is little incentive for making the repairs, so they are left undone—contributing to a self-fulfilling prophecy of substandard quality. Ultimately, when considering housing standards, it is almost impossible to discuss the condition of housing without regard to its larger social and physical environment: the neighborhood of which it is a part.

Housing Supply

The relationship between housing standards and the neighborhood environment is intertwined with normative issues about the housing supply. Any housing policy must consider supply, because the population is expanding and because existing housing eventually wears out. That is, the need for housing increases geometrically in terms of both growth *and* replacement. The greater the population, the greater the supply of housing that must be created each year. Judging from these two standards alone—growth and replacement—a critical housing shortage already exists. Crises in housing supply are compounded by the time lag required for construction and the tremendous capital costs associated with development as a whole. Housing represents an immediate need, but also one that projects commitments into the future.

Hence discussion arises as to how the housing supply should be created—by construction of new housing, or rehabilitation of worn-out housing? If both, in what combination? And should it be created by the private market, or the government? And if both, in what balance?

New housing lasts a long time, and it can be constructed with current, "state-of-the-art" materials. Moreover, the costs of building new housing, as compared with rehabilitation of older housing, may be quite reasonable, particularly in the middle cost ranges. But new housing does not take into account the costs of housing amenities that go beyond the physical construction of a particular building. New housing is usually created in undeveloped areas—outside cities or in the suburbs. Land in these areas tends to be cheaper, precisely because a community infrastructure has not been developed there. Roads and transportation systems may be incomplete, shopping resources scarce, schools and churches unplanned, even water and sewer systems may be available only in selected areas. This cheaper environment makes new housing economically competitive with more established housing on property that has already appreciated in value.

Rehabilitating old housing poses different problems. Old houses are usually in old neighborhoods, and rehabilitation of a few structures has little impact on the housing supply unless blocks, and sometimes whole neighborhoods, can be rehabilitated. Rehabilitation costs may be comparable with new construction costs, but overall there are fewer indirect costs associated with developing or renewing the service infrastructure. It is true that old neighborhoods often are plagued with high crime rates and deteriorated public amenities, but bringing neighborhood services into line with community expectations is less costly than developing them from scratch.

Choosing between new construction and rehabilitation may depend on whether it is more important to expand the existing stock of housing or to use what already exists more efficiently. Arguments for new housing derive from the housing needs of an expanding population: more people need more units. Arguments for rehabilitation derive from changes that take place within the population: young couples have children and add rooms to housing; older people with grown children may seek smaller homes or apartments; a family's home may need renovation to accommodate a disabled child or parent. Obviously both choices are desirable. The decision should depend on the expected use for housing in particular contexts.

Who should develop housing, the private or the public sector, is not as debatable as the question of who should ultimately own the housing. In practice a "trickle-down" theory of housing development has undergirded American housing policy since the federal government first became involved in housing in the 1930s. This rationale assumes that new housing is built by people with capital to invest, and then gradually passed down through resale to those with less capital as it ages and becomes less valuable, until, in the end, zero-value housing is available to people with zero capital.

But in fact housing seldom approaches zero value, and consequently the poor have no chance of owning, or in most cases even using, housing that in theory should have become valueless. Thus, in order to house the poor, government must either build housing, or pay housing costs for the poor, or subsidize private housing so that the poor can afford it. No one debates the necessity of government intervention in housing markets as a means of aiding the poor. There is room, however, for considerable disagreement about the scope of this government intervention and the form it takes.

Housing Subsidies

The "scope" of government intervention in housing refers to its association with private industry to develop housing within the context of a free-market economy. Determining an acceptable scope of intervention is not easy. Government intervention on behalf of the poor is clearly acceptable, but as with policy for income-maintenance programs, it is difficult to define who the poor are.

Publically supported housing policy rests on an assumption that housing should consume 25 percent but not more than 30 percent of a household's after-tax income. This benchmark has received widespread acceptance not only as a threshold to eligibility for government-assisted housing programs but also in less restricted private-sector transactions such as approval of consumer loans for mortgages. Costs in excess of 25 percent of after-tax household income are often termed a "housing gap." This gap can be measured as the monetary difference between 25 percent of after-tax household income and the cost of housing available to the household. In theory, at least, government extends its intervention in the housing market to close the gap—to provide housing that meets the 25 percent guideline when it cannot otherwise be achieved. Government might construct housing, charging no more for rent than 25 percent of each household's income, on an individualized sliding scale. Or it might supplement household income to make up the difference between the 25 percent guideline and the actual cost. Or it might supplement private builders, so that the housing constructed could be offered more cheaply, at prices consistent with 25 percent of people's incomes.

The problem with this formula lies in its application. If the 25 percent guideline is applied uniformly, many middle- and upper-income households also have a housing gap that may amount to several thousand dollars per year. Proponents of restricted government intervention would argue that efforts to close the housing gap should be applied only to those with very low incomes. Advocates of expanded government scope would counter that the housing supply is limited for middle-income households as well and that it is now almost impossible to find safe and sanitary housing for middle-income families because of a housing gap. In this view, government should act to reduce the cost of housing overall, or should provide public subsidies to everyone with housing gaps regardless of income, until the market makes housing available to all at affordable prices.

In sum, normative debates over distribution of housing subsidies range over the type of subsidies that should be offered, who the recipients of the subsidies should be, and the amount of the subsidies themselves. The need for subsidies derives from the general understanding that government must be involved in housing markets. But governments should be involved unobtrusively, so as not to upset the capitalist market system. The most unobtrusive type of government intervention is through the construction of housing. Government may build housing itself, or help the private sector build housing.

The way subsidies are distributed determines who benefits from them and how much the subsidy will be (see table 8.1). Although most critics of housing subsidies agree that people who need housing, particularly those with low incomes, eventually benefit from subsidies, no matter who gets them originally, the most direct beneficiary of most housing subsidies is apt to be the de-

Table 8.1: Federal housing subsidies and their beneficiaries.

Form	Direct beneficiary	Present source of policy[1]
Reduction of interest rate	developer/tenants	Secs. 235, 238
Increased loan coverage	developer	Sec. 221
Payment of principal and interest on housing loans	tenant/owner	Sec. 2; public housing
Payment of capital grant to developer	developer	—
Housing allowances to tenants	tenant	Sec. 8
Housing allowances to owners	owner	Sec. 2
Allocating housing for general income maintenance	low-income tenants	—
Allocating housing in public assistance	low-income tenants	AFDC, assistance programs
Tax deduction of mortgage interest and property taxes	owner/developer (middle-income)	tax codes
Accelerated depreciation	developer	Sec. 236, tax codes
Reduction of local property taxes	owner/tenant	Sec. 2
Reduction of land costs	developer/owner	Community Block Grant (Housing Act)

1. Section numbers refer to the Federal Housing Act.

Source: Anthony Downs, *Federal Housing Supplements: Their Effectiveness and What We Should Do about Them.* Washington, D.C.: National Association of Home Builders, (1972), 18.

veloper or builder (see table 8.2). Most housing subsidies take the form of tax credits rather than direct expenditures. By far the largest federal subsidy is the exclusion from capital gains tax that usually goes to developers, followed closely by the income tax deduction for interest on homeowners' mortgage payments. The larger the development, the higher the capital gain, and the greater the tax saving. The higher the mortgage payment, the greater the tax deduction. Thus higher-income people are likely to receive higher benefits from these policies.

Low-income people can and do receive housing sudsidies directly through rental assistance programs, (see table 8.2) and indirectly through public housing programs and the housing allowance built into cash grants in need-based income-maintenance programs. About one-third of the cash grant in the AFDC program, for example, is presumed to go toward housing. Yet subsidies for low-income people are modest when compared with the total housing subsidy, and these people are dependent on "trickle-down" housing to meet their needs. And even with such housing, they are likely to experience a housing gap.

Both tables 8.1 and 8.2 show that most of the subsidies are provided to developers. Consequently present policy stimulates new construction and may have little benefit for people who need good-quality, affordable housing.

Table 8.2: Direct and indirect (tax credits) federal housing subsidies.

Direct expenditures	
Housing assistance	7.95%
Mortgage credit and insurance	2.44
Community development	2.95
Regional development	1.92
Subtotal	15.26%
Indirect expenditures (tax credits)	
Dividend exclusions	4.29%
Interest on consumer credit	11.28
Mortgage deductions	17.24
Property-tax deductions	6.47
Capital gains exclusions	18.53
Capital gains deferment (elderly)	0.58
Investment credits (rehabilitation)	16.35
Accelerated depreciation (rentals)	6.67
Corporate (housing) income	3.33
Subtotal	84.74%
Total	100.00%

Source: U.S. Budget Receipts and Outlays, 1986. Washington, D.C.: U.S. Government Printing Office, 1991.

The social value of housing subsidies may be understood better in terms of their different fiscal functions: some are intended to alleviate initial housing debt; others are geared to closing the income gap.[2] Debt-tied subsidies include interest-rate reductions, modifications in loans, capital gains exclusions, and capital grants. Income-gap subsidies are rent supplements and housing subsidies that form part of need-based income-maintenance programs. Because they focus benefits on low-income households and provide housing more economically on a unit-cost basis, income-gap subsidies may seem to offer the best housing assistance to those who need it, but they may have several latent disadvantages. When housing costs accelerate more rapidly than incomes— for example, during periods of inflation—the costs of income-gap subsidies will rise proportionately. Moreover, costs of income-gap subsidies may be greater in the aggregate (even though unit costs may be lower), because they create no incentives to keep housing costs low, and they require continuous administrative monitoring and supervision. The greatest disadvantage of income-gap subsidies may be that although they provide greater purchasing power, they contribute very little toward increasing the overall housing supply. Thus, direct government housing subsidies to low-income people may end up costing more in the long run than debt-tied subsidies that create more housing for the poor.

The normative issues that drive housing policy span a wide range of topics, not all of them concerned with developing better and more affordable housing. Housing standards involve considerations about the kinds of communities people prefer. Decisions about where housing is built, and how it is built, cannot be made properly without attendant decisions about services infrastructure—schools, roads, transportation, health and social services, fire protection, and public safety. Housing policy also interlocks with local political decisions about taxes, land use, and the enforcement of housing codes. These are classic issues that are explained in detail in chapter 3.

Improving the housing supply requires not only projections of housing needs but also long-term political commitments to achieve targeted construction goals. For example, in an effort to close a looming housing shortage caused in part by the post–World War II "baby boom," Congress in 1968, set a goal of developing 26 million housing units by 1978. To achieve this goal, Congress created the Department of Housing and Urban Development (HUD) and gave it comprehensive program and funding authority to subsidize private housing development. But in 1973 President Nixon ordered a review of national housing policy, enforced a moratorium on housing development, and impounded funds already authorized by Congress that were necessary to achieve that goal. Private subsidized housing starts, which had averaged 1.75 million units per year during HUD's first several years, dropped gradually to

1.1 million in 1982. By 1992 the Government National Mortgage Association reported providing the capital to finance or refinance 1,135,000 units. Thus government-subsidized housing continues to fall short of stimulating the development of housing to meet national goals, because the long-term funding commitment was not matched with political commitments to implement the policy through succeeding administrations.

Finally, housing policy aimed at expanding the supply of housing has dramatic implications for the banking and construction industries. Not only is considerable individual wealth held in housing, but corporate wealth as well is heavily invested in all kinds of housing. Mortgages comprise about 90 percent of all savings and loan companies' portfolios of assets, and housing-related loans constitute as much as half of all commercial banking activity. The entire construction industry, which ranges from the fabrication of building products to consumer products and home furnishings, from the tradesmen and their unions to the real estate salespeople who handle final transactions, is dependent upon housing. This vast housing industry is extremely sensitive to policy changes that may affect any of its parts. Labor problems may disrupt construction or increase costs. Increased interest rates may dampen consumer demand and inhibit construction of new housing. Changes in direct housing subsidies or in tax laws that reduce special tax treatment of housing may cause investors to invest their capital elsewhere. Any of these changes can set in motion a chain of reactions that are difficult to reverse, particularly since housing policy requires such long-term commitments.

In such an environment housing policy cannot be approached solely in terms of the development of housing units. Viable housing policy depends not only on how normative questions about housing are answered but also on how other public concerns interlock with housing issues. From this perspective any analysis that focuses only on issues of developing housing for the poor is likely to be incomplete. On the other hand, approaching housing policy from the perspective of all the interrelated interests is a much too comprehensive strategy for most policy analysts. The analysis of housing provided later in this chapter tries to keep interlocking factors in mind while focusing on housing's most obvious social welfare issues.

The Context of American Housing Policy

Although the first national housing legislation was adopted in 1933, the basis of present housing policy was created with the Housing Act of 1937. This act was designed primarily to stimulate growth in private housing through various subsidies: loan guarantees, special tax treatments, and assurances for construction. The act (and its subsequent changes) did not place the federal government in the position of building housing, but rather made it a stimulator, guarantor, and insurer of efforts undertaken in the private sector. Nor did the federal government use this power to concentrate its efforts on the creation of housing for poor people. Rather, federal support of housing then and now continues to be directed primarily toward ensuring that private housing markets perform sufficiently well that housing will eventually filter down to low-income citizens.

The context for American policy is thus the free-market mechanism of American capitalism. Indeed, economic analysts often use housing policy as an example of the efficiency of unregulated markets. There is, they say, a house for everyone at exactly the price that that person can afford. This filtering or "trickle-down" concept of housing development is a fundamental theoretical framework frequently used to dispute the necessity of public involvement in private affairs, and its operation with respect to housing bears closer examination.

In general, the theory argues that people who have capital to invest in housing put their money into *new* housing, usually in undeveloped areas where land costs and taxes are low. Once the housing is built and used for some time, its value (but not its market price) begins to decrease; to protect their capital, the owners sell, usually to people with less capital, as the value of the housing is now less. The sellers develop new housing somewhere else. The new owners hold the existing housing until its value declines to a point where they in turn decide to sell, again usually to someone with less capital to invest. Eventually the housing should reach zero value and thus be available to people who have nothing to invest. In the United States, the usual lifespan of housing (down to zero value) is calculated at approximately forty years. In practice, the market value of housing (resale value) is always greater than its "real" value.

Of course, this theory of housing does not operate as efficiently as its proponents may argue, nor does it operate in such a way that low-income people eventually get housing they can afford. Because housing development is so dependent on capital, slight fluctuations in money markets have immediate effects on housing production; larger fluctuations, such as 4 to 5 percent increases in interest rates, can disrupt the entire chain of housing production so seriously that it may take years to reestablish suppliers, builders, and other related businesses in a good balance. Moreover, the United States continues to experience a severe housing "shortfall" of about 2 million to 3 million units per year. If macroeconomic events, such as the 1981–83 recession or the 1990–91 high interest rates, continue to disrupt the housing chain, which is also bound by more and more stringent housing standards, this shortfall is likely to increase. In the present tight market, most low-income people have already been squeezed out of the housing chain entirely.

Table 8.3 summarizes housing resources as they exist for certain population groups in America. (It has been impossible to obtain numbers for table 8.3 that describe projected housing shortfalls for the 1990s. Given the slowdown in housing construction, the high interest rates for the early 1990s, and population increases as documented by the 1990 census, housing shortfalls in numbers are probably greater, reflecting about the same percentages found in table 8.3.) According to the 1983 housing census there were more than 84.6 million units available to house about 86.3 million households. This meant a housing shortfall of about 1.7 million units. Price preferences, location and related conditions discussed above influence the distribution of available housing among various population groups. Of the units available, 72.6 million were essentially for 73.2 million white households (a shortfall of .6 million) and 12.1 million were for 13.1 million black and other minority households (a shortfall of 1.1 million). This meant that about 14.3 percent of households (blacks and other minorities) bore the brunt of 63.3 percent of the shortfall. Looked at another way, in terms of shortfall per available households for each group, the crunch for minority households was nine times as great as it was for white households. Reliable figures for low-income households are harder to determine, but the estimate provided at the bottom of table 8.3 suggests a very bleak picture

Table 8.3: Summary of national housing distribution, 1983.

Population group	Households[1]	Housing units[2]	Shortfall	Owner-occupied[3]
White	73,173,000	72,562,000	611,000	
	84.7%	85.7%	36.7%	67.7%
Black	9,020,000	12,076,000	1,056,000	
	10.5%	14.3%	63.3%	46.2%
Hispanic and other	4,112,000			
	4.8%			
Total	86,305,000	84,638,000	1,667,000	
	100.0%	100.0%	100.0%	64.7%
Low income	10,357,000	1,270,000*		
	12.0%	1.5%		

Source: All notes refer to Housing Census of 1983.
  1. Extrapolated from Table 56.
  2. Table 1285
  3. Table 1297
  *Includes 1,262,500 units of public housing and 7,500 units of Section 8 housing.

indeed: public housing constitutes about 1.5 percent of the nation's housing supply, for the 12 percent of households that live in poverty. Although no figures for
home ownership among low-income people are given in table 8.3, it can be presumed that people at or below the poverty line would generally be unable to
qualify for mortgages, at least by FHA standards. According to the Department
of Housing and Urban Development's 1994 annual report, 87 percent of all private homes are financed by mortgages; 71 percent by conventional mortgages;
9 percent by FHA mortgages; and 6 percent through Veterans Administration
loans. About one-third of the conventional mortgages are issued by FHA. The
housing shortage would not be the same, however, in the case of older people
who have paid for their homes before entering low-income retirement.

The context of housing policy in America is framed by larger macroeconomic concerns that shape money markets and the construction industry, and
public efforts toward the development of housing must interlock with these
traditional and powerful private-sector activities. Pressure for government involvement in housing thus comes from two sources: (1) from housing deficiencies that have developed from long-term policy based on the
"trickle-down" principle and from attendant inequitable distributions caused
by inefficiencies in the private sector; and (2) from the private sector's need
for an adequate money supply, at attractive interest rates, to stimulate private
capital investments in housing development at all levels. In other words, housing policy in the United States attempts both to satisfy redistributive concerns
and to maintain an adequate housing supply for everyone.

Both of these normative positions have guided policy efforts to manipulate
the housing market. Competition for scarce public resources has often bred antagonism over which of these positions should be maximized, but in reality the
overall objective—decent housing—is compatible with both. As a result of
this tension, housing policy has evolved unevenly, sometimes concentrating
on redistributive objectives, sometimes emphasizing efforts to support the
present housing flow.

The Housing Act of 1937, the cornerstone of housing policy in America
today, has gradually been molded into a leviathan that provides public support
toward both these policy objectives. The housing legislation of 1933 committed government protection to housing lenders against financial losses during
the Depression. The act of 1937 added to this the Public Housing program (a
redistributive policy) and Federal Home Mortgage insurance, designed to
stimulate lending for private-sector housing construction.

By the end of World War II a severe housing shortage was evident. A need
for temporary shelter had arisen during the war itself for people who were re-
located to defense plants, military bases, and other strategic locations. But few
materials for permanent housing construction were available, and new hous-

ing starts dropped practically to zero. After the war, thousands of returning ser-
vicemen wanted to establish new households. To meet this need, the Housing
Act was expanded to include the Veterans Administration (VA) loan program,
which guaranteed mortgages to veterans, underwrote some of the share of interest, made it possible to extend the term of the loan, and subsidized the
amount of down payment necessary to secure the loan. These changes in housing policy provided a tremendous boost to the housing industry. Largely stimulated by the VA loan programs, housing starts doubled from 1945 to 1946 and
reached 1.9 million annually by 1950. More than 90 percent of these were sin-
gle-family houses. Home ownership increased from its prewar level of 44 percent of all households (in 1940) to 62 percent in 1960. The American housing
dream was well within reach.

Interestingly enough, the public housing program was almost scrapped during this period, as an unnecessary effort, and no public housing initiatives were
undertaken to respond directly to the housing needs of the poor. In fact, between 1945 and 1960, virtually no attention was given anywhere to subjects of
poverty. The Depression was history. The war had stimulated prosperity.
Poverty no longer existed.

In 1949 further amendments to the Housing Act set a new course for housing policy by recognizing that housing development was a broader issue than
a multiple of individual transactions in the housing market. Costs and benefits
of housing affect residents in a community regardless of whether they are involved in current transactions, and the problems of housing "extras"—the
need for roads, schools, and public services in new developments, and for improving slums and run-down neighborhoods in old developments—became a
public responsibility. "Urban renewal" entered the vocabulary of housing policy in this 1949 legislation. By making federal funds available to local governments, the Urban Renewal program was intended to help cities revitalize
areas "blighted" by "urban decay."

Urban Renewal supported local programs designed to eliminate deteriorated housing and replace it with new housing. Public Housing was promoted
as the flagship of Urban Renewal programs. The 1949 Housing Act authorized
the construction of 810,000 public housing units during the next six years, but
despite these commitments, the fate of that program was questionable from the
start. Initial lack of enthusiasm for public housing continued into and throughout the debate over the 1949 amendments, and only by linking the program
with Urban Renewal was enough support gained to preserve public housing as
part of the nation's housing policies. However, joining the two in legislation
and official policy was not sufficient to inspire the same results in redevelopment plans of local communities. Individual communities were not motivated
to build public housing, and by and large Urban Renewal funding was used for

other purposes, mostly rehabilitation and expansion of the middle-income rental housing supply.

The Housing Act of 1954 expanded Urban Renewal policy to include commercial redevelopment. Although Urban Renewal projects had spread rapidly as a means of revitalizing deteriorating urban residential areas, commercial redevelopment was an even more profitable scheme. By contrast, President Eisenhower's austerity budget held authorizations for public housing at a minimum. By 1960 only 250,000 public housing units had been built since the 1949 legislation was passed, bringing the national total to 478,200, well behind the 1949 policy goals. By 1980 the total had increased to only 1,281,900, about 1.5 percent of all occupied housing. By 1992 there were 1,323,000 public housing units, of which only 1,199,000 were occupied. Age of dwellings and years of abuse have taken a toll on America's public housing program.

Amendments to the Housing Act in 1957 permitted federal support for private housing rehabilitation as a means of keeping the focus of redevelopment on residential housing and of refocusing Urban Renewal toward its original emphasis on housing. This effort was too little, too late, and too unimaginative. Most existing housing in eligible areas was beyond rehabilitation, and the little that was worth saving often stood amid blocks and blocks of empty lots that had fallen to the bulldozers. The plan, which had called for revitalization (mostly of black neighborhoods on property owned by suburban whites) but lacked the capacity to develop entirely new housing for residents of demolished buildings, was a dismal failure. Urban renewal became black removal. In many instances the vacant land was ultimately deemed economically unsuited for redevelopment in housing, and it was retargeted for commercial development as the only way to save local governments from huge financial losses from their original investments in Urban Renewal programs.

Housing policy met with further disappointments through the 1960s. The bitter experiences with Urban Renewal and the general lack of adequate housing for blacks contributed significantly to urban unrest and rioting.[3] Criticism of Urban Renewal continued to undermine all efforts at residential redevelopment. Rehabilitation of the urban infrastructure became a more pressing aspect of the problem. Cities were not able to improve police and fire protection, area schools, or cultural and recreational opportunities, without massive public assistance. Thus the Housing Act was modified in 1968 to include funding for upgrading the infrastructure of Urban Renewal areas; this was the Model Cities program. That year also saw the founding of the Department of Housing and Urban Development; Robert Weaver, the nation's first black cabinet member, was appointed its first head.

However, housing policy had again shifted in focus away from residential development. Once again the modifications provided too little support, after most of the damage of Urban Renewal had been done. Model Cities did little to reverse the growing housing shortage. A new interest-rate subsidy program (Section 235), designed to help low-income families become owners of their own homes, had even less success among the increasing numbers of people who were abandoning their properties in central city areas.

By 1970 the Senate Banking Committee had opened hearings to obtain information about the dearth of housing for the poor (particularly in the wake of urban riots). Concern focused strongly on the deterioration of the American city.[4] The hearings sorted out bitter complaints from all quarters. Public housing was in serious trouble. Too few units were available, and the occupants seemed to be all too representative of a subculture of poverty: black and single mothers with young children. Public housing was blamed for creating urban segregation, a reversal of the intention of the 1937 act. Urban Renewal was judged a failure, and some of the programs that it had bred—Section 235 and Model Cities—were condemned as compromises geared toward the middle and upper classes and far removed from the fundamental problems of decent housing.

Reformulation of housing policy emerged slowly from this public scrutiny, but finally, in 1974, Congress legislated modifications of the Housing Act that gave housing policy its present form. Unable to resolve all the conflicts that had developed over Urban Renewal and Model Cities, Congress acted in predictable fashion by turning all these functions over to the states through the much-heralded Community Development Block Grant program. The other programs under the Housing Act were preserved in their existing forms, and a new program, Rent Subsidy (Section 8), was added as a companion program to Public Housing. The Rent Subsidy program provided federal funds to local housing authorities to pay the difference between what would be a fair rent for housing, and what a low-income person could afford to pay.

Existing Housing Programs

In summary, present housing policy falls into four areas (see table 8.4). (1) Housing programs comprise all the housing subsidy programs administered by the Federal Housing Administration, including loan insurance guarantees to individuals, as well as loan programs to developers under Section 202 (housing for the elderly and disabled), Section 235 (middle-income housing subsidies), Farmers' Home Loans, and Section 8 (low-income rent subsidies); Public housing, a separate entity, includes all federal assistance to low-income public housing construction and rentals under the supervision of local housing authorities. (2) Community planning and development is essentially the Community De-

velopment Block Grants that provide financial support to states for local rehabilitation projects, including private housing redevelopment and renewal and
improvements to the infrastructure of local communities. (3) The Government
National Mortgage Association (GNMA), the fiscal arm of housing policy,
manages the large loan portfolio of the government's support of essentially
private-market housing programs. In 1984 it had a budget of $6.2 billion. In
FY 1992 GNMA had a housing portfolio of over $72 billion in mortgages. (4)
Solar Energy and Energy Assistance funding supports efforts to develop alternative energy sources and to help low-income people cope with energy-related
housing problems. (5) In response to the public outcry in the late 1980s over
homeless individuals and families, Congress amended the housing act to provide funding for temporary shelters for the homeless. Although slow getting
off the ground, the McKinny Act has been able to provide funding for homeless in almost every municipality. In FY 1992 Housing and Urban Development provided $73.2 million to 372 shelters in cities to improve the conditions
of shelters, sold or leased 2,400 properties to various not for profit homeless
providers, and extended the use of Section 8 rental assistance for use of the
homeless in Single Room Occupancy (SRO) facilities.

How well these programs work toward meeting the primary objectives of
housing policy is debatable. Table 8.4 shows that housing for low-income people and the aged and disabled receives attention in several areas of housing
policy. However, among direct federal expenditures, "housing assistance" to
the poor comprised less then 10 percent of the annual federal housing budget
in 1986. Table 8.3 reminds us that the shortfall of public housing for low-income people is drastic, and the history of housing legislation sketched above
explains that incentives for local communities to construct public housing
have been low, even when federal policy has offered the opportunity. If federal housing policy is regarded entirely in terms of aid to the poor, this is a dismal record indeed. But, as mentioned earlier, since its inception in 1937,
federal housing policy has evolved amid the tension of two overall aims: assistance to the poor and support of adequate housing for all. Because emphasis on either of these normative positions alone tends to undermine the
integrity of the other, evaluations of housing policies and programs are best
approached through an understanding of the dual context of housing policy as
a whole. In the present context, for example, it must be remembered that much
government support of housing in general is aimed at reducing shortages that
would create even greater competition for adequate housing for everyone, with
the result that low-income households would be forced into even more des-
perate circumstances.

As it presently exists, housing policy spills into private-sector concerns in
great volume. The macroeconomic implications of this have been charted only

Table 8.4: Programs under the Housing Act.

Program	Primary focus	Beneficiaries
Housing programs		
Section 202	new construction and rehabilitation	aged and disabled
Section 235	new construction	middle-income renter
Section 8	rental assistance	low-income renter
Farmers' Home Loans (FHA)	new construction	rural low- and middle-income
Public housing	new construction	low-income
Community planning		
Community Development Block Grants	rehabilitation and urban renewal	usually targeted at low-income neighborhoods
Government Mutual Mortgage Association		
Various programs	loan management	banks and lending institutions
Solar Energy and Energy Assistance		
Activate energy	new energy sources	everyone
Energy assistance	cash support for high energy bills	low-income
Weatherization	rehabilitation	low-income

vaguely, and then only during periods of economic crisis. The "multiplier effects" of housing policy are difficult to determine even during normal economic cycles. For example, whether housing subsidies reduce housing costs or drive them higher remains an unresolved economic debate. It is also clear that housing policy straddles many such partly public, partly private issues. Even if the main normative issues could be restructured, and even if analysis of housing policy could be confined to its possible effects on a clearly delimited public sector, normative issues surrounding distribution of benefits might remain problematic. Products of housing policy actually seem to be distributed on an uneven geographic basis, rather than, for example, according to a nationwide standard of need.[5] Assisted housing in particular tends to be clustered in urban areas, as opposed to rural areas; regionally it clusters in the Northeast and on the West Coast, as opposed to the Midwest and South. These patterns may be a function of spillover economic effects, or may be due to a number of factors not directly related to housing, such as geopolitical administrative boundaries. Any analysis of housing policy, in sum, is apt to be severely compromised by latent or unforeseen anomalies within normative contexts.

Policy Analysis

The criteria-based model is especially helpful in analyzing housing policy because the values that surround housing policy as a whole are so diverse and because the programs have policy consequences that overlap in complex ways. The normative issues and the existing housing alternatives shown in table 8.5 have been discussed above. Consequently the table contains no surprises. Tax incentives and mortgage guarantees maximize universal values, particularly for efficient, stigma-free housing of personal choice. They also contribute to expanding the housing supply, although not for low-income people. Housing subsidies target resources better, particularly for improving housing and directing housing resources at low-income people. Community development alternatives have very little relevance to selective or universal housing criteria. Public housing and Section 8 subsidies have the greatest number of low evaluations on the table, even though these programs best target housing for low-income people. This evaluation of public housing and Section 8 programs confirms the historical development of housing policy: housing targeted for the poor, though a continuing issue, has never been a high priority. To state this in slightly different terms, policymakers who favor housing carefully targeted for low-income people might do well to seek a different policy arena altogether, in which this value has greater potential for realization—such as income-maintenance policy, through which housing could be offered as a highly valued in-kind benefit. (See chapter 6.)

Conclusion

Perhaps the major issue in all of housing policy is the duality of normative orientations toward the whole subject of housing. Certainly the normative issues outlined and discussed at the outset of this chapter present a complex orientation to housing in America that tends to deemphasize the government's direct creation of housing, particularly for the poor, preferring an emphasis on economic stimulus to housing in general. Nevertheless housing policy debates

Table 8.5: Alternative policy and program approaches for housing (criteria-based model).

ALTERNATIVES

Normative orientations	Tax incentives	Housing subsidies				Mortgage guarantees	Community development
		Sec. 235	Sec. 236	Public housing	Sec. 8		
Universal criteria							
Equity							
Horizontal	Hi	Lo	Lo	Lo	Lo	Hi	Lo
Vertical	Med	Hi	Hi	Hi	Hi	Med	Lo
Efficiency (low cost/high value)	Hi	Med	Med	Med	Med	Med	Lo
Nonstigmatizing	Hi	Med	Med	Lo	Lo	Hi	Lo
Preference satisfaction	Hi	Med	Med	Lo	Lo	Hi	Lo
Policy-specific criteria							
Expand housing supply	Hi	Med	Med	Hi	Hi	Hi	Lo
Improve housing quality	Lo	Lo	Lo	Lo	Lo	Lo	Hi
Improve housing supply	Hi	Lo	Lo	Hi	Hi	Med	Med
Protect financial markets	Lo	Med	Lo	Lo	Lo	Hi	Med
Stimulate the economy	Hi	Med	Med	Med	Med	Med	Med
Aid low-income households	Lo	Lo	Med	Hi	Hi	Lo	Med
	Hi = 7	Hi = 1	Hi = 1	Hi = 4	Hi = 4	Hi = 5	Hi = 1
	Med = 1	Med = 6	Med = 6	Med = 2	Med = 2	Med = 4	Med = 4
	Lo = 3	Lo = 4	Lo = 4	Lo = 5	Lo = 5	Lo = 2	Lo = 6

continue to raise the question of what *should* be the normative orientation to housing policy. For example, should housing policy be directed toward providing more units at government initiative, primarily for the poor, at the potential risk of driving up housing costs generally? Or should housing policy stress government subsidies and market stimulus strategies that would foster competition and some price control, but leave inadequate supplies, particularly for those who most need help with housing?

The analysis of housing policy presented in this chapter suggests two guiding principles that must be applied to any housing policy choice. First, the macroeconomic impact of any housing policy choice must be calculated. Housing policy operates in a vast nationwide environment of lending institutions, large federal, state, and local programs, the construction industry, and a complex network of related service industries. Even the slightest alteration in housing policy is likely to create ripples throughout these interrelated economic spheres. Second, developing and implementing housing policy requires prolonged "lead time." Like the docking of giant ships, housing policy moves slowly, and considerable leeway must be allowed for the execution of even the most modest maneuver. In this view, it may be wisest to insist that whatever course housing policy takes, it may be more important to stay on that course than to tinker with the policy in order to achieve marginal objectives.

Chapter Nine

CHILD WELFARE

Introduction

The welfare of children holds an exceptionally important place in American public policy. Until the Social Security Act established the contemporary framework for child welfare policy, children's concerns were met in a variety of ways. Even before the reform movement of about 1890–1910, voluntary agencies and local communities had mobilized resources to protect and aid children. During the late eighteenth and early nineteenth centuries children without parents (orphans) were placed in public homes or farmed out as apprentices in exchange for room and board. In 1853 the Reverend Charles Loring Brace founded an emergency "child-saving" movement with the formation of the New York Children's Aid Society, whose primary responsibility was collecting orphaned and deserted children from the streets of New York and other cities and transplanting them to farms of the American Midwest. Dorothea Dix's celebrated state-by-state visitation of county almshouses and local jails (1845–1854) uncovered abusive treatment not only of the mentally ill but of children as well. The New York Society for the Prevention of Cruelty to Children was formed in 1870 after public outcry over the case of Mary Ellen, an abused child, who had less public protection than many of New York's animals. This first "child protection" agency was legitimated by the English and American legal doctrine *parens patriae*, which held that public courts have surrogate parental authority to protect the property rights (and now all rights) of children when those rights can no longer be protected by their natural parents.

The reform movement directed much of its energy toward engaging state governments in the provision and supervision of programs for children. States developed mechanisms to ensure that local care of homeless and dependent children was humane and consistent with child care standards of that day.

States also developed legislation that gave legal recognition to differences between children and adults. Illinois created the first juvenile court in 1899, and half the states had laws regulating child labor by 1900. Beginning with Illinois in 1911, states initiated financial aid programs to support dependent children in their own homes.

The suffrage movement gave further thrust to public policy for children. As women organized to obtain the right to vote, they also advocated strongly for the rights of children. The first White House conference ever called by a President was one concerning children convened by Theodore Roosevelt in 1909, and the delegation of hundreds of national leaders who attended the meeting generated enough concern to create the Children's Bureau in the U.S. Department of Labor in 1912. In 1921 women won a long-fought struggle to convince Congress to approve a health program for new mothers and their newborns.[1] This, the Sheppard-Towner Act, was a prototype of future social welfare programs. The Maternal and Child Health program (discussed below and also in chapter 7) became its lasting legacy.

By 1935, when the Social Security Act was legislated, the architecture for modern child welfare programs had been partly established. Because state-supervised and state-administered programs of financial aid were already in place, the child welfare policy of the Social Security Act layered federal funds over existing state-level foundations. The child welfare programs created by the Social Security Act thus were new only to the extent that they established a uniform framework for administration, to which a specified number of existing state programs were required to conform. These programs comprised a mixture of services for dependent children—foster care and health services, for example—and income support for them in the form of "pensions" for mothers, which became Aid to Dependent Children under the federal act.

Normative Issues

Four normative issues have shaped child welfare policy and programs today and perpetuate crosscurrents of debate in child welfare policy analysis: (1) parental responsibility versus children's rights, (2) protection versus liberation, (3) need-based versus universal services, and (4) services versus income maintenance. Although these normative concerns are similar to many of those related to income-maintenance policy, with respect to children they take on a unique significance.

Parental responsibility versus children's rights

These two conflicting issues arise from two different conceptions of childhood. Prior to the nineteenth century, children were perceived as miniature adults and were expected to become part of the adult world as soon as they were physically able. "Childhood" was restricted to the helpless and dependent phases of infancy and the very early years. This did not mean, however, that children achieved true independence and autonomy at an early age. A unique feature of family history throughout much of the world is the amount of legal authority fathers have traditionally possessed over the lives of family members. Decisions about children have been an important part of this system of family authority. These dual conceptions of child and family have shaped child welfare policy that distinguishes sharply between children who are in families where fathers are present, and children who are not.

Law and custom have shaped theories of parental responsibility for children. If a child damages property, parents are held liable. Parents are responsible for their children's school attendance, and they are expected to ensure that their children satisfy other social obligations. In exchange for compliance with such basic social expectations, parents are left free to deal with their children as they see fit in almost every area of physical and social development. The welfare of the child is the responsibility of the parent. From nutrition to dating, from health care to school achievement, from clothing and dress to decisions about the family car, parents are responsible for their children.

In the nineteenth century, with the spread of the Romantic movement and its ideas, a new concept of separate identity in childhood initiated new views about children. Children were seen as good, innocent, and subject to corruption and danger from an otherwise evil society. Thus childhood problems and problem children could be corrected, and children were held in high esteem as the salvation of future generations. According to one theorist, it was this reformed view of children that led to "child-saving" activities such as those undertaken in New York by the Reverend Mr. Brace, which were designed to rescue children from the evils of society.[2] The obligations of society to protect and nurture children, together with the reformed view of childhood as a period of innocence, led to the idea that children not only had rights, but rights peculiar to the status of childhood. Paramount among them, social reformers argued, were the right to an education, the right to life and good health, the right to play, and the right to make their own choices.

Whether rights exist for anyone, and what limitations are placed on them if they do, is an important philosophical question that has intricate overtones in child welfare policy. The emerging idea of children's rights collided sharply with earlier views of parental responsibility. If children had rights independent of their status in the family, how were these rights to be protected and asserted? If children's rights were to prevail, some greater force had to exist outside the authority of the family, and this force was government. Because the "best interests of the child" were placed before the authority of the child's parents, efforts to promote and protect children's rights on this basis raised—and still raise—serious questions of conflict between personal individuality and the privacy of the family.

Protection of children versus their liberation

The newly perceived status of children prompted considerable activity during the reform movement. Not only were public policies designed to embrace children's rights, but a vast array of public and private programs were developed that served to protect and promote their interests. Juvenile courts were established to deal with violations of the law in nonadversarial, nonpunitive ways, and in an environment designed to correct delinquent behavior and help young people develop into productive members of society. When children were found guilty of crimes for which adults would be punished, rehabilitation and treatment were substituted for fines and incarceration. After the Mary Ellen case, states moved quickly to adopt laws to protect children, giving power to state agencies to remove children from their homes if they were abused, neglected, or financially deprived. Families were expected to care for their children in acceptable ways, and if that care could not be provided, public agencies would provide it. Special treatment units for children, with recreational activities, were created in general and psychiatric hospitals.

Such efforts to protect children, to enhance the virtues of childhood, and to reform children's alien and antisocial behaviors into socially acceptable ones, began to conflict with the very rights that child advocates had sought to identify and protect. As new protective programs were introduced, the new definition of childhood came under attack: if children did indeed have rights, would it not make better sense to liberate them to enjoy their rights, rather then enforce their rights upon them? From this distinction developed two views of childhood that continue to influence child welfare policy today.

> The *institutional* concept [of childhood] is a legal or quasi-legal one in which in modern society childhood is usually determined by age. . . . The *normative* concept is connected with certain [childhood] capacities, the acquisition of certain elements of knowledge and experience, expertness and possession of certain ethical interests, or reasonable expectations about a person's likely behavior at certain stages of development.[3]

The products of this normative definition of childhood have left a legacy of policies and programs with diffuse, often conflicting, goals. For example, public policy now supports early-childhood development programs, programs for culturally disadvantaged children, programs for adolescents, preadolescents, postadolescents, and so on. These normative child welfare policies all hinge on somehow defining children's functional capacities to use available resources without limiting their access to those resources by specific age boundaries. In contrast, the products of institutional definitions of childhood—such as mandatory public education, child labor laws, and certain legal privileges (voting, driving, public drinking)—are defined by specific age, without regard to functional ability. In effect, normatively produced policies support activities that liberate children from traditional roles, whereas institutional, age-limited programs focus on protection, promote constraints, and communicate traditional paternalistic messages. As programs developed from normative views of childhood have become interlayered with age-specific programs, the purposes of child welfare policies and programs as a whole have become very confused, and all types of programs have lost some—or much—of their clarity and focus.

For example, confusion may abound over which programs are best suited for a teenage parent, who can be viewed normatively as an adult but still be defined institutionally as a child. Or suppose a retarded couple in their twenties wish to marry and raise a family; institutionally they are adults, but normatively they may still be children. What policies should apply to them? Allied to these exceptional examples is the almost universal complaint: "If I'm old enough to fight and die for my country, I ought to be old enough to drink."

Need-based versus universal services

This issue pervades the two preceding ones: parental responsibility versus children's rights, and protection versus liberation. The recognition that childhood is a special condition would certainly argue for special services for all children, placing special demands on all parents and familes to satisfy those special circumstances. Children are expensive, particularly when they are not allowed to support themselves financially until age 16 (or longer in many cases). Some nations, including Great Britain and Canada, provide financial allowances for children. The United States provides a standard income-tax deduction for each family dependent. Such policies—essentially a variety of income maintenance—give some public sanction to the idea that all children have special needs.

Income maintenance becomes a very controversial topic, however, when it is especially administered to children who live in low-income families. A reasonable question may be: "Can parents fulfill their responsibility to their children when they do not earn enough money to maintain their children at acceptable social standards?" In the eighteenth and nineteenth centuries, children could indeed be removed from their families for financial reasons, but modern child welfare policy does not support such practices. Nevertheless the adequacy of parental care for children in low-income families is frequently questioned even today. These children do not benefit from community resources as much as children from families with adequate income. They are at higher risk of accidents, delinquent behavior, poor school performance, and teenage pregnancies. Children with nutritionally inadequate diets do not learn well in school.

In that sense it would be fair to say that poor children require more intense and more specialized services, many designed to protect them or intervene in their lives—in sharp contrast with normative views about freedom and liberation. For example, studies of child abuse and neglect continue to find a close association between parents' low income and poor child care, and between family stress (as expressed particularly by separation and divorce) and child abuse and neglect.[4] Social programs of family intervention and child protection, which have a universal legal responsibility, usually have a heavy caseload of low-income clients. The success of a program like Head Start, which attempts to mitigate the impact of poverty on learning, is undermined when low-income families are unable to stabilize the home learning environment for their children.

As it presently exists, child welfare policy includes activities to satisfy both sides of this issue. Some programs, such as public education, are clearly universal, whereas others, like Head Start, are need-based. Yet in most instances the issues are not so clearly separated. For example, policymakers remain undecided as to whether birth control information and supplies should be available without charge to all teenagers who request it. Such information and material is provided without charge to children from low-income families, but critics have objected that these services (whether universally offered or not) bypass parental authority. Other services, such as preventive health service, generally are available to all children, on a cost basis. However, because many low-income families cannot afford routine medical care, many poor children go without some basic health services. For example, a child may not receive standard immunizations against serious chidhood diseases until about to enter school. (By state laws, vaccinations are prerequisite for enrollment.)

Services versus income maintenance

Income maintenance for a child is always provided through an adult, usually a parent. Consequently normative concerns about parental responsibility ver-

sus children's rights and about protection versus liberation are also complicated by questions of how benefits should be provided—as outright monetary
support, or in kind? If parents effectively control the use of income-maintenance resources, particularly for low-income children, will those resources be
used for products most necessary for the child's well-being? In-kind products
do ensure better targeting of resources, and a decision about the first two normative issues may determine the normative orientation for this one. If, for example, one decides to act in the best interest of the child, might not in-kind
benefits achieve this objective better than income maintenance?

If the child is considered in the context of the family, the principle of family
privacy would seem to dictate that the family knows best how to use income resources to answer the child's needs. This assumption falters, however, when
faced with children who are under public charge—who have no families or cannot live with their families. In those circumstances in-kind benefits may seem
the safest and fairest alternatives, even though they may override the opportunity for the children, or the adults who attend them, to make their own choices.
Hence, in practice, income maintenance and autonomy have become the prime
policy choices for children who are within families, whereas in-kind services are
preferred for children who are outside the protective influence of the family.
This division seems to apply regardless of whether the family does in fact serve
the interests of the child, or whether the child has been removed from the family's protection due to his or her own activities or to some other factor.

Child welfare income-maintenance issues have become more complicated
as more children live in single-parent, female-headed households. Although
public income-maintenance programs exist for these children, critics have
long questioned the propriety of supporting children when parents are unable
to contribute financially to their care. The issue of parental responsibility is
thus joined forcibly with policy choices concerning income maintenance and
in-kind products. The AFDC program had been juggled to make it an income-
maintenance program that tried to maximize parental responsibility by forcing
work on mothers and taking fathers to court when they did not support their
children. As appropriate as work and child support obligations are in their own
right, mixing them into income-maintenance policy has resulted in complex
and confusing policies that fail to respond to the larger child welfare issues. In
other words, adequate family income is important, and parental responsibility
is also highly valued, but neither assures the welfare of the child. In-kind products can.

Most normative debates over child welfare policy can usually be summarized in terms of children's rights versus parents' responsibility, public protection of children versus public liberation of children (issues that affect
definitions of childhood), universal versus special public services for children,

and the nature of special services—whether they should be income-maintenance or in-kind benefits. Child welfare policy in its present state has not clearly distinguished these normative questions, and consequently, it sustains and creates policy products that often have arisen from conflicting normative bases. A profile of American children may give some objective vantage point for reviewing these normative issues and policies against the current state of child welfare across the nation.

A Profile of American Children

The basic normative issues reviewed above ultimately revolve around the conditions in which children actually live, and public expectations about them. The following profile of American children suggests some areas of special concern for child welfare policy. Table 9.1 presents a composite view of children that highlights their social and economic status. Children under age 18 comprise about 26 percent of the total population. To suggest a child welfare policy that would serve all children would cover a lot of people—over 64 million. Thus, at the outset, any comprehensive child welfare policy is likely to be very expensive, and indeed most are. In fiscal year 1994, federal funds for educational activities for children in public primary and secondary schools totaled almost $28 billion, 4.4 percent of the entire federal budget; but even this large sum amounted only to 10 percent of all federal expenditures on children's education. Total educational expenditures for elementary and secondary education in 1992 amounted to $256.2 billion and many experts believe education is still underfunded in the United States.[5]

Children in Poverty

Because of the potentially high costs of any policy that serves all children, most child welfare policy is directed toward special groups of children, most usually children who seem particularly in need of something. Table 9.1 suggests that children in single-parent, female-headed families are likely to be poor and likely to be black—two special overlapping classes of children for whom child welfare policy can have very significant effects. Research on children over the years suggests that children in single-parent, female-headed families are more likely to do poorly in school and display more antisocial behavior (including tendencies toward delinquency and difficulty in social adjustments),[6] problems complicated by their poverty. Overall, their poor performance may be due as much to their poverty as to their family situation.

Table 9.1: Profile of children in the United States (1989).

Population group*	Number	Percent
Children under age 18	64,083,000	100.0
(25.8% of the U.S. population)		
Male	32,821,000	51.2
Female	31,262,000	48.8
Total		(100.0)
Children under age 5	18,752,000	100.0
(29.3% of children under age 18)		
White	15,050,000	80.3
Black	2,890,000	15.4
Other	812,000	4.3
Total		(100.0)
Children under age 18 living in families	63,637,000	100.0
(99.3% of all children)		
Living with both parents	46,592,000	73.1
(White–79.6%)		
(Black–38.0%)		
(Other–67.0%)		
Living with mother	13,682,000	21.5
(White–16.1%)		
(Black–51.1%)		
(Other–27.8%)		
Living with father or other relative	3,373,000	5.4
Total		(100.0)
Children living below poverty level	13,918,000	100.0
(21.7% of all children)		
In white families	7,165,000	51.4
In black families	4,257,000	30.6
In Spanish or other families	2,496,000	18.0
Total		(100.0)
Children under 18 by presence of parents		
White mothers:		
Married, spouse present		79.6
Divorced or widowed		9.2
Married, spouse absent		4.0
Never married		2.9
White fathers only		2.7
Neither		1.6
Total		(100.0)

Table 9.1: *(continued)*

Population group*	Number	Percent
Black mothers:		
Married, spouse present		38.0
Divorced or widowed		11.6
Married, spouse absent		12.1
Never married		27.4
Black fathers only		3.4
Neither		7.5
Total		(100.0)
Hispanic and other mothers:		
Married, spouse present		67.0
Divorced or widowed		9.1
Married, spouse absent		10.3
Never married		8.4
Hispanic and other fathers only		2.7
Neither		2.1
Total		(100.0)

*Excludes women in the military
Source: U.S. Census. STI3A (1990).

The fact that children are two-and-one-half times as likely to be poor if they live in single-parent, female-headed families is a special concern. About 24 percent of all children live in such families, and almost all of them have living fathers, who by law are required to provide financial support for them. Uncollected child support is one of the most pervasive child welfare problems today. As mentioned in chapter 5 in the only study of parental failure to pay child support that has examined fathers' financial capacity to pay, researchers found that $26.6 billion in child support was owed and could be paid by absent fathers in 1984. Only $6.1 billion was actually paid, leaving $20.5 billion uncollected.[7] By 1992 $32 billion in child support was owed, of which approximately $24 billion went uncollected. If this $24 billion were distributed equally, this amount would provide every child living with one parent (poor or not) $1,444 per year, or every poor child $1,647 per year, or every poor child living in a single parent family $2,978 per year. The average amount of child support received by a single-parent family in 1989 was $2,995, according to the U.S. Bureau of the Census, and this amount provided about 19 percent of the family's income.

The Racial Factor

Table 9.1 also highlights a striking difference in family structures for black and white children. About half of all black children are living in single-parent, female-headed households, and many of those live with women who have never been married. The poverty rate among these children is twice as high as that for children in similar white families; about one out of three black children in single-parent, female-headed homes are living in poverty; only 19 percent of white children in such families are poor.

For these and other reasons over the years, scholars and analysts have debated how the differences between black and white family structures may affect the rearing of children. Writing in the 1940s, Gunnar Myrdal identified this difference as a continuing product of the American system of slavery, which had deliberately destroyed family bonds and established the black matriarchal family.[8] Two decades later, in 1965, a critique of the black family by Patrick Moynihan, written while he was an assistant director of the Office of Planning and Policy of the U.S. Department of Labor, stirred considerable controversy. Moynihan identified high rates of out-of-wedlock births, dissolved marriages, and the relatively high proportion of female-headed families among blacks as a cause for alarm and argued that the black family was no longer able to rear children properly.[9] Many black social scientists had expressed concern about black family structure before Moynihan issued his report. Most notable was the social psychologist Kenneth Clark, an influential scholar whose work helped shape civil rights laws and policy of the 1960s.[10]

More recently the black scholar Andrew Billingsley and the white anthropologist Carol Stack have presented research that confirms important differences between white and black family structures.[11] This does not mean, however, that black families are somehow inadequate or are unable to raise their children properly. Research has also shown that black women may rely more customarily on the extended family for surrogate parenting resources, an option that may not be as commonly available among white families. In other ways, black family structures serve important functions for blacks that are not necessary for the white family, and that should not be minimized: "Negroes have created . . . a range of institutions to structure the tasks of living a victimized life and to minimize the pain it inevitably produces. Predominant among these institutions are those of the nuclear family, the social network— the extended kinship system . . . by which they instruct, explain and accept themselves."[12]

On the negative side, however valuable they are to black families, these important structural differences continue to isolate blacks and their children from the mainstream of American life, which has provided the energy for upward mobility for other American minorities. The difficulty and appropriateness of developing public policy designed deliberately to modify forms of family life raises huge issues of ethics and public expense. Because so many public child welfare policies do indeed have an influence on various forms of family life, it might seem tempting to suggest new policies that would modify present forms of black family life as one means of addressing the degrading experience of poverty that more than half of all black children undergo. From the perspective of policy analysis, however, family policy and child welfare policy are two separate issues, and they must be addressed independently of each other. Focus on the family as the subject for policy analysis raises a host of normative issues, which differ profoundly from those surrounding child welfare policy. For that reason, analysis in this chapter concentrates on the problems of children. Thus it is important to digress briefly here to consider conclusions drawn from research about family patterns generally and specifically about the black family. The alternative patterns so evident in black family structure have not deprived children of basic maternal care, but serious doubts about that care must be raised when adequate funds to support this and other analogous forms of maternal care are not available, and when women are poorly prepared for the maternal roles that today's complex urban society forces upon them.

The Changing Character of American Families

The changing character of the American family, so dramatically portrayed by our gradual recognition of special black family structures, has had a significant impact on child welfare in many other ways. More women are working than ever before. They presently compose half the civilian labor force, which means, among other things, that many more mothers are working. In fact, maternal employment is now greater than at any time since World War II. Table 9.2 provides some information about maternal employment and women's participation in the work force that has direct bearing on child welfare.

Married women compose almost half of the female labor force. Married women who work and have children of school age make up over 65 percent of all married women with school-age children. Many studies have explored why women work and the impact of their changing roles on families and on the care of children. In general, women work because they need money and are seeking meaningful lives. Work itself does not diminish women's maternal interests and abilities. However, lack of supportive resources for working mothers makes mothering more difficult. Perhaps because women traditionally have

Table 9.2: Women in the labor force.

Category	Number in labor force	Percent of category	Percent of total labor force
Total women in the labor force (57.9% of all women)	58,407,000	100.0	100.0
Single women	14,624,000	66.4	25.0
Married women	31,978,000	59.4	54.8
Widowed and divorced	11,805,000	47.1	20.2
Married with children to 6 years	7,300,000	59.6	
Married with children 6-17 years	9,700,000	74.9	
Single with children to 6 years	1,100,000	47.4	
Single with children 6-17 years	700,000	70.2	
Widowed, divorced, or separated			
with children to 6 years	1,200,000	60.0	
with children 6-17 years	3,000,000	78.3	

Source: Statistical Abstract of the United States (1994), Tables 625 and 626.

been expected to stay home and provide nurturing and care for children and spouses, few public resources have been developed that substitute for traditional maternal activities during mothers' working hours.

But not all mothers have a choice about whether to stay home and provide child care. Poor mothers, in particular, are expected to work, and from time to time poor mothers who receive welfare support will be required to work as the 1995 welfare reform amendments are implemented. But conflicting messages are expressed when enforced work policy fails to anticipate the kinds of resources necessary to support employment for mothers who wish to work and for those who are forced to do so by other policies. Working mothers destabilize child welfare policies in today's social and vocational context. Daycare for children becomes a critical issue, particularly for poor mothers who cannot afford to purchase such services. By 1990, the Congressional Budget Office states, there were 2.8 million children under age 6 living in poverty in female-headed households.[13] At present publicly funded daycare can serve only about 10 percent of these children. Welfare mothers who work are permitted to deduct child care expenses from gross earnings, which provides in most cases only a partial subsidy for that expense. And although welfare will guarantee daycare to mothers who are required to work, finding adequate daycare may be difficult for all mothers, regardless of their ability to pay for it. From the standpoint of child welfare, maternal employment without an adequate infra-structure of reliable and trustworthy daycare services and an infrastructure of other family support services for mothers and children is a questionable pol-icy option.

Special Issues of Health and Social Welfare

The health status of children was discussed to some extent in chapter 7. Poor mothers are more likely to bear low-birth-weight (premature) babies, who in turn are at risk of frequent and serious childhood health problems. This is a critical issue not only of early childhood welfare, but also of the welfare of older children who themselves bear children. Teenage pregnancy and motherhood is a serious problem for both mother and child. The birthrate had dropped from 1 birth for every 1,000 women age 10–14 in 1950, to .8 in 1965, but it rose to 1.3 in 1975 and has stabilized at 1.1 in the 1990s. An unusually high percentage of these births were children with low birth weights, born to mothers without financial and social resources to care for them adequately.

A number of other health problems of older children have not been ad-dressed adequately by child welfare policies generally, or by public health pro-grams specifically. Drug use, auto accidents, and suicides are persistent problems that ignore boundaries of class, race, or economic status. Emotional health, both immediately and in the long term, may be greatly affected by suc-cess or failure in school and its influence on employment. Black children and poor children are more likely to drop out of school before they complete high school. The nationwide dropout rate among white teenagers is currently about 7 percent, for black teenagers, about 15 percent; these rates tend to be higher in impoverished areas.

This profile of American children suggests that traditional issues of rights and responsibilities, protection or liberation, universal or specialized services, or choices between in-kind services and income maintenance are amplified by the present status of children. In particular, changes in family roles and struc-tures have severely strained child welfare policies that originally emerged to deal with children in traditional contexts. Single-parent, female-headed fami-lies are seriously limited financially in caring for their children. Families with working mothers may have increased difficulty finding adequate child care and other supportive services. Black children, in particular, are at great risk of poverty and resulting inadequate care. These facts raise concern about how well children really are being protected from a variety of social risks, how well parents are capable of meeting traditional child care expectations, and how well current social services and income maintenance programs provide protection for all children, but especially the poor ones.

Policy Background

As indicated above, child welfare policy has a rich history of efforts to protect and promote the welfare of all children. Of particular significance for this policy analysis is the contemporary policy background directed at disadvantaged American children. One analyst has put the picture in somewhat reductive terms:

> It may develop that private families really are not equipped to meet most children's needs. . . . Unless and until that case is made more persuasively than it has been, however, a children's policy will be successful enough if it concentrates on ways to compensate demonstrably unlucky children whose bodies or minds are sick, or whose families are unstable or in poverty.[14]

Table 9.3 gives an overview of current child welfare policy for the disadvantaged and comparable expenditures for each program. The number of children served and the amount of federal money spent on them suggests that, except for Social Security benefits to the retired and disabled, children's policies constitute in aggregate the nation's most expensive federal welfare program.

The Social Security Act and Child Welfare Policy

Most child welfare policy is part of the same legislative act as the Social Security program. At present the Social Security Act contains eight program titles that have some bearing on the welfare of children (see table 9.4 and figure 9.1). One of these, Title IV, composes the fundamental federal child welfare policy for disadvantaged children. The 1995 welfare reform legislation modifies the program elements of the Social Security Act, but not its basic structures.

Social Security Benefits (Title II)

Title II of the Social Security Act, which provides benefits to the retired and disabled—what most people mean when they say "social security"—also benefits many children, a fact that has gone relatively unnoticed in current Social Security debates. Children to age 18 are covered under Social Security if their

Table 9.3: Federal expenditures on programs that primarily affect the disadvantaged child.

Program	Number 1985	Number 1992	Expenditures (in billions) 1985	Expenditures (in billions) 1992
Total civilian population	238,648,000	253,493,000	$10.7	$13.6
Total children	66,372,000	61,166,000	14.4 (1984)	22.0
Social Security	3,319,000	3,391,000		
AFDC recipients	10,921,000	13,384,000	11.1	20.9
AFDC families[1]	3,721,000	4,936,000	5.5	3.7
Food stamps	20,000,000	25,369,000	20.1	25.2
School lunch and other subsidized needs	24,600,000	24,546,000	22.1	27.2
Unemployment insurance (per week)	2,800,000	3,245,000	1.2	2.8
Medicaid	22,500,000	22,240,000	555 (million)	2.8
Public housing	1,300,000[2]	1,323,300		
Headstart children	430,000	621,000		

	Social Security beneficiary breakdown 1986	Social Security beneficiary breakdown 1992
Total	37,058,000	41,507,000
Retired	22,432,000	25,758,000
Wives/husbands	3,375,000	3,382,000
Children	3,319,000	3,391,000
Disabled	—	3,468,000

1. Average monthly family payment = $385.00
2. Total units, 1980 census
Sources: Statistical Abstract of the United States (1985), Tables 588, 611, 619, and 622; (1994), Tables 2, 162, 577, 582, 590, 597, 600, 601, and 1227.

parents are covered. This eligibility may have happened as a result of a covered parent's retirement, death, or disability. Because Social Security has become so universal, children are protected by its "safety net" feature. Social Security was intended to perform this function for children, with the expectation that the need-based program, AFDC (see Title IV below), would eventually become unnecessary. AFDC was, in fact, designed as a temporary program; Social Security was expected to carry the burden of income maintenance for children. AFDC's origin as a temporary measure is important to recall for later discussion.

Table 9.4: Children's focus under the Social Security Act.

Title	Function	Children's focus	1995 welfare reforms
Social Security (Title II)	social insurance	in covered families	unchanged
Unemployment insurance (Title III)	social insurance	in covered families	unchanged
Aid to Families with Dependent Children (AFDC):			
• Assistance in payments (Title IV-A)	income maintenance	cash for dependent children in own homes	block grant
• Child welfare services (Title IV-B)	social services	dependent children in foster or adoptive homes	block grant
• Demonstration and training (Title IV-C)	social services	work programs and demonstrations	block grant
• Child Support Enforcement (CSE) (Title IV-D)	social services	child support collections for poor and nonpoor	unchanged
• Permanency planning (Title IV-E)	social services	home finding and placement	block grant
• Jobs Program (Title IV-F)	services	put parents to work	block grant
Maternal and Child Health (MCH) (Title V)	health services	health care for children and others	unchanged
Supplemental Security Income (SSI) (Title XVI)	income maintenance	for severely disabled children	unchanged
Medicaid (Title XIX)	health income	health care for poor children	unchanged
Social Services Block Grant (SSBG) (formerly Title XX)	social services	various services	unchanged

Source: U.S. House of Representatives. *The Green Book* (Washington, D.C.: Government Printing Office, 1993). U.S. House of Representatives, Sub-committee on Human Resources, July 1995.

Figure 9.1: Programs under the Social Security Act.

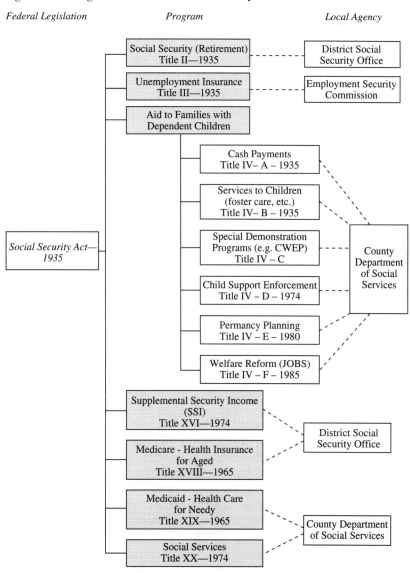

Federal Legislation   *Program*   *Local Agency*

Source: Conference on Poverty, *Community Social Program Inventory.* Chapel Hill, N.C., September 1994.

229

Unemployment Insurance (Title III)

Unemployment insurance, discussed in detail in chapter 6, provides income maintenance to children when they are part of a family in which the wage earner becomes unemployed through no fault of his or her own. There is no clear figure for how many children are covered under this program, but by counting the number of families who receive the service, one can estimate that a great many children must benefit. Single-parent, female-headed families are covered if the woman is employed in covered employment. The way the program is set up, however, makes it difficult for many low-income, single-parent, female heads of families to qualify for unemployment insurance, for many of them are employed in jobs that are not covered by unemployment insurance laws. On the other hand, because unemployment insurance is not means-tested, its universal applicability provides important income protection to many children.

Aid to Families with Dependent Children (Title IV)

As table 9.4 shows, Title IV has had a prominent position in child welfare policy, since it authorizes both income maintenance and social services on behalf of disadvantaged children and their adult caretakers—usually their mothers, but also foster and adoptive parents and institutions. Title IV contains subtitles all specifically directed at poor children. (In some cases other children are eligible.) The legislative development of Title IV is worth noting because it exemplifies many practical confusions of the normative questions discussed at the beginning of this chapter. Also, as noted above (and in chapter 6), the program was originally designed as a temporary program, because it was assumed that as the social security program expanded its coverage, public aid for dependent children would not be necessary. In this context states were given great discretionary authority over setting payment standards and criteria for eligibility. This was in keeping with the fact that all states had public programs to support dependent children before 1935; the new federal program was essentially intended to provide additional funding to brace these earlier efforts.

Title IV began with three parts. Part A was the financial assistance program, Part B was child welfare services, and Part C was demonstration and training. The financial assistance program (Part A), originally called Aid to Dependent Children (ADC), made matching federal funds available to states, provided that state programs met uniform federal administrative standards. Fourteen original standards—modified frequently over subsequent years—established a federal context that protected individual rights from possible infringements during the process of providing assistance. Nevertheless, noneconomic standards for determining eligibility often crept into the administration of the program. For example, in 1956 Louisiana established a condition of eligibility that denied ADC to mothers who had a second out-of-wedlock birth. The federal government threatened to withdraw funds from Louisiana's program, which appeared blatantly prejudiced racially, but Louisiana contested the case in court. A compromise was reached before a court decision was made, but the case clearly illustrated states' ability to set ADC policy that could circumvent guarantees established by federal statute. Child welfare policymaking continues to be a joint responsibility shared by the federal government and the states.

In 1959, after six years of increased attention to matters of the family, Title IV as a whole was renamed Aid to Families with Dependent Children (AFDC), signifying a movement away from its original, more exclusive emphasis on the child. The late 1950s brought a spate of studies that linked family welfare to child welfare. The most important one, conducted by the American Public Welfare Association in 1956, established the importance of families to healthy child development and documented a strong association between families who received social service counseling and had shorter stays on welfare.[15] These and similar findings of the period led to the development of a new policy for children that included federal funding for social services designed, in the words of the 1962 amendments to the Social Security Act, "to maintain and strengthen family life for children."[16]

Bringing a focus on the family into child welfare policy through the AFDC program seemed a logical extension of child welfare policy: Protect the family, and you protect children; strong families provide strong children. Thus there developed perceptions that policy did, could, and should manipulate the family to achieve wide-ranging public goals, including improved child welfare. At the programmatic level, the changes introduced into Title IV during the 1950s and 1960s were designed to deal, directly, with family issues. Provisions were made to provide financial support for unemployed parents (usually fathers), to keep the family together through casework counseling, and to establish programs of work training and placement to help families become economically self-sufficient. The change in name reflected a substantial shift in the direction of child welfare policy.

Despite this strong interest in "family impact statements" and family policy studies, the Orwellian overtones of such efforts did not go unnoticed by public critics.[17] Nor, for all the additional assistance children and their parents received through these special services programs, did AFDC caseloads decrease as hoped. Not only did the number of AFDC recipients increase during the 1960s, but also more and more AFDC families were becoming financially dependent because a parent was absent from the home, due to out-of-wedlock births, desertion, or informal separation. Welfare critics blamed AFDC for causing "family breakup" and argued for stronger policy to keep families together. Amid all this clamor the welfare of children, the original purpose of Title IV, seemed to have become lost, so much so that the seventh decennial White House conference on children, proposed for 1979, was modified to become a conference on the family. But even then, preliminary discussion could not establish a definition of the family, and under a wave of discontent, the conference was canceled—nor has a White House conference on children been held since.

There is little doubt that the family is an important institution in America, but there is still little professional or public consensus on just exactly what a family is. The disagreements early on in the White House conference on the family opened a Pandora's box of normative issues. The planners initially defined a family as a husband who probably worked and a wife who usually stayed at home and took care of (approximately) two children—despite the fact that less than 10 percent of American families then fit that stereotype. But women in particular objected to having single-parent, female-headed families categorized as "broken" families. Many separated and divorced women argued that they had much more "intact" families than they had while they were married. Religious organizations, however, could not accept single-parent families as "full-fledged" families, any more than they could accept the idea that homosexual couples (even those with dependent children) should be included in the cornucopia of wholesome American families.

It is impossible to make good policy for an abstraction. The concerns of women's advocacy groups over new family policies did help redirect attention of Title IV back to children's financial concerns. The increase of absent and nonsupporting fathers became viewed less as a problem of "family breakdown" and more of an issue of financial support for children that might lift them out of poverty, or keep them off welfare in the first place. In 1974 a fourth part was added to Title IV—Part D—known also as the Child Support Enforcement Program (CSE). In 1984 this program was enlarged and broadened to give it more authority over collecting financial support owed to children from absent parents.

CSE represents a departure from original child welfare policy under Title IV, in two ways. First, the federal government provides help to the states in their effort to collect child support. All states have statutes that make parents' failure to support their child a crime, and all states have procedures enforcing these statutes. CSE policy requires, as a condition of receiving welfare, that the applicant (usually a mother) sign over to the state his or her right, *and the right of the dependent child or children,* to support from the absent parent. The state then collects the support from the absent parent and uses the collected funds to *lower the state's share* of welfare costs. If the family is eventually able to leave the welfare program, the support payments revert to the family. But as long as the family is on welfare, the state keeps the collections. This is an important shift in policy: the state "owns" the right to child support payments for welfare families; the money owed belongs to the state and the federal government.

Second, through CSE the federal government provides funds to help parents and children who are not on welfare collect any child support that might be due to them. This also departs from traditional Title IV policy, which was applicable only to poor children. Consequently this new policy creates considerable confusion in program administration. States do not benefit directly from child support collections on behalf of non-welfare families because those collections go directly to the families. Hence states have been slow to spend their own resources to help collect money that goes to someone else. States may levy a fee on these services, but fees are apt to discourage those who need the service from using it. The fact that the greatest amount of uncollected child support (about $24 billion in 1992) is owed by parents whose children are not on welfare has presented a serious obstruction to implementing CSE successfully. States are reluctant to help collect child support for these children because it costs states more than they are repaid for their services. Thus a potentially important child welfare policy that would help all children has become seriously compromised in its administration by a normative conflict over whether different standards should apply when all children or only needy children are served by it.

Title IV-C, like Titles IV-A and IV-D, is designed to provide financial support for children who live with their own families. Originally instituted to provide funds to states to educate child welfare workers, Title IV-C now provides funds for demonstration and training. When work programs were first required in the 1960s, they were also put under this subtitle. The work programs administered under Title IV-C were administered by Title IV-F, the JOBS program created by the 1988 welfare reform amendments. The 1995 welfare reform lumps this program into the overall welfare block grant. Work programs have had many individual successes but limited universal application. For parents who have a foundation of education and skill and strong work motivation, work programs have been helpful stepping stones for getting back into the work force. But for those who have little employment potential the program has no meaning. More than 60 percent of all adult welfare recipients either have never worked or have not worked in the five years prior to receiving welfare. The creation of a single new job may require as much as $5,000 to $10,000 in capital investment, another $2,000 to supervise that job for a year, and about $5,000 to train a person to do the job. At this rate a newly created job may take five to ten years to pay for itself.[18] Welfare reform does not provide funding for these purposes, and consequently work programs have poor potential for assisting welfare parents and their children. One recent study of work demonstration programs has found that only 7 to 10 percent of welfare beneficiaries who participate in such programs do find steady jobs.[19]

The other two of the five subtitles of Title IV—IV-B and IV-E—provide funding for the care of children who do not live with their own families. Title IV-B (usually called child welfare services) provides funds to states to protect the welfare of children from a variety of circumstances such as abuse, neglect, exploitation, and unnecessary separation from families. These funds are used to support foster care, adoptive placements and services, and care of children in nonhome environments such as group homes and institutions. It also provides funds for diagnosis, counseling, and treatment for children who are experiencing difficulty in their own homes or the homes of others, even though they are otherwise ineligible to be served under this program. There are no federal income eligibility requirements for the receipt of Title IV-B services. These programs would become part of the proposed child welfare block grant.

Title IV-E (often called permanent planning) was created in 1980 as an extension of the IV-B program. Because out-of-home care is expensive and has always been considered a temporary alternative to care at home, concern was voiced in Congress during 1976–79 that not enough effort was being put forward to establish a permanent home environment for many of the children served with Title IV-B funds. In particular, many children with special medical and psychological problems were maintained in "temporary" environments for long periods and frequently shifted from one such setting to another. Black children were especially often kept in these uncertain settings, in many cases for the whole of their childhoods. Title IV-E was created to motivate states to review the status of children supported by IV-B resources, and to develop permanent plans for all of them, emphasizing adoptive alternatives or return to their own rehabilitated homes. The program requires the recruitment of adoptive homes and also assistance to families who may, with some adjustment, be able to accept their children back into the original home.

Title IV-E has probably already achieved the maximum benefit of its policy objective. States quickly developed classification systems for reviewing the status of AFDC children in foster placements and made dramatic strides to provide permanent homes for children. Out-of-home child care populations decreased in 1981, stabilized in 1982, but then began to rise again. Since 1990 there has been a steady increase in both the number of children in foster care and adoptive care under the IV-E program. Foster care cases increased from 168,000 in 1990 to 233,000 in 1993, a 29 percent increase in four years. IV-E adoption assistance cases increased from 44,000 in 1990 to 81,000 in 1993, a 46 percent increase. Thus while the Title IV-E program has succeeded in getting children into permanent homes, it has not reduced the number of children in foster care. At present there are about 390,000 children in foster care, and 20,000 awaiting adoption in both the Title IV-B and Title IV-E programs.[20]

If the Title IV-E program has not significantly reduced the substitute care population, it has provided an unusually good understanding of the problems of this group of children. More than 75 percent of children in substitute care have been there for two or more years; 60 percent have special physical, mental, or emotional problems; 39 percent are black; and 69 percent are more than six years old. The discovery that so many children need substitute care because of abuse and neglect provided firm evidence of the seriousness of child abuse and neglect in the general population. Federal legislation under Title IV-B was strengthened in 1984 to provide the funds to identify abuse and neglect among dependent children and to provide assistance to abused and neglected children. More recently, this legislation has given special attention to child sexual abuse and, after the publicity given to the "Baby Doe" case, medical abuse. For children whose substitute care is terminated successfully in a permanent home, the IV-E program is invaluable, but the program has not efficiently reduced the use of or need for substitute care.

Maternal and Child Health (MCH) (Title V)

MCH was also discussed in chapter 7. Federal funds for this program are distributed to the states through a block grant. Although children with special medical problems, such as crippling conditions, are identified in the block grant as a specific service population, the states otherwise use MCH funds in widely divergent ways. Because all states provide a complex mixture of types and amounts of health care services for mothers and children, funds from MCH frequently are used to supplement programs that states are already providing. In most cases services that are supplemented with MCH funds are provided at local (usually county) departments of health. Such programs include pre- and postnatal care and child health follow-up services for preschool children.

As mentioned above, MCH and other public health programs that serve children have thus far given comparatively little attention to problems of older children, such as alcohol and drug abuse, auto accidents, suicide, and teenage pregnancies (although many teenage mothers do receive help as mothers of children themselves). Although MCH funds could be used for services that could deal with the variety of teenage problems, the lack of specificity in the use of these funds perpetuates financial support for existing service programs rather than encouraging ventures in new directions.[21]

Medicaid (Title XIX)

Like MCH, Medicaid has been discussed in detail in chapter 7. Table 9.3 shows the importance of Medicaid for needy children. One little noted section of the Supplemental Security Income (SSI) program, discussed in chapter 6, allows income maintenance from SSI to children with medically handicapping conditions. Because SSI payments are larger than AFDC payments, and because many medically handicapped children require social services but may not meet AFDC eligibility requirements, the SSI program is important for this very small group of children.

Social Services (Formerly Title XX)

Social services for children are provided under the Social Services Block Grant (SSBG), earlier, Title XX of the Social Security Act. SSBG provides states with funds for a wide variety of services that may be initiated at their own discretion. Although there are no services that states are required to provide for children under SSBG, well over half of services that states do provide with SSBG funds are directly or indirectly for children. Since SSBG services do not have to be means-tested (restricted for use only by the poor), many SSBG programs provided for children complement and extend services offered under Title IV. For example, adoption, foster care, residential care and treatment, and protective services are provided by most states in harmony with services supported with funds from SSBG, with the net effect of developing an infrastructure of services for all children that is not possible under the Title IV program alone. At the same time, states have used SSBG to develop services not likely to be funded through other sources. Daycare, for example, is the most commonly provided such service, because SSBG funding permits widespread support for daycare programs and subsidies—though not nearly enough to meet the growing demand for more daycare.

Both social services and Maternal and Child Health programs are funded with block grants. The block grant method of financing social programs is itself an important policy issue with a number of normative questions of its own. These issues were discussed thoroughly in chapter 3, but child welfare policy provides a good practical illustration. Among other issues, the block grant virtually eliminates any federal authority over decisions about what kinds of services states may provide, or under what circumstances. Block grants allow states to shift funds around as the need arises. This increased flexibility has been accompanied by decreasing federal financial support for these programs. Several studies have demonstrated that, in turn, state service patterns have changed as a result of block grant funding. For example, the policy infrastructure of service, which had had some commonality from state to state, has been eroded, and decisions about what services should be provided have shifted from professional groups to political forums.[22] Moreover, although states generally have made up for federal funding decreases, they have modified their programs, shifted programs to other federal funding sources, restricted eligibility for services, and eliminated some programs completely, both to save money and to make the services more consistent with their political realities.[23]

A wide array of policies and programs are available for a wide range of children's needs. These programs engage many of the normative issues inherent in child welfare policy. For the most part these policies are directed toward poor children, which is consistent with the general policy orientation of Title IV of the Social Security Act. Additionally, child welfare policy has become increasingly intertwined with normative views of the American family, making it very difficult to develop child welfare policy independent from efforts that seek to modify the American family to stereotyped, idealized forms. The extent to which child welfare policy is viewed in traditional or contemporary contexts may determine its effectiveness in coping with child welfare problems.

Policy Analysis

The long-standing and traditional national experience with child welfare policy, the relative clarity of the normative issues, and the lack of marginal utility for many of the policy alternatives already in place suggests that analysis of child welfare policy would best be assisted by the behavioral or "rational" model. Despite some disagreements, the amount and depth of consensus on normative issues of child welfare indicate that child welfare policy first considers the best ways to protect children through maximizing parental responsibility, buttressing this protection with programs of income support and social services that can be made available to all children when needed. The major question in policy analysis here is not so much what kinds of policies and programs are needed, but how to modify the existing ones, within the normative environment discussed above, to deal more satisfactorily with circumstances in which children presently live. Under the behavioral model we might thus see the analysis in terms of three major alternatives, each with measurable subsets.

1. Protection of children
    a. Protection of income
    b. Protection of health
2. Parental responsibility
    a. In two-parent traditional families
    b. In alternative family forms
3. Income maintenance and service mix
    a. For poor children only
    b. For all children

These alternatives can be analyzed by examining their subsets and setting the costs of policy alternatives against their benefits to illustrate which choices would most likely realize the best benefits for children generally. The analysis is based on an understanding of existing programs, as described earlier in this chapter. Because the behavioral model may identify several "best" alternatives, more than one recommendation may be suggested for child welfare policy.

Following are alternatives:

Protection of children

Income protection. There were 14 million children living in impoverished households in 1991. Assuming a median family size of 3.23 persons, there would be approximately 4.4 million families needing incomes of about $12,320 per year in order to stay out of poverty. This would mean that about $54 billion would be needed in the aggregate to keep all these children and their families above poverty. According to current estimates, one-third of all poor families have at least one family member working full time (see chapter 5). Assuming this work to be at minimum wage, 1.45 million families would earn about $14.3 billion, leaving a poverty income gap of $39.7 billion.

There is no good way to estimate how much earnings from part-time work contribute to eliminating the poverty gap for poor children. Experience suggests that such work is usually below the minimum wage and is intermittent. Assuming that 17 percent of poor families have one member working at least part time, and assuming that this part-time work would be valued at two-thirds of full-time work, this would add another $2.8 billion to earned income for poverty families, leaving a poverty deficit of $36.9 billion. The Earned Income

Tax Credit (EITC) would add around $9.5 billion at current spending levels reducing the poverty deficit to $27.4 billion.

Income maintenance on behalf of children and its impact on the income deficit below the poverty line can be estimated from table 9.3. Depending on state support for the welfare block grant, welfare will provide about $22 billion toward this purpose; state and local expenditures contribute another $2.1 billion, and food stamps add another $25.2 billion. Child support presently collected by the CSE program for non-AFDC families amounts to about $10 billion and assuming that about 75 percent of these funds goes to poverty families, the poverty deficit would be reduced further. Furthermore, if one-fourth of the $24 billion in unpaid child support could be collected on behalf of poor children, the poverty deficit could be reduced even further. These analytic projections suggest that perhaps little or no new spending could eliminate poverty for children in America, if all potential resources for these purposes were pooled and carefully focused. Of course this aggregate estimate does not account for uneven distributions, for instance, from state to state. But on the other hand, it does not include the cash value of all in-kind services either. However, it does seem possible to eliminate poverty among children via better income protection programs. The problem seems to be less one of insufficient spending, and more one of whether spending is well focused on existing problems.

Health protection. Protecting the health of children is more difficult to calculate in terms of costs and benefits. The analysis of health policy presented in chapter 7 mentions the high benefit and low cost of pre- and postnatal care programs for children. A further expenditure of $3.5 billion on MCH and WIC would double the funding of these programs and open them to more women and children, as well as enriching the benefits of the programs for those who receive them.

Taken together, an additional $2.4 billion for direct income support and $3.5 billion for health care—a total of $5.9 billion in extra funding—would considerably strengthen existing programs designed to protect children.

Parental responsibility

Parental responsibility for children would require analysis of traditional families—mother, father, and children living together as a primary social and economic unit—and nontraditional families (all other kinds of families). The costs of promoting and protecting the traditional family structure would have to be weighed against the benefits—social development of children, happiness of children, and so forth. Discussion above, however, has suggested that although the traditional form still dominates the national ideal, nontraditional families also provide viable structures for realizing parental responsibility to children. The single-parent, female-headed family and the matriarchal extended family are two family structures that depart significantly from traditional ideas of family structure, but there is no evidence that parenting responsibility is better or worse in these families. These two dominant nontraditional family forms are both characterized by absent fathers; in the case of the single-parent, female-headed family, the father is most likely known. In the matriarchal extended family, the father is most likely unknown.[24]

There are currently about 9.4 million single-parent, female-headed families. The proportion of matriarchal extended families in this group is hard to determine. However, 18.9 percent of all births are to unwed women. For whites this percentage is 11.6; for blacks it is 56 (see table 9.1). This evidence supports the idea that the form of black American families differs significantly from that of other American families. Thus most efforts to reestablish traditional families in America would have to take place in the black community, and would be extremely difficult to accomplish by public policy.

There is no good way to measure either the costs or the benefits of reestablishing traditional families in America, if indeed such a social objective is desirable or possible. From time to time social critics have suggested that some policies may encourage the development of nontraditional families. During the 1950s, for example, AFDC was blamed for breaking up families because fathers had to be absent before the family could become eligible for benefits. Some states consequently amended their AFDC programs to permit eligibility for benefits without the absence of a parent; but the number of absent-parent families has not diminished perceptibly as a result. The Guaranteed Annual Income studies completed in the 1970s provided evidence that middle-income families that received income maintenance tended to separate more frequently than families that did not receive such support.[25]

Such findings may simply illustrate what is already known: the family, however it is defined, is an economic as well as a social unit. Hence economic changes result in change in family form, just as social changes do. In other words, the form of families can be manipulated by financial incentives. Whether policy should try to change the form of the family remains an unresolved normative issue.

Although it is virtually impossible to establish the costs and benefits of maintaining the traditional family as an American ideal—except for purely economic benefits—it is possible, and appropriate, to discuss parents' *financial* responsibility under this rubric. This can be measured. Statistics mentioned earlier in this chapter (and also in chapter 5) amply demonstrate the immense difference that efficient retrieval of uncollected child support payments from absent parents could make in child welfare—perhaps to the point of virtually eliminating childhood poverty. The costs of obtaining this child support may in some cases exceed the financial benefits of collecting it, particularly for financially marginal families. At least one study has found, for instance, that low-income, absent black fathers did not appear to have sufficient earnings to make collection efforts fiscally beneficial to their children. The same study also demonstrated, however, that low-income black fathers took considerable parental responsibility for their children, even if that did not take the form of paying much child support.[26]

Although this analysis suggests that by maximizing parental financial responsibility in the aggregate, money could be made available to provide much more support to children, the distribution of such funds might not result in a benefit to children who are most in need of financial protection. Black families are most in need of financial support, but white, upper-income fathers owe by far the greatest proportion of the unpaid child support. Pressing black fathers to become more financially responsible would not necessarily generate sufficient funds to aid poor black children, at least in overall terms.

To the extent that more child support can be collected through the assistance of programs like CSE (Title IV-D), all children will benefit. Encouraging parental financial responsibility in the process may be desirable in its own right. However, as the situation now stands, it may not be cost-effective to pursue CSE collection efforts. Low-income families do not have enough money to make the program work for poor children. States find the costs of collecting support payments for other families so great that they are discouraged from pursuing the program, and even new policy initiatives such as wage garnishment requirements have failed to generate additional collections.

Income maintenance and in-kind services for children

This policy alternative might be the very best to pursue at this time. Discussion above has suggested that the income gap for children in poverty might be eliminated, and that expanded health services could be offered for $3.5 billion. This, along with slight modifications in other services for children, could realize significant improvements in child welfare. CSE in particular could be modified to increase its efficiency among non-welfare households that need the service. Less emphasis could be given to collecting child support from low-income absent parents. Additional services might be provided through SSBG, especially expanded child care and better vocational training for the working poor. Because one full-time job at the minimum wage currently pays only 60 percent of the poverty index for a family of four, raising the minimum wage could have an important influence on reducing poverty, without additional outlays in public funding.

From the normative perspective some decision about what kinds of services should be given to which children is a problem that is difficult to resolve. From a financial perspective, the cost of such a policy would be extremely high, making the policy less desirable than one that focused primarily on poor children.

A summary of the conclusions from this brief analysis appears in table 9.5. Protection of children's income and health, and income maintenance for poor children seem the best alternatives. Parental responsibility in alternative family forms is also an intriguing possibility, but normative controversies about alternative family forms would probably inhibit effective implementation of such a policy.

Conclusion

Child welfare policy covers a wide spectrum of public efforts on behalf of children. Child welfare policy is also the best-developed sector of public policy. Consequently child welfare is difficult to analyze, and recommendations for policy choices are often laden with implications for other policy sectors. This analysis has attempted to focus child welfare considerations around two normative issues—protection for children, and parental responsibility—and to restrict the scope of analysis to matters of health and economic welfare for poor children. (The full scope of child welfare policy often necessitates an ex-

Table 9.5: Summary of child welfare policy analysis, using the
behavioral model.

Alternative	Benefit	Cost
1. Protection of children		
a. Protection of income[a]	High	Low
b. Protection of health[a]	High	Low
2. Parental responsibility		
a. Two-parent families	Low	High
b. Alternative family forms	Medium-High	High
3. Income maintenance and services		
a. For poor children[a]	High	Low
b. For all children	High	Very High

a. Best alternatives.

amination of other policy sectors; policy on childhood education is an obvious example.) Within these limitations, and on the basis of data mentioned in discussion above, analysis yields a series of "best" alternatives that can be recommended.

First, there is an income gap for families in poverty, but it is a manageable one. The AFDC program (Title IV-A) is now being modified by the block grant to make welfare spending more effective, and this modified distribution mechanism could well be used to distribute additional funds without significantly greater costs. Current proposals to make welfare a program of exclusively state responsibility would be appropriate, so long as provisions were made to ensure that adequate funding existed.

Second, children would be served better at less cost by preventive health care services. Funds spent on pre- and postnatal care for mothers and infants already contribute to reducing short- and long-term medical costs, as well as improving the welfare of all participating children significantly.

Third, parental financial responsibility has become a more important issue as nontraditional families have become more common in American society. Collection of unpaid child support, an important element for parental responsibility, clearly has great potential for substantially decreasing childhood poverty. However, unless there is greater public acceptance for nontraditional families, collection and distribution of such resources will probably be used to achieve social conformity, and will have little impact on the children who need financial resources.

Chapter Ten

OLDER ADULTS

Introduction

If policies for children have a long and rich tradition in America, dating to the nineteenth century, policies for older people have been perhaps the most lasting legacy of the Great Depression's New Deal. During the 1980–83 recession, unemployment offices were jammed with people filing claims; but during the Great Depression there was no unemployment insurance. There was no Social Security and no Medicare. And the 1980–83 recession did not send crowds of older adults into shantytowns and the streets in search of shelter and sustenance. For the most part, older adults were spared the worst suffering of the 1980–83 recession, even as they were the greatest victims of the 1929–34 Depression. In 1980–83 there was an economic safety net that did not exist in 1929–34, and that safety net held.

That this remarkable development in public policy for older people could take root in less than fifty years is due almost entirely to growing political pressure from older adults. Unlike children, older adults vote, and they vote in greater numbers than any other age group. The increase in the number of older people and the emergence of new, politically oriented groups of older people provided the energy for the creation of Social Security and Aid for the Aged (1935), Medicare (1965), and the Older Americans Act (1965). Once slighted by public policy, today older people, both independent and dependent financially, are treated to a cornucopia of benefits through public policy.

On the one hand, then, public policies have developed significantly for older people. But, on the other hand, severe and lasting problems for America's older people persist. Consider this kind of all too frequent problem that continues to plague the elderly, in spite of the many important policy advances that have taken place over the past sixty years.

Haddie Wilson had been living alone for the past two years after her husband died. At age 82 she was able to take care of herself in her own home since her children stopped by each day and generally helped her with shopping and other things she could not always do for herself. She still smoked a pack and a half of cigarettes a day, stayed up for the late news, and thought any form of exercise was a mortal sin. Her 78-year-old sister usually came to Haddie's every afternoon, stayed overnight, and returned to her own apartment at about ten o'clock the next morning. Sarah said the arrangements kept Haddie from getting scared at night, but, in truth, Sarah was often frightened at night when she was alone in *her* apartment, so the arrangement seemed to have great value for both sisters.

Early one morning, Haddie had a heart attack and was rushed to the emergency room. Open-heart surgery was deferred in place of angioplasty, a procedure Haddie had undergone three years earlier. Her recovery was perilous, then slow, and when it looked as though she would survive she was moved to the local nursing home. Although she suffered a small stroke, and her memory began to fail more rapidly, gradually her health improved. As she improved, she was moved to intermediate care, and, day by day, her health continued to improve so that within three months after her heart attack she had pretty much recovered most of her physical abilities. Her mental condition, however, remained weak and at times borderline.

With two sons, living and with local, grown-up families, and with two daughters, also with adult families, and with the attention of Sarah who had become more or less a live-in sister, it seemed like Haddie could leave the nursing home and return home, providing adequate in-home care and support could be found. Money was not a problem. Haddie had a comfortable estate left by her husband. Finding help was not a problem. A number of persons answered ads for live-in homemaker at a reasonable monthly salary. Additional in-home nursing care was also available as needed.

The problem was that the children did not want the responsibility of arranging and supervising the plan to move Haddie out of the nursing home and into her own home. Sarah was willing to continue to spend nights with Haddie, but she felt she was too frail herself to be responsible for her sister. However, homemakers were available to stay overnight with both of them. The youngest daughter was willing to arrange, and even supervise, the in-home living plan, but the other siblings expressed their reluctance to become too involved, fearing that their commitments to an in-home plan would increase as time went on. And the longer Haddie stayed in the nursing home, the less dissatisfied she became with it. The screaming, putrid odors, bland food, and constant intrusions that bothered her so much at first became commonplace in her life as she began to settle into the nursing home routine.

The nursing home was one of the best in the city, yet it was a depressing place. Sometimes wheelchairs so clogged the hallways that it was impossible to walk through them. Other days the smells were so overpowering one almost gasped for breath. Yet more than half of those who spent their lives in this nursing home were like Haddie. They had been sick. Their health had returned to the extent that they no longer needed the kind of care offered in a nursing home, but there was no plan for them to go anywhere else, and they had adjusted to nursing home life.

Although this is not a true story, similar situations are repeated day by day across the whole United States. This story does help to identify the most important problems facing older adults today.

Normative Issues

Three normative issues dominate policy debates about older adults: (1) adequacy of postemployment (retirement) income, (2) independence for self-maintenance and care, and (3) overall quality of life.

Postretirement Income

Adequacy of resources may be the most significant normative policy question that concerns the welfare of older adults, especially because it influences definitions of adequate income in retirement. Except for those who have amassed large fortunes, most older people live on much less income than they were accustomed to during the years immediately preceding their retirement. In theory, reduced retirement income is justified on the grounds that everyday costs of living are less after retirement. The house is probably paid for, and the state may grant a tax exemption for it. Children are grown. Cars are paid for.

But the economics of retirement must take into account the overall standard of preretirement living. People who have enjoyed a high or modest standard of living before retirement might reasonably expect to continue a similar level of existence during retirement; hence questions of income adequacy interlock with normative concerns about equity and quality of life. For example, suppose that during the working years a family manages to live comfortably in a very nice house and maybe even manage to purchase a summer cottage at the lake, with a boat and near a golf course. In fact, the family anticipates retirement as a time when they will be able to enjoy more fully what they have obtained. This family can look forward to retirement income from personal savings, Social Security, and reduced taxes. From one standpoint of equity, it might be asked why this family should benefit from public funds and live very well, when a retired family in the city slums has barely enough food to eat. It might also be asked, however, why a lifetime of inequity should be adjusted only after retirement: doesn't the comfortable family deserve what it has earned? Or, should the public largesse be shared with this comfortable family when it is needed more by the poor family?

The *source* of retirement income, therefore, is an issue closely related to questions of adequacy of income. Retirement income usually is a mixture of funds from three major sources: Social Security, earnings, and income from savings, in the form of annuity programs or interest (see table 10.1). Although no exact formulas for estimating retirement income have ever been established, President Roosevelt seemed to suggest one when he commemorated the Social Security Act in 1945:

> It seems necessary to adopt three principles for old age security: . . . old age pensions for those unable to build up their own pensions . . . compulsory annuities which will in time establish a self-supporting system for those now young and for future generations . . . and voluntary contributory annuities by which individual initiative can increase the amounts received in old age.

He also warned that Social Security "does not offer anyone either individually or collectively an easy life—nor was it intended to do so."[1] Social Security was originally meant to be a major source of retirement income, but not the *only* source.

Table 10.1: Percent of income from various sources for family units with all members age 65 or over

Percent income from	Poor	Non-poor
Earnings	1.5	11.5
Social Security	69.6	40.2
Other pensions	2.8	19.9
SSI/Public assistance	10.1	0.4
Interest income	4.2	25.6
Food stamps	1.9	0.0
Housing assistance	8.1	0.3
Other	1.8	2.1
Mean income per family member	$4,851	$16,188

Source: U.S. Congress, Committee on Ways and Means. *Overview of Entitlement Programs (The Green Book).* (Washington, D.C.: U.S. Government Printing Office, 1993), p. 1297.

Nearly 98 percent of all retired people in the United States receive Social Security. But, as discussed in chapter 6, Social Security payments may be quite modest, often less than enough to keep recipients above the poverty line. In many instances Social Security amounts to less than half of a person's retirement income, yet the other sources that contribute to that income may not be sufficient to bring the total up to the poverty line, or to any other agreed-upon definition of adequate resources. Table 10.1 summarizes the sources of income for older adult families—poor and non-poor. From this table it can be seen that the income from Social Security is the most important income source for older people, but it is not the only source. For the poor, social security provides 69.6 percent of their income, but only 40.2 percent of the income for the non-poor. For the non-poor, other pensions, usually private pensions, make up 19.9 percent of their income. Earnings also constitute 11.5 percent of the incomes of those over 65 who are not poor.

Figure 10.1 shows the distribution of married couple families age 60 and older by income categories. Over 80 percent of these families have incomes over $15,000. In fact about 22 percent of these families have incomes of $50,000 and over. This general distribution remains consistent for all age groups, including families with the householder age 75 and older.

Independence for Self-Maintenance and Care

Independent living is an important normative issue that concerns policy for older adults. It stems from deeply held, traditional American values of freedom and independence, as well as the contemporary emphasis on self-sufficiency that permeates the whole of public domestic policy.

Drastic changes in the structure of the American way of life have taken place in the middle decades of the twentieth century. Not only are there increasing numbers of single-parent, female-headed families, as outlined in chapter 9, but the extended family, a prominent social structure well into the present century, has almost disappeared since World War II. Some explain this change by saying that the extended family ceased to be an efficient economic unit, whereas the smaller, one-generation family unit that is most common today functions more efficiently in the modern American economy.[2] Others have argued that children sought to be free of the burden of their older adult relatives; still others hold that older adults wanted to be free of their children. From whatever perspective, generationally independent households are highly prized today in America. Few modern households contain more than one adult generation.

To the extent that *cohorts* of people (age-linked groups such as the "Sixties Generation") share similar experiences and carry these experiences with them

Figure 10.1: Income of married-couple families (age 60 and over) by income categories.

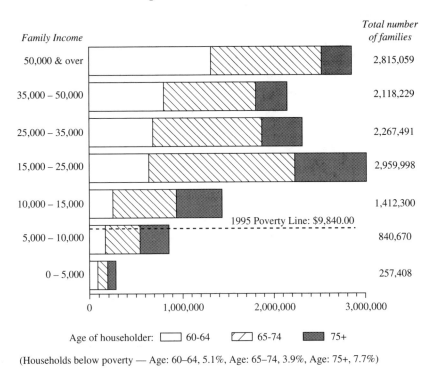

Source: U.S. Census, STF3A (1990).

throughout their lives, there may be a cohort effect that currently supports independent living as a normative policy issue. Table 10.2 demonstrates how this phenomenon may have led current generations of older people to value highly independent lives.

Everyone who is 65 years old today, or older, experienced the Great Depression in some way. The depression was such a profound economic crisis that it had some influence on all who lived through it. Those who are now 65 years old would have been just born during the most severe part of the depression. They may remember their parents struggling to make ends meet, and they may recall their own personal sacrifices as their families began a slow economic recovery.

Table 10.2: Cohorts of older adults.

Age at time of critical events

Age in years 1990	World War I (1914-1917)	Great Depression (1929-1935)	World War II (1942-45)	"Baby Boom" (1946-50)
85 (b. 1905)	9-12	24-30 Young families	37-40 Possibly in war	41-45 Steady period
75 (b. 1915)	1-2	14-20 Older children in Depression era families	27-30 Probably in war	31-35 Raising families
65 (b. 1925)	—	4-10 Young children in Depression era families	17-20 Probably in war	21-25 Starting families
55 (b. 1935)	—	—	7-10 Living with Depression era parents	11-15
45 (b. 1945)	—	—	—	1-5 "Baby Boom" generation

Those who are now seventy-five years old, however, had different experiences, with perhaps more chilling and more devastating effects. During the height of the depression these people were young adults, possibly married, perhaps even with a family of one or two small children. Already on tight personal budgets, with great responsibilities, they faced the depression under severe personal stress due to total loss or serious reduction of income. They had babies to feed and clothe, without any public resources. For assistance they may have stood in line for free food. The specter of hunger, sickness, and perhaps even the death of loved ones is not fantasy for this cohort. Having had some personal financial security before the depression and suddenly having it disappear through no fault of their own left a profound psychological impression on many of them. They experienced a loss of self-sufficiency in a most personal way. On this basis it is easy to understand the fierce sense of personal independence that is virtually the hallmark value of this cohort of older people today.

Those who are fifty-five years old today and just facing the prospect of retirement were small children during the depression. They had few personal experiences of the economic crisis that were bad enough to have a lasting effect
on their lives. They heard stories from their parents, perhaps, but they are a cohort with a different orientation. Instead they probably recall—vividly—
World War II. That event made a strong impression on them and is likely to
influence how they view the problems and challenges of older age.

Another factor that increasingly affects policy founded on normative concerns for self-sufficiency is that older people are living longer than ever before. As discussed in chapter 7, the tremendous improvements in medical
science over the course of this century not only keep more people alive longer,
but keep older people in better health (see figures 10.2 and 10.3). At the turn
of the century an average person could expect to live to age forty-seven. Today
the average life expectancy is seventy-four years.

Increased longevity means that older people have many years for independent activities after the usual retirement age of sixty-five. In 1990 the average
sixty-five-year-old American could expect to live another 17.3 years. Many
older adults today begin second careers or undertake activities that engage
them in a broad range of social and vocational pursuits. Often these activities

Figure 10.2: Life expectancy for older adults.

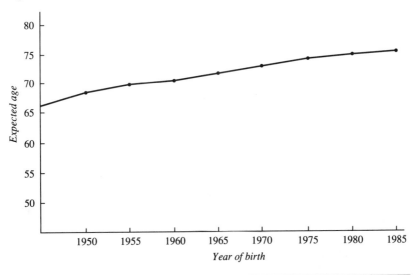

Year of birth

Source: Statistical Abstract of the United States (1988), Tables 105 and 108.

Figure 10.3: Survival rates in the United States by age.

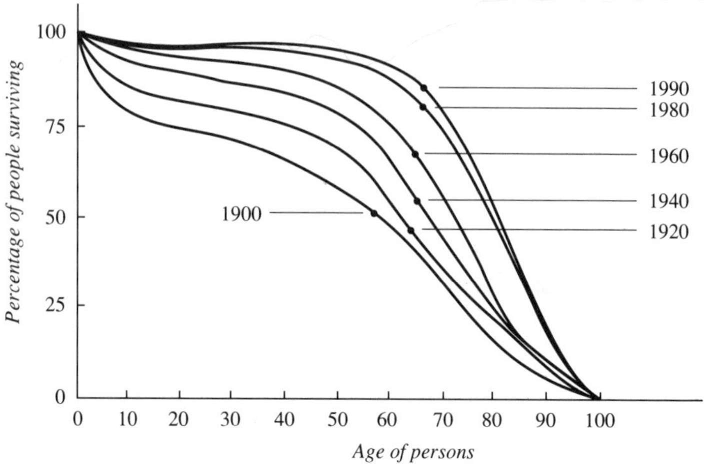

Source: Department of Health and Human Services, Office of Health Statistics (1990).

have considerable economic and social value for their communities as a whole.

Living independently, however, requires more than sufficient financial resources alone. Social supports are also necessary, particularly if health begins to deteriorate. In-home services such as chores services, shopping assistance, and companionship have become increasingly essential to helping an aging population stay in its own homes and communities, where it wants to be. When such support services are available and accessible, the cost of living independently remains far less than the cost of living in dependent care facilities.

Quality of Life

With increased longevity has come increased concern for the quality of life for older people. Personal well-being and personal satisfaction contribute greatly to how well older people live within the resources available to them. Key elements are a sense of safety and security, the opportunity for personal choice, and a sense of contentment. Quality of life can only be defined very subjectively by each individual, but several important social conditions contribute to circumstances that improve the quality of life for older people.

Where people live determines the context of the quality of life. Although as many as 65 percent of all older people live in homes that they own, free of debt, nearly 20 percent live in housing that is not appropriate to their present needs. Many lack the financial resources to purchase or rent more appropriate housing. About 70 percent live in urban areas, 35 percent specifically in central city areas. The urban elderly are more likely to live in older neighborhoods; even if the housing in which they live is adequate and appropriate to their needs, their surroundings may have become undesirable and unsafe. It is not uncommon for older people to remain virtual prisoners in their city homes and apartments, not because of physical limitations, but because it is not safe to venture out on the streets. Even when the threat of crime is minimized, urban environments can challenge older people in many ways. Congested sidewalks, which may be cracked and crumbling; wide, busy streets without monitored crosswalks; and difficult access to public transportation all contribute to stressful living conditions. Lack of access to public facilities may be more troublesome for these older people than for their counterparts in rural areas, who have never had such resources to rely upon in the first place.

Housing contributes to or detracts from quality of life in another way. Housing is more than shelter. It constitutes a base for emotional security, a feeling of being at home and close to one's own. It accords a sense of independence and mastery. Unfortunately, maintenance, high utility costs, and rapidly escalating taxes force many older people to relocate to housing that is presumed to meet their economic needs but often fails to meet their emotional and aesthetic needs. Even when older people move from less to more appropriate and desirable housing, they may suffer a sense of dislocation and emotional trauma and loss. Thus there are no clear-cut choices for improving the quality of housing for older people. In some cases the familiarity and security of a long-time home may more than offset the dangers of an undesirable physical environment. In others, the comfort, convenience, and safety of new quarters may soon overcome the sadness of leaving an old home behind.

Finally, the use of postemployment time has become one of the most complex issues in quality of life for older people. In most cases older people suddenly find inordinate amounts of extra time in their daily lives when they retire from full-time employment. Not only is more time available, but it is available during periods of the day that previously were occupied by other activities. All too often preretirement dreams of unfettered leisure are quickly transformed into a postretirement reality of boredom, aimlessness, depression, and subsequent frustration and personal deterioration. Many older people are unprepared for these increased amounts of personal time, and many come to realize that retirement is not a long vacation, as they may have anticipated during their working years.

In short, work is still an important factor in quality of life for most older people. Older people want and need work opportunities to enhance the quality of their lives. Work for wages has been discouraged by public and private employment policies, yet many older people would prefer to continue working at their jobs—and many do. Many others seek second careers by going back to school and by exploiting hobbies and productive activities, transforming them into vocational pursuits. And for many older people, especially craftsmen, writers, artists, and various professionals, some of the best, most creative, and most useful work comes in later years, when some of life's pressures are reduced.

Planning ahead can enhance the quality of use of retirement time and help identify personal and interpersonal problems that might arise after retirement. For example, one spouse may look forward to retirement as a time for increased recreation; the other may view the additional time as an opportunity to pursue a new career. Without prior discussion and planning, these different expectations may cause serious conflicts during the early retirement years. Quality of life for older people would be improved considerably if the public and private sectors offered routine counseling for employees about the use of time after retirement. Such counseling would, on the average, cost less than the traditional "gold watch" and retirement luncheon, but it would be much more valuable to the person who retires.

Normative issues in aging policy focus on adequacy of income in retirement and its sources, on self-sufficient, independent living, and on quality of life. To a great extent the policies that have developed for older people since the 1930s have dealt with these concerns, and new policy efforts for older people must continue to do so.

Policy Context

The contemporary context of policy for older people is found mostly in the Social Security Act, the Older Americans Act, special provisions in the Health Services Act, and the Housing Act. Other policies are scattered through state and local programs. Health services and housing policies for older adults have been discussed in earlier chapters of this book, as have relevant sections of the Social Security Act. Title II, Social Security (retirement) and Title XVI, Supplemental Security Income (SSI), were analyzed in chapter 6. Title XVIII, Medicare, was featured in chapter 7. The policy context on aging created by these programs is briefly described below, as it reflects normative concerns differently from policy oriented solely toward income maintenance or solely toward health or housing. A full discussion of the Older Americans Act, not previously mentioned, completes the review.

Policy for Older People under the Social Security Act

The original Social Security Act contained two financial support programs for older people: Social Security (then called Old Age and Survivors Insurance, OASI), an insurance program; and Aid for the Aged, a welfare program. Social Security benefits were to be based upon contributions to the Social Security System. Aid for the Aged benefits were to be based upon financial need. The federal government administered Social Security, but Aid for the Aged was administered cooperatively by the federal government and the states. Because of intense political pressure from older people during the formative years of Social Security, these two programs were developed as the first titles of the Social Security Act. Aid for the Aged was Title I, Social Security was Title II. Thus at the outset two categories of the financial assistance were available to older people: one for the poor, the other for those who were not. Social Security was provided not only to retirees but also to spouses, children, and survivors of retirees. Partly from political motivations, and partly from practical considerations, scales of payment under Aid for the Aged were established by the states. Although the federal government would have preferred to set national standards for Aid for the Aged, as it had with Social Security, Congress opposed efforts that appeared to override state authority. Instead Congress agreed to let states control the payments as long as they were of amounts sufficient to meet a "standard of health and decency," though it did not stipulate what constituted those standards.

These ideological differences extended to program financing. Social Security was financed by a tax on employers and employees, with revenues reserved exclusively for the Social Security program. The constitutionality of this tax was upheld in 1937. Aid for the Aged was financed by a categorical grant-in-aid similar in pattern to the one devised for the Aid for Dependent Children (ADC) program. States were free to choose whether they wanted to have the program, as well as the level of support they wanted to provide. Thus separate financial issues affected each program. Although states were more or less forced to participate in Aid for the Aged, they still had options about their level of participation.

Medical coverage for older people was added to the Social Security Act in 1965 as Medicare. A separate payroll tax was established to support Medicare, and a separate trust fund was established to secure employer and employee contributions. The name of the program absorbed OASI to become Old Age and Survivors Disability and Hospital Insurance (OASDHI). In 1972 Congress modified the original Aid to the Aged program by combining it with aid for the blind and disabled, into a consolidated program called Supplemental Security Income (SSI), incorporated under Title XVI of the Social Security Act.

Social Security (Title II)

Social Security under Title II of the Social Security Act is available to older people under a variety of circumstances. Currently there are more than thirty-five different criteria by which people may become eligible. In 1992 there were 25.7 million retired workers who were receiving Social Security benefits, comprising 62 percent of all Social Security beneficiaries. (Table 6.9, based on slightly earlier figures, shows a general breakdown. Social Security benefits to others, especially children of covered retirees and disabled, are discussed in chapters 6 and 9.)

Supplemental Security Income (SSI) (Title XVI)

SSI was created by Congress in 1972 by combining Aid for the Aged (Title I) with Aid for the Disabled and Aid for the Blind. Thus, in principle, SSI operates for older people in the same way that Aid for the Aged did. It was presumed that, generally, fewer and fewer older people would need public assistance of this kind because they would be increasingly covered by Social Security, and indeed the number of older people receiving SSI is comparatively small. In 1992 only 6.5 percent of all persons over the age of 65 were receiving SSI, but 54 percent of all poor elderly received SSI payments.

About 65 percent of all SSI recipients also receive a Social Security benefit. SSI is a means-tested program, and Social Security benefits are counted as part of income when determining an applicant's eligibility. Any resulting SSI benefit is reduced by the amount of Social Security the beneficiary receives (with a $20 "pass-through" exclusion). As discussed at some length in chapter 6 (see especially table 6.8), this policy poses a problem in that it essentially devalues Social Security. A person who has worked to earn Social Security will receive little more in combined Social Security and SSI than will a person who receives SSI only.

The Older Americans Act

Unlike the Social Security Act, the Older Americans Act is not a policy instrument designed to transfer funds or resources to older people. Instead it provides legislative authority for combining and organizing a variety of public resources for older people. Legislated in 1965, the Older Americans Act was part of the Great Society programs, which provided income support, housing, food, jobs, self-help, and medical care to poor people with the full support and assistance of the federal government. In particular the Older Americans Act was designed to provide governmental authority for coordinating these apparently abundant resources in order to make them more effective for older people. That the federal government should provide resources for such coordinating activities represented considerable ideological development beyond the philosophy that supported the Social Security Act. The Older Americans Act stated that federal funds would be used to excite, stimulate, and encourage the development and refinement of efforts to get greater shares of the social welfare "pie" for older people.

The Older Americans Act has a number of provisions, but Title III has the greatest importance as policy. It contains four subparts: (1) Area-wide Agencies on Aging (AAAs), (2) social services, (3) senior centers, and (4) nutrition services.

Area-wide Agencies on Aging (AAAs)

The AAA is the crucial policy structure under Title III. Each state is required to establish distinct planning and service areas in which the details of Title III mandates will be carried out. These planning and service areas may be geographically or politically defined regions, general-purpose local government centers, or other subsections of state and local administrative structures. As illustrated in chapter 3, the AAA may be a public or a private, nonprofit, organization. Thus, even though each state must designate AAAs, each AAA is different.

The AAA's main purpose is to develop for its service area an "area plan" that is submitted to the state. These area plans generally tell how the services available to older people in each area will be prepared and presented. In practice, the work of the area-wide planner is to make some judgments about which agencies and organizations within the area will receive funds for providing the services that are covered under the act. The planner must take into account the extent to which resources and services, *overall*, will be improved for older people by choosing one local organization as opposed to another, as the recipient of funds provided through Title III.

Social services

Specific social services are provided through the Older Americans Act, even though their exact form may vary from place to place. Some of these services are available to meet specific objectives, others meet general objectives. Services to meet specific objectives—health education, training, "welfare," information, recreation, homemaker-aides, counseling, referral, and transportation—are funded discretely. Although the names of these services are very clear, the elements that constitute the actual services may vary greatly from place to place. Usually area-wide planners decide which sets of activities qualify as services according to the act. For example, are inoculations against influenza and discussions about body care both health services? If they are, which service is more likely to achieve the objective of a health service? The degree of interpretation of services varies so widely that ultimately no one exact pattern of social services is provided under the Older Americans Act.

Services designed to meet general objectives include those that encourage older people to use other services, those that help them attain adequate housing, crime prevention programs, victim assistance programs, and similar programs, including, to round out a list of fourteen such general programs, "any other service . . . necesary for the welfare of older individuals." As a result of this latitude in the scope of the policy, each community and each social service agency competes vigorously for funds available from the Older Americans Act. In many cases, however, the decisions are based on political expediency. There are no established standards that could guide decision making.

Senior centers

Senior centers are developed as "focal points" and operate as informal community resources where older people can come for planned services or just drop in for fellowship. The National Council for Senior Centers has established elaborate criteria for development of such centers, and these are frequently used as standards for evaluation and funding. The programs offered at senior centers vary from community to community. In most cases the resources and services of the centers are available to all older people without charge.

Nutrition services

Ideally, the senior center provides nutrition services, and nutrition services are the center of activity at the senior center. Nutrition services essentially consist of three distinct activities rolled into one: (1) a hot meal (usually lunch) served in a group environment, (2) nutrition education, aimed at instructing older people about good eating habits, and (3) a program designed to help older people learn about other resources in the community that would contribute to a satisfactory life. The meal is available without charge, although participants are encouraged to make a contribution to defray some of the expenses. The meal must meet nutritional standards established by the National Academy of Sciences. Although some of these meals may be delivered to older people who are unable to leave their homes, most of the meals must be provided in a friendly and inviting group environment.

Despite its fairly clear policy guidelines, the purpose of this program has often been misunderstood. Because it is available without charge, it is *not* a means-tested program, yet it is an in-kind program. The purpose of the program is to use the meal as an inducement to get older people out of their homes and into some healthy social interactions with others, as well as to link them to useful information that affects their well-being. Therefore nutrition services are available to anyone age 60 and older, and to their spouses, even if the spouses are not yet 60 years old.

Other Services and Programs

The programs discussed above constitute some of the major efforts to assist older people in their retirement years. These programs cover a wide array of resources available in one form or another across the United States. But because both the needs and interests of older people are so varied, programs other than those discussed above may also be available in different localities, and under different circumstances. For example, many localities offer abuse and protective services for older people, in-home care services to help elders remain at home, and chore services to help with minor household maintenance. These and other specialized services would likely be provided with funding from the Social Services Block Grant (Title XX of the Social Security Act.)

More and more elderly are concerned about prolonging their lives with artificial life support systems, beyond a time where life as we usually think of it no longer exists. Recently states are beginning to face legal challenges to acts such as "assisted suicide," "living wills," and other documents that give authority to guardians to discontinue life support systems. While popular among many elderly, and legal in most states, these measures designed to prevent routine efforts to prolong life at all costs, contribute greatly to the enhancement of independence and self-determination among today's elderly.

But in spite of the expanded use of home care, in lieu of nursing home care, and various forms of respite care that are now available, sometimes supported by Medicaid and Medicare, sometimes not, the problems faced by persons like Haddie continue. In the face of expanded policies and programs for older people, there remain a reservoir of problems of later years that cannot be solved by public policies, but, instead, are problems that must be dealt with by individual, private decisions.

Summary and Overview

The programs offered to older people under the Social Security Act and the Older Americans Act provide a rich array of income support services and social services to needy and nonneedy older people. Consequently, policy for older adults has sometimes been criticized as contributing to a mass distribution of resources to older people at the expense of children.[3] Whether or not such a competitive situation exists, public priority for older people has caught up to other policy sectors in comprehensiveness in a relatively short period of time.

Policy Analysis

Taking into account the normative issues involved and the varied centers of policy-making that serve older people, policy directed at the welfare of older adults might best be analyzed using the criteria-based model. Of particular relevance are normative issues pertaining to adequacy of income, independence, and quality of life. Table 10.3 offers a policy analysis geared to those issues.

As one might expect, Social Security does the best job of meeting the universal criteria outlined in the table, whereas programs under the Older Americans Act are best at meeting the program-specific criteria. All the means-tested programs—SSI, Medicaid, and existing housing programs—satisfy very few criteria, because policy for poor older adults must consider, in a comprehensive way, the needs of all older adults to some extent. From this analysis it appears that if Social Security could be improved to provide greater income adequacy, and if some of the services of the Older Americans Act could be expanded, policy for older adults could be improved considerably.

Attention to the normative issues of existing policy alternatives, particularly those that would enhance the policy-specific criteria, is especially crucial in view of the rapidly expanding older adult population—called by some the "graying of America." In other words, the increasing proportion of older people in American society means that policy for older people has a special obligation to consider income adequacy, independence for self-maintenance, and quality of life. Without attention to these normative concerns, policy for older adults will become as inflexible as policy for children has become under current income-maintenance programs.

Adequacy of Income

Perhaps the most significant fact of most older adults' income is that it was fixed upon their retirement and remains fixed through the retirement period. Therefore, older people are usually not as well off financially as the adult population as a whole, and without deliberate policy efforts, adequacy of income

Table 10.3: Analysis of policy for older adults, using the criteria-based model.

ALTERNATIVES

	Income-maintenance programs		Older Americans Act				Health services		Other
Normative orientations	Social Security	SSI	AAAs	Social services	Senior centers	Nutrition program	Medicare	Medicaid	Existing housing programs
Universal criteria									
Equity									
Horizontal	Med	Lo	Med	Med	Med	Hi	—	Hi	Hi
Vertical	Hi	Lo	—	Lo	Med	Lo	—	—	—
Efficiency (low-cost/high value)	Hi	Lo	—	Lo	Med	Lo	Lo	Lo	Lo
Nonstigmatizing	Hi	Lo	—	Hi	Med	Hi	Hi	Lo	Lo
Preference satisfaction	Hi	Lo	—	Hi	Med	Med	Hi	Med	Lo
Policy-specific criteria									
Income adequacy	Hi	Lo	—	—	—	—	—	—	Med
Independence for self-maintenance	Med	Med	Hi	Hi	Hi	Hi	Hi	Med	Med
Quality of life	Med	Lo	Hi	Hi	Hi	Hi	Hi	Lo	Lo
	Hi = 5	Hi = 0	Hi = 2	Hi = 4	Hi = 2	Hi = 4	Hi = 4	Hi = 1	Hi = 1
	Med = 3	Med = 1	Med = 1	Med = 1	Med = 5	Med = 1	Med = 0	Med = 2	Med = 2
	Lo = 0	Lo = 7	Lo = 0	Lo = 2	Lo = 2	Lo = 2	Lo = 1	Lo = 3	Lo =4

will deteriorate. Economic disparities among older people are striking. There are approximately 65,000 men and women in America who are worth more than $1 million, and of these, 50 percent—28 percent men, 22 percent women—are more than fifty years old. Yet in 1991 the average family income in older adult families was only $20,467 per year (based on an average family size of 1.4 persons). Forty-one percent of this annual income came from Social Security retirement payments. Net worth is another way to look at income adequacy for older people. In 1988, for example, the average net worth of an elderly married couple householder was $124,400, but $78,500 of this was in housing, leaving only about $45,800 net worth in liquid assets. By today's standards, if Social Security retirement was discontinued, the average elderly household would exhaust liquid assets in about 6 years and would probably have to sell its home, or get a loan to live on during the additional 11 years of its life expectancy. This scenario does not take into account increased living expenses that might be brought about by illness.

For these and other issues related to income adequacy, older people, as a group are getting poorer. Statistics from 1990 indicate that 12.6 percent of all Americans over age 65 live in poverty—up one percentage point since 1978. This is a little lower than the rate for the nation's population as a whole (14.0 percent) and lower than the rate for children (20.1 percent).[4] And, as mentioned earlier in this chapter, a great many more older people live on incomes just above the poverty index, with another cluster in the higher income brackets. This pattern bespeaks an inequity in the distribution of income among the nation's older population, despite the presence of Social Security as a major source of income maintenance for retirees over the past half-century.

Serious economic inequities can be observed for many kinds of people in America—the young, minorities, the poor, women—but the inequities that older adults confront are striking. Most older people are retired and are not part of the labor force. Their income must come from prior savings, income from stocks and bonds or similar investments, rents, support from children or other relatives, or government income transfer programs. By comparison, as much as 93 percent of all income for individuals and families under age fifty-five comes from earned wages and salaries in the work force. For those over age 65, earned income has decreased to the point that it composes only about 30 percent of total family income. Depending on the health and previous employment pattern of the older person, earned income may be at best an unstable and unreliable source of income. More than 95 percent of all older adults have worked at some time, or have, or had, spouses who have worked in the past. This degree of attachment to the work force conveys something of the magnitude of the loss that results from the cessation of earned income—which must be made up by other resources.

The single greatest source of wealth among older people is their homes. This wealth does provide some income protection in old age, but it lacks liquidity, and from a personal standpoint it is not a reliable form of income support in old age. For people whose savings are mostly personal real estate, Social Security is a much better investment. A worker who entered the Social Security system in 1937 contributed $20,741 toward his (not her) retirement and would have $186,000 (average) in benefits in 1986, amounting to about 6 percent of total earnings of more than $3 million.[5] The same $20,741 invested in a home would have yielded assets upon retirement valued at approximately $65,000. In this view, "contributing" to Social Security is more valuable than building retirement assets in housing.

Cash programs such as Social Security and SSI are also essential because they provide maximum autonomy to older people. With cash, the older person can satisfy personal preferences in meeting particular needs, wants, and desires. The use of cash is compatible with the economic system to which most older people have become accustomed. In-kind programs, on the other hand, may seem an alien resource. Since Social Security is the mainstay of retirement income, it must be adequately funded to preserve adequacy of income. That a large number of Social Security beneficiaries must accept SSI because their Social Security benefit is so low also attests to the importance of assuring adequate income through Social Security. Table 10.3 suggests that enhancing Social Security would provide the best opportunity to realize a number of the most important policy goals for older adults.

Independent Living

Presently it is estimated that 32.15 million older people are covered by Medicare, representing about 85 percent of the older population and about 92 percent of older, eligible Social Security recipients. However, only 21 percent of those covered will receive reimbursed services. The amount of medical treatment costs paid by Medicare and Medicaid is astonishing. In 1993 Medicare expenditures were $144.6 billion, with $74 billion spent on hospital based care (51 percent of all expenditures). Reimbursements for physicians' services amounted to 24.7 percent of the rest of Medicare costs. Only 21 percent of those covered under Medicare received reimbursable services. The average reimbursable cost for in-hospital care (Part A) was $2,552 while reimbursable costs under Part B averaged $1,157. By contrast, costs for home health care are about 10 percent of the costs of in-hospital care, yet most medical services cover expenses other than in-home care. Even with these levels of expenditure, only 77.4 percent of total physician costs and 55 percent of total outpatient hospital costs were reimbursed through Medicare. The balance was paid by the individual, either through private insurance coverage or out of pocket.[6] By these standards the cost of medical care for older people is truly alarming.

Most of the Medicare payments to older people are used to reimburse hospitals, nursing homes, intermediate care homes, and group homes, for prolonged care of older people in those facilities. Recent studies by the federal General Accounting Office substantiate, however, that in many circumstances home-based care could substitute for these various forms of institutionalized care. Not only would the costs be more reasonable, but the care itself would be more personalized and, in most cases, more desirable from the patient's point of view inasmuch as home offers a base of emotional security and a vantage point for maximizing independence. Yet the rules for Medicare reimbursement do not permit routine payments for in-home services, since most of these services are not identified as "medical" in the strictest sense of "treatment." They belong more to the category of "care" during convalescence or terminal illness—a distinction discussed at some length in chapter 7. Thus older adult policy would be enhanced by modifications in Medicare that would permit greater use of in-home services and encourage independence and personal autonomy.

Quality of Life

Where older people live determines the context for quality of life. In 1990 there were 15.5 million owner-occupied housing units held by owners age sixty-five or older. As many as 65 percent of older adults live in homes that they own, and of these, 85 percent are free and clear of mortgage debt. Most owner-occupied and rental property in which older people live is older housing; 95 percent is fifteen years old or older.[7] This housing is likely to need repair or renovation to enhance its comfort to the aging resident. Lacking special architectural features such as grab-bars, handrails, accessible electrical light and wall outlets, wide doorways, and special-height toilet bowls, older housing may not always contribute to the quality of life for people with even minimal physical impairments. Instead, rather than enhancing life, this housing often presents a series of obstacles with which older people must learn to live.

Table 10.3 does not rate housing alternatives for older people very high in terms of important normative issues. Because housing policy in general offers so little opportunity for improving the housing stock for disadvantaged groups, improving housing for older people through existing housing programs does not seem to be a viable alternative. However, improved housing is important if older adults are to maintain decent quality of life and reasonable independence. This issue will grow in importance as the population of older adults continues to swell in succeeding decades. Rather than seek housing improvement for older people through existing housing programs, policymakers might investigate the possibility of making housing services available to older people through modifications in Title III of the Older Americans Act. If this housing emphasis could be shifted to Title III services, in combination with changes in Medicare policy that would permit reimbursement for in-home care on a broader basis, quality of life for older people could be improved substantially.

Conclusion

Unlike policy for children, policy for older adults has a more focused context. Three specific normative issues—adequacy of income, independent living, and quality of life—have the greatest salience in policy directed at older people. Fortunately, a strong base of public policy exists for older people, which is already capable of addressing these normative issues. Among the major recommendations from analysis of existing programs for older adults are (1) ensuring that Social Security is financed and administered sufficiently to provide the foundation for an adequate income for all older people, (2) redirecting Medicare reimbursements for older people so as to cover a greater number and variety of at-home care services, and (3) developing housing policy efforts directed specifically at bringing the home situation for older people in line with other support for at-home care and independent living in general. The second of these recommendations is consistent with a recommendation in chapter 7 that proposes a general shift in public medical expenditures away from treatment and cure and toward prevention and care. The third recommendation might be accomplished by diversifying social services under Title III of the Older Americans Act to accommodate home improvement and similar home-based services. Improving the physical living environment of older people means improving their quality of life as well.

Public policy for children must ensure an opportunity for full growth and development. Public policy for older people must act to protect and enhance what these citizens have already obtained. In this view policy for children does not compete with policy for older people, but rather both sets of public policy, together, offer opportunity to construct a safety net for two vulnerable populations. Both, too, are based on a respect for the dignity of individuals regardless of limitations imposed by age.

Chapter Eleven

A FOUNDATION FOR PUBLIC POLICY: ANALYSIS AND CHOICE

Policy Overview

Part I presented policy analysis as an applied social science discipline. The analyst may be in any one of the many private or public units where policy is shaped, refined, and partially, at least, made. The policy analyst may be the policymaker, but it is most likely that the policy analyst will be asked to provide systematic information to policymakers. The policy analysis is most useful when the information it provides helps policymakers as they reach for a decision. The lament, "they had all the information in front of them and made the wrong decision anyway," is much more an indictment of the policy analyst than of the policymaker, because such statements bring into question whether the information was provided in a useful way. Policy is made in a unique political environment in America. There is no clear center of policy decision. Rather, policy is made and remade in a constant stream of decision making.

Despite such complexity in policy making, it is possible to identify focal points of policy activity—executives, legislators, administrators, judges, private organizations—and the patterns of interaction among those centers give definition and clarity to a policy process at a particular point in time. Thus, policies become settled. Programs flow from the policies. Professional people make the programs come alive by connecting people with the programs that assist them. Therefore, a policy analysis necessary at one policy focal point is likely to be different from that necessary at another policy center. But while no single approach to policy analysis is likely to satisfy these divergent requirements, a range of models is available to guide the analyst in organizing, ex-

266

amining, and presenting information useful to the policy decision process. Most of the necessary information already exists in some form. Sometimes new information has to be created. But whether new or old, the information has to be communicated, unencumbered and clear.

Part II identified the five most significant sectors of social welfare policy. A brief policy analysis was undertaken in each sector, not only to demonstrate the methods of policy analysis, but perhaps more significantly, to acquaint the policy analyst with the basic shape of each of these sectors. Because policy locates the public interest, reflects the time in which we live, or charts a course for action by allocating resources, normative views about the times in which we live and the problems we face shape both the ways we understand our problems and how we go about solving them. Particularly in a diverse nation, it is not at all unusual for people to see the same things differently. For some the issue of children's policy may be seen as a responsibility of the state to protect children from harm. Others may see the critical issue in children's policy as an erosion of parental responsibility. Policy analysis must provide information that will illuminate how one set of choices will enhance resolution of one set of normative positions or another.

Because policy is a reflection of our current social world, changing times bring restructuring of policy contexts in which problems are viewed and addressed. Policy contexts that have been shaped over many years, such as income-maintenance policies, have a rich tradition of policy and programs. Unfortunately, policies and programs that are products of these contexts contain divergent, often conflicting directions, since the way a problem was seen and resolved in one historical context may not fit in another context. Thus a good bit of policy analysis, particularly at the administrative level, is directed toward how these widespread policy mandates can be harmonized and redirected to fit with the ways issues are presently understood.

The Unresolved Policy Agenda

An emphasis on five policy sectors, even though these sectors are fairly comprehensive of current policy, leaves many public welfare policy issues unattended. Some attention is given to some of these issues in other policy contexts. But in other ways the policy problems raised by contemporary social issues have not been addressed. For example, abortion is a highly volatile policy issue. In *Roe vs. Wade,* the U.S. Supreme Court ruled that state laws could not interfere with a woman's choice to have an abortion. But striking down the illegality of abortion laws has not resolved the policy debates over abortion. In 1978, the Hyde amendment to federal spending bills, another form of public policy, did not resolve the controversy either. In fact, more than half the states continued to provide publicly funded abortions after the Hyde amendment. Then, in 1987, the Department of Health and Human Services (DHHS) proposed requirements that would have terminated all federal funding to any program providing abortions, even if the abortions were a separate program activity funded by entirely separate funds. Under these policies a hospital could lose all its federal funds if it provided abortions. At present, courts have made policies that say these administrative policies are illegal. Just when some balance seemed to be achieved with respect to abortion policy in America, the issues resurfaced in the 1995 welfare reform debate—same problem, but in a different policy context. Thus a consistent reshaping of normative orientations to problems (i.e., government should not pay to support children born out of wedlock, but we don't want women to have abortions to stay eligible for welfare) forces policymakers to revisit problems that, although seemingly resolved in one policy context, present continuing unresolved issues in a different policy context.

Abortion policy is a good example, then, of a normative concern that does not have its own clear policy context. Some abortion policy exists as set by the courts, but abortion policy is also played out in a newly established policy area, as in welfare reform or health policy for example. A clear policy environment about abortion, however, does not exist, because the normative questions surrounding abortions have not been sufficiently understood and clarified. For the time being, abortion policy is addressed as a health issue, even though "right to life" groups argue that abortion is a moral issue, and "freedom of choice" groups argue that abortion is a constitutionally guaranteed right. Since only health policy context exists, until the normative orientations of the adversary groups can find a more appropriate policy context for their policy debates, public policy over abortion will remain unresolved, and tension and conflict over abortion is likely to continue.

There are other unresolved policy problems like abortion that do not have sufficient independent policy contexts to permit discrete policy analysis. Since the implementation of *Brown vs. Board of Education* (1954), the Civil Rights Act, and its subsequent amendments, and the Voting Rights Act, acts of racial and sexual discrimination have become less pronounced, although they still exist. While a policy context exists in which issues of discrimination can be addressed, the actual practices of discrimination have shifted. Discriminatory treatment of minorities, mostly blacks in the urban Northeast and rural Southeast, Latinos in the West and Southwest, and Native Americans in the Southwest and northern plains, continues to plague American public policy efforts. Minority concerns seek special attention in well-established policy sectors such as child welfare, health, and housing, even though these traditional policy sectors may be ill equipped to deal with problems of discrimination.

Sexual discrimination against women had tended to concentrate within the context of the workplace and is most evident in the fact that women in the aggregate earn about 60 percent of what men earn for similar work. But despite the existence of a policy context, little policy has been developed to address sexual discrimination because the normative issues are clouded. Traditional views of the family and the role of women generally continue to conflict sharply with current social realities. Thus George Gilder, for example, argues that women do not want social or economic parity with men.

[G]overnment may not be discriminating against women and private companies may not either. Let us at least consider the possibility that many women, desperately rejecting the values of male careerists, are discriminating against the job "rat race" and in favor of their families.[1]

Getting on the Policy Agenda

Although policy issues and concerns must have some policy context before they enter the stream of policy-making, the processes by which public issues become subjects for policy analysis remain vague. Sometimes public debates become so polarized that conflict develops. Conflict, usually over the allocation of resources, propels such issues onto a public agenda. Policies are then demanded to guide the use of resources. Analysis is undertaken, and a policy process is underway.

Sometimes issues are propelled onto a public agenda by social science findings. For example after World War II there was a general concern about poverty, and as discussed in chapter 6, the social science findings of the American Public Welfare Association not only helped to rediscover poverty, but also prompted policy analysis about how the aid to dependent children program could be improved to combat poverty more effectively. In a similar way the findings of Michael Harrington in *The Other America,* and subsequent research by Richard Cloward and Lloyd Ohlin, reintroduced poverty as a public issue. This led to poverty being placed on a policy agenda and the Economic Opportunity Act and its many programs being created by President Johnson and the U.S. Congress.

Sometimes governments initiate public policy agendas independent of conflict or social science discoveries. Often government-initiated policy agendas are products of social and physical planning. Local governments, for example, are engaged in planning land use, transportation, housing, and the need for various public utilities—clean water, waste disposal, communication, schools, and health services, for example. When a particular issue suggests the need for

269

policy, government may initiate a policy process. A local government may initiate a school bond issue, or it may decide to create an urban transportation system. The 1988 welfare reforms were largely initiated by Congress after prolonged frustration over growing welfare needs in the face of increased welfare spending and an environment of fiscal austerity.

Despite these suggestions about how issues become part of a policy agenda, why some items become policy subjects and others do not is not always clear. Robert Eyestone identifies an "Issue Transition Process" in which he describes how an issue becomes transformed to a policy subject:

1. A problem is
2. perceived by groups, and
3. others join groups with related but differing objectives until
4. the problem becomes a social issue.
5. The issue finds some place on some public agenda, due to
6. activities of "issue entrepreneurs" (advocacy groups) and
7. the issue becomes part of a formal policy process.
8. A policy decision of some kind is made encouraging
9. groups to pursue similar or related issues or
10. wait until the "next round."[2]

Of course, Eyestone also notes that not all issues have to follow the transition pattern he outlines, suggesting that such global formulations do not always explain systematically how public policy issues emerge or how the policy process really operates. The materials in part I of this text, however, suggest a systematic framework for abstracting the reasons why some issues *do not* move onto a policy agenda and into policy-making processes. The following constitute conditions that prevent issues from becoming policy concerns:

1. Normative issues may be lacking in clarity so that no firm views can be generated about the problem or concern.
2. There is no policy context in which the issue can be addressed. The issue just does not seem to fit.
3. There is insufficient public concern, or if there is public concern, it is not strong enough to command the resources necessary to develop policy about the issue.
4. The problem area has not become recognized as a public one. In other words, the problem is seen as a private rather than a public concern.
5. The problem has been addressed by an element of policy process that is not appropriate to develop policy on that particular problem. For

example, the federal government may be engaged to assist in developing more effective elementary education, when in reality states and local communities have policy authority over this issue. Or DHHS may try to resolve abortion issues through administrative policy, when the matter is really one for the U.S. Supreme Court.

As discussed in detail in earlier chapters, whenever one or more of these conditions exist it is unlikely that an issue will be transformed into a policy question. Unfortunately, it does not follow that if all these conditions are met, the issue *will* emerge on a policy agenda.

The Intellectual Foundation of the Policy Process

Many of the basic ideas presented in this book may appear equivocal. When a policy-making process is presented, it is accompanied by cautions that not all processes operate the same way in the complex American system. Policy analysis procedures are modified by warnings that the exact procedures depend upon the expectations of the policy-makers. And the major social welfare policies do not include many of the public social issues churning throughout American society today. These constant cautions are designed to remind analysts that much of the energy behind policy analysis is generated by a distinctly American political and economic tradition.

This tradition in public policy analysis and development emerges from the tension created by the interplay of American capitalism and democratic political principles. The American economic system is based on a free-market economy in which the accumulation of capital is left in the hands of private individuals. The American political system is based on a system of representative democracy in which individuals exchange a measure of individual freedom for protection and pursuit of common, nation-enhancing goals. The tension between these two systems creates the need for public policy and its accompanying policy analysis. As chapter 1 illustrates, public policy is the way questions are resolved by the allocation of political and economic power between individual pursuits and public goals.

As public policy has become a more familiar element in American society, functional distinctions between public and private spheres of activity have become less clear. Consequently, as discussed in chapter 3, functional distinctions in the scope of public policy have been replaced by a more dynamic interaction between public and private interests. Recently, serious debate over the question of the scope of public policy has spawned widespread political assaults on the entire social welfare policy enterprise that has been crafted since the Great Depression. Particularly, as articulated by President Reagan's neo-conservative supporters, a series of reevaluations of the scope and justification of public welfare policy has raised serious doubt in the minds of many about the wisdom and appropriateness of pursuing nation-enhancing social welfare goals at the expense of reduced personal liberties to do as one sees fit with one's own private wealth and property. The 1995 welfare reforms are part of this tradition.

The Neoconservative Position

Charles Murray in *Losing Ground* and George Gilder in *Wealth and Poverty,* present widely read critiques of American social policy today. Both Murray and Gilder argue that the products of social policy—contemporary social programs—do not provide a substantial social benefit and that there is little justification for government to provide them. The substance of the Murray and Gilder arguments derives from the neoconservative view that the federal government has no authority to provide social welfare benefits, and that this form of public policy represents an unwarranted intrusion on the rights of people to do what they please with their possessions.[3]

Another neoconservative critic, Richard Epstein, dean of the University of Chicago Law School, presents a more substantial critique of social welfare policy than Murray and Gilder. Basing his argument on an "original intent" interpretation of the U.S. Constitution and subsequent constitutional law, Epstein says that social programs constitute an unjustified "taking" by the federal government and that therefore Social Security, medical insurance, workers' compensation, and welfare payments should be abandoned.[4] "The fundamental problem in a system of welfare is that it conflicts with a theory of private rights that lies behind any system of representative government. There is quite simply no private cause of action for want of a benevolence that remotely resembles those causes allowable under the domain actions of tort, contract and restitution."[5]

Epstein's arguments are unequivocal. Unlike Murray and Gilder, Epstein develops both a social and a legal theory to support his contentions. Epstein argues that the "just compensation" clause of the U.S. Constitution in Article V of the Bill of Rights should be the controlling constitutional element for examining the legitimacy of a welfare function. A welfare function represents a "taking," without satisfying a definition of public use and without just compensation, Epstein argues; welfare is an unconstitutional taking of property, with no support in legal doctrine or social theory.

Economic Challenges to the Expression of Social Welfare Policy

Neoconservative economists object to social welfare programs, particularly those discussed in chapter 6, because they do not meet economic conditions that usually justify the public use of private property. It is at this point that economic neoconservative welfare critics discuss specific social programs as if they are similar in public purpose and rest on similar economic foundations. The discussion in part II of this book demonstrates the wide economic diversity among social programs offered by the federal government and those offered cooperatively with states and local governments. Differences abound among programs such as insurance programs, worker protection programs, social services programs, and cash assistance programs. The unwillingness of neoconservative economists to distinguish among these programs leads them to criticize all social welfare programs as if they served the same economic purpose and as if they were, therefore, founded on the same economic principles.

For example, chapters 3 and 6 discuss how welfare cash payments are cooperative policies funded through the states. The federal government makes grants for many social purposes. It seems specious to isolate welfare cash payments for special criticisms when highway and airport construction, education, law enforcement, environmental protection, and a variety of other domestic programs are funded similarly with federal grants.

If neoconservative economists mean to criticize only those welfare cash programs administered directly by the federal government, this criticism should be limited and directed to Social Security, unemployment insurance, and Supplemental Security Income. But neither Social Security nor unemployment insurance are "welfare takings." They are insurance programs in which beneficiaries pay into the program and receive benefits from the program. The economic justification for these programs reflects the same macroeconomic necessity as other federal government policies that provide a range of federally guaranteed subsidies, such as the U.S. Postal Service, Conrail, Fannie Mae, farm and oil price supports, and the Chrysler bailout. These macroeconomic necessities stem from the public need to protect economically fragile industry. Social Security protects economically fragile people.

In fact Social Security and unemployment insurance meet one of the best economic tests used to distinguish between public and private activities—market externalities, sometimes called "spillover" effects. As the policy analysis in part II identifies, external but often hidden costs are part of the real costs of a product that for many reasons are not reflected in the price of the product. For example, scarce resources may be used to produce a product without acknowledging their replacement costs, as in the case of oil depletion, or costly by-products of production may not be included in production costs as in the case of environmental pollution. In the same vein, the true value of any product must also include a true measure of the costs of labor. True labor costs include the cost of maintaining an adequate labor supply during times when prices of products force the firm to save by laying off personnel. The unemployment tax levied against the employer, therefore, ought to be reflected in the overall price of the product—and it is, through the unemployment tax levied on employers. In this view the unemployment tax is a legitimate cost of producing a particular product. It does not represent a taking of private property.

The best justification to support externalities, neoconservatives argue, is a measure of their efficiency. However, neoconservatives such as Charles Murray contend that only externalities that demonstrate highly favorable cost/benefit ratios (highly efficient) are appropriate candidates for public support. In practice, however, the level of efficiency necessary to justify a public use function is, itself, a normative issue. Although a private firm may fail when it provides inefficient products, populations frequently are willing to pay for a collective good even though they receive absolutely no benefit from it—a case of little or no degree of efficiency to that population. Economist Peter O. Steiner affirms an economic justification for income redistribution under such circumstances as a public use function when overall patterns of consumption are considered *along with* patterns of distribution, and when efficiency issues are used as the criteria for justification of public use.[6]

The Neoliberal Critique

Liberals have been quick to defend contemporary social welfare policy from neoconservative attacks. Stung by the Reagan administration's successful policy retrenchments, a number of well-known liberal policy analysts seek to neutralize growing dissatisfaction with social welfare policy by restating time-worm liberal dogma. Robert Morris, for example, asks for a return to "traditional" values of justice and mutual obligation.

> Welfare becomes a proxy term for values, a lightning rod for differing views about the obligations we owe each other, the virtues of selfishness, the limits of obligation, and political behaviors which will either unify or further divide a multiethnic population. Though limited in its singularity, social welfare provides a means of addressing certain questions related to human values and their expression in our society.[7]

With a similar plea, Alvin Schorr chides the policy objectives of the Reagan administration and urges a return to decency and just treatment. "Next to the discovery of sex and the invention of money, the Reagan administration will rank high in history as a force in the promotion of selfishness."[8] Schorr concludes his liberal defense of social welfare by writing:

> If we will express decency through policy as well as in personal relationships, if we will understand that in the modern world one affects us as deeply as the other, and if we will call on the skill and sophistication that are widely available, we may yet build a society that is just and fraternal."[9]

The difficulty with the neoliberal position lies in the high value given to individualism in liberal thought. While liberals and conservatives both agree that social policy should pursue just and decent social goals, neither liberals nor conservatives are likely to agree on what constitutes either justice or a decent society. Jeffrey Galper put the liberal dilemma in perspective several years ago when he wrote:

> Twentieth century liberalism has developed in a collectivist fashion. Individual well-being is pursued through state intervention, the welfare state being the limiting case. Despite the collectivist superstructure, however, modern liberalism retains its individualistic bias. Our welfare state, consequently, does not generally establish specific policy goals for the society as a whole. Rather, public policy establishes a framework for individual effort.[10]

Theodore Lowi offered the most salient critique of liberalism some years ago, pointing out that the individualism of traditional liberalism had become infested with special interests—interest groups—and no longer offered consensus about social goals, such as justice or a decent society. "Modern [liberal] policymakers have fallen into believing that public policy involves merely the identification of problems toward which government ought to be aimed. It pretends . . . that the unsentimental business of coercion need not be involved and that the unsentimental decisions about how to employ coercion need not really to be made at all."[11]

Social Welfare and American Political Institutions

American political institutions were established within the intellectual tradition of the seventeenth century—reason, enlightenment, individual dignity, and human rights. Perhaps more than any other, it was the political philosophy of John Locke (1632–1704) that inspired the form of America's political institutions as we know them today. In particular, the foundations of the modern constitutional state were drawn from Locke's expression of individualism, which he called popular sovereignty, and his theories of the social contract.

Personal property provided the most tangible expression of Locke's theories of individuality. Personal property was a novel idea in Locke's times. The prevailing theories, then, rejected claims of individually determined rights to property, supporting instead the "divine right of kings" doctrine which argued that the king, or God, was the only property owner. Locke's belief in individual property rights was an important part of his political philosophy.

Locke's idea of a social contract was also an important part of his political philosophy. According to Locke, the civil society is created when a group of people enter into a contract with one another, and by their consent create a governing order, or as we would say today, a government. Locke foresaw numerous kinds of government, all with sovereignty limited to their specific purposes, coexisting and semi-independent of one another. Thus American government as described in chapter 3 is consistent with Locke's political ideas.

The great theoretical problem for Locke continues to this day: How is it possible to have personal rights and to have an ordered society at the same time? If all citizens do as they please, how are the rights of some protected against the abuses of others? As far as public policy is concerned, the question is raised sharply by the neoconservative social welfare policy critics. How can my private property be taken and given to others in the form of welfare benefits with no compensation to me?

Locke found the answer to this question in the social contract. Societies are created for specific purposes by the contract which also provides rules by which members of the society agree to live. These rules, according to Locke, are needed to achieve the purpose for which the society was created. Locke wrote:

> Whosoever therefore out of a state of Nature unite into a *Community* must be understood to give up all power, necessary to the ends for which they unite into society ... and thus that, which begins actually *constitutes any political society* is nothing but the consent of any number of free men . . .[12]
>
> But because no *Political Society,* can be, nor subsist without having in itself the power to preserve the Property and in order there unto punish the office of all those of that Society; there and there only is *Political Society,* there everyone of the Members hath quitted this natural Power, resigned it up into the hands of the Community. . . .[13]

Locke understood the development of the state, or the commonwealth, as necessary to protect private property through a contractual process in which individuals exchange exclusive rights to property that existed in the state of nature for rights determined by the commonwealth. Locke writes, "The laws regulate the right of property and the possession of land is determined by positive Constitutions."[14]

Locke visualized civil societies that had obligations to its citizens. He did not think civil societies could agree to make all kinds of rules, particularly rules that offended personal rights. Locke thought that all rights were limited by social obligation, and in particular, the right to own and use private property was limited by the social obligation of charity. Locke stated the conditions of charity on the use of private property quite clearly when he wrote:

> But we know God hath not left one Man so to the Mercy of another, that he may starve him if he please . . . [H]e has given his needy Brother a Right to the Surplusage of his Goods; so that it cannot be justly denied him, when his pressing Wants call for it. . . . As *Justice* gives every Man a title to the products of his honest Industry, and the fair Acquisition of his Ancestors descended to him; so *Charity* gives every Man Title to so much out of another's Plenty as will keep him from extreme want, where he has no means to subsist otherwise; and a Man can no more justly make use of another's necessity to force him to become his Vassal, by the withholding that Relief . . . than he that has more strength can seize upon a weaker . . . and . . . offer him Death or Slavery."[15]

Locke's idea of charity derives from the inclusive right to property and the claim right to property held in common by all. "Charity gives every Man Title to so much of another's Plenty." James Tully, a Locke scholar, says this about Locke's limitation of private property: "If a case or need arise then *ipso facto,* one man's individual right is overridden by another's claim and the goods become his property."[16] Locke's idea of charity would prevent society from using want or need to force someone to work, and stands in sobering opposition to the neoconservative ideology articulated by Gilder, Murray, and others. Labor, for Locke, was the way one laid claim to property, not the foundation for a vassal-master relationship. The work-incentive program and other efforts to deny welfare to those unwilling to work find no support in Locke's theories. Locke states clearly that a claim right exists to the property of others: "A man may labor for himself or he may work for another but only if an alternative is available. If it is not, he cannot labor for himself and he cannot be forced to work for another; he is simply given the necessary relief.[17] Locke's theories were the original "contract for America." It might do well to review his ideas in the closing of the twentieth century.

The Contributions of Policy Analysis

Thoughts concerning what our country is all about, from intellectual perspectives to the public media debates, fall short in explaining day-to-day life in America. While the basic issues continue to exist—for example, how to exercise one's freedoms in the collective community—these fundamental issues of American society have taken on an additional complexity. Much has been said and written about the erosion of "American" values, and, indeed the values that undergirded the early development of the American state have changed dramatically—eroded, according to some. The strong Judeo-Christian ethic that played such an important, although unrecognized part, in the creation of America, has been challenged, repudiated, and replaced by other values.

Government is about values; policy is about values. Thus, rather than seeing present debates over values as destructive, it is also possible to see these debates as necessary to clarify our twenty-first century American values. Taking this perspective, policy debates that deal with contestable issues, such as the welfare reform debates of 1995, are positive steps in the reformulation of American values. For as much as we may bemoan the loss of traditional values in the shaping of American policy, it is impossible to return to those values to energize the tasks facing Americans today. Policy analysis cannot address directly either the neoconservative criticism of social welfare policy development or the helplessness of neoliberal efforts to reestablish an authority for further policy development. Policy analysis can, however, bring clarity to the issues being faced by American society in the last decade of the twentieth century. When policy analysis is undertaken as discussed in part I, it achieves three purposes: (1) it clarifies normative positions, (2) it offers alternatives which can be adopted through the political process, and (3) it attracts public attention to issues that may have been obscured by their uncertain normative contexts.

Policy analysis requires information that can be shared. A democratic political system needs information if it is to address problems. Good policy analysis provides good information—usable information—which enhances the process of policy-making, even when political processes do not operate flawlessly. By its nature, policy analysis becomes involved in ideological struggles, not theoretically or philosophically, but by providing information to policymakers as to which choices might best achieve sought-after political objectives. These political choices must be just, and while policy analysis cannot define justice, it can provide information that helps separate just from unjust alternatives. For example, policy analysis can show that enforced work programs have neither reduced welfare caseloads nor put welfare recipients to work. Consequently, enforced work programs must serve other purposes. Policymakers then can evaluate whether these other purposes are just or not.

Policy analysis provides an essential product in the American system. Despite the complexity of the policy-making process, and in spite of its lack of specificity, policy analysis takes confusing information about highly emotionally charged subjects, sorts out important considerations from unimportant ones, and then provides information that will enhance the quality of policy decisions. Without policy analysis it would be difficult to determine the relative value of the ever-increasing numbers of conflicting choices. Without policy analysis it would be difficult to categorize the many normative orientations to many policy options. And without policy analysis, the American political system would fall far short of meeting its commitments to its citizens.

The continued development of social welfare policy as it is known today finds strong intellectual support from those economic, political, and legal actions that were so critical to the founding of the contemporary American state. Through careful policy analysis, progressive social policies can be realized that are consistent with the American economic and political systems.

NOTES

Chapter 1: Understanding Public Policy

1. Congressional Quarterly Weekly Report, "House Passes Welfare Bill; Senate Likely to Alter it," March 25, 1995, p. 872.
2. Vee Burke, "Cash and Non-Cash Benefits for Persons with Limited Income: Eligibility Rules, Recipient and Expenditure Data, FY 1990–92" (Washington, D.C.: Congressional Research Service), September 1993.
3. Jack A. Meyer, "Health Care Policy: Historical Backgrounds and Recent Developments," in J. Meyer, ed., *Incentives vs. Controls in Health Policy* (Washington, D.C.: American Enterprise Institute, 1985), pp. 1-9.
4. Harold Wilensky and Charles Libeaux, *Industrial Society and Social Welfare* (New York: Free Press, 1968), pp. 138-47.
5. *Messages of the President,* Articles of the United States, vol. 24 (1964).
6. Frederic N. Cleaveland, *Congress and Urban Problems* (Washington, D.C.: Brookings Institution, 1973), pp. 279-310.
7. *Messages of the President,* Articles of the United States, vol. 24 (1964).
8. C. Wright Mills, *The Power Elite* (New York: Oxford, 1956), p. 187.
9. Amitai Etzioni, *Modern Organizations* (Englewood Cliffs, N.J.: Prentice Hall, 1963), p. 16.
10. Ibid., p. 67.
11. Ibid., p. 71.
12. Edward Banfield and Martin Myerson, *Politics, Planning and the Public Interest* (Glencoe, Ill.: Free Press, 1955), p. 287.

13. Mel Scott, *American City Planning Since 1890* (Berkeley: University of California Press, 1969), p. 88.
14. Ibid., p. 75. *Recent Economic Trends and Recent Social Trends* were documents produced by the Hoover administration's Research Committee on Social Trends.
15. 45 *CFR* 1331. All policy students should become familiar with the *Code of Federal Regulations,* the repository of all policy of the administrative agencies of the federal government.
16. *Executive Order of the President 12291,* Feb. 7, 1981 (Washington D.C.: Government Printing Office, 1983).
17. Howard Ball, "Presidential Control of the Federal Bureaucracy," in Howard Ball, ed., *Federal Administrative Agencies* (Englewood Cliffs, N.J.: Prentice Hall, 1984), p. 224.
18. Theodore Becker, *Comparative Judicial Politics* (Chicago, Ill.: Rand McNally, 1970), p. 137.

Chapter 2: The Process of Policy-Making

1. Andrew Dobelstein, *Politics, Economics and Public Welfare* (Englewood Cliffs, N.J.: Prentice Hall, 1985), p. 57
2. See John Palmer and Isabel Sawhill, eds., *The Reagan Record* (Cambridge, Mass.: Ballinger, 1984), chapters 6 and 7.
3. K. J. Meir and C. G. Nigro, "Representative Bureaucracy and Policy Preferences," *Public Administration Review,* 36 (1976): 458-69.
4. Roger H. Davidson, "Representation and Congressional Committees," *Annals of the American Academy of Political and Social Sciences,* 12 (Jan. 1974), p. 49.
5. See, for example, Hanna Pitkin, *The Concept of Representation* (Berkeley: University of California Press, 1972), pp. 144-67.
6. James Madison, *The Federalist Papers* (No. 48).
7. Woodrow Wilson, "Public Administration," *Political Science Quarterly,* 2:4 (June 1887), p. 128.
8. Herbert Simon, "Comments on the Theory of Organization," *American Political Science Review,* 54:2 (1954), p. 157.
9. Paul Appleby, *Big Democracy* (New York: Knopf, 1949), p. 39-47, 128-34.
10. Dwight Waldo, *Public Administration in a Time of Turbulence* (Scranton, Pa.: Chandler Pub. Co., 1971), pp. 108-15.
11. Robert Dahl and Charles Lindblom, *Politics, Economics and Welfare* (Englewood Cliffs, N.J.: Prentice Hall, 1953), pp. 88-104.

12. Wallace Sayre, ed., *The Federal Government Service* (Englewood Cliffs, N.J.: Prentice Hall, 1965), p. 6.
13. Glendon Schubert, *Judicial Policy-Making* (Chicago, Ill.: Scott, Foresman, 1965), pp. 11, 85.
14. *Gilliard v. Craig, 272 U.S. Fed.* (1972).
15. U.S. Congress, House of Representatives, Committee on Ways and Means, *Overview of Entitlement Programs (The Green Book)* (Washington, D.C.: Government Printing Office, 1993), pp. 781, 798, and 803.

Chapter 3: Policy-Making at the Local Level

1. See Andrew Dobelstein, *Politics, Economics, and Public Welfare* (Englewood Cliffs, N.J.: Prentice Hall, 1980), pp. 64–72.
2. *City of Clinton v. The Cedar Rapids and Missouri River Railroad* 24 Iowa 455 (1868).
3. *Akins v. Kansas* 191 U.S. 207, 220 (1903).
4. See, for example, Martin Grodzins, "The Federal System," in *Goals for Americans* (Englewood Cliffs, N.J.: Prentice Hall, 1960), pp. 265-82.
5. Deil Wright, *Understanding Intergovernmental Relations* (Monterey, Calif.: Brooks/Cole, 1982), p. 69.
6. Ibid., pp. 307-9.
7. U.S. General Accounting Office, *Block Grants: Overview of Experiences to Date* (Washington, D.C.: Government Printing Office, 1985), pp. 14-17.
8. Andrew Dobelstein, "The Bifurcation of Social Work and Social Services," *Urban and Social Change Review,* 18:1 (1985), p. 13.
9. David Easton, *The Political System* (New York: Knopf, 1964), p. 129 ff.
10. Randall Ripley, Grace Franklin, William Holmes and William Moreland, *Structure, Environment and Policy Actions: Exploring a Model of Policy-Making* (Beverly Hills, Calif.: Sage, 1973), esp. pp. 13-17.
11. Randall Ripley and Grace Franklin, *Congress, the Bureaucracy and Public Policy* (Homewood, Ill.: Dorsey Press, 1984), p. 10.
12. Ibid., pp. 11-12.

Chapter 4: Methods of Policy Analysis

1. Robert Mayer and Ernest Greenwood, *The Design of Social Policy Research* (Englewood Cliffs, N.J.: Prentice Hall, 1980), p. 20.

2. John Hallowell, *Main Currents of Modern Political Thought* (New York: Holt, Rinehart and Winston, 1960), p. 292.
3. Ibid., p. 307.
4. Andrew Dobelstein, "The Bifurcation of Social Work and Social Services," *Urban and Social Change Review,* 18:1 (1985), pp. 12-17.
5. Sheldon Danzier, "Statement," in U.S. Congress, Joint Economic Committee, *New Federalism: Its Impact to Date* (Washington, D.C.: Government Printing Office, 1983), pp. 444-66.
6. C. Arden Miller, "Infant Mortality in the United States," *Scientific American,* 253:1 (July 1985), p. 31.
7. John Palmer and Elizabeth Sawhill, *The Reagan Record* (Cambridge, Mass.: Ballinger, 1984), p. 345.
8. Stewart Nagel and Marion Neef, *Social Policy Analysis* (Beverly Hills, Calif.: Sage, 1979), p. 11.
9. Herbert Simon, "A Behavioral Model of Rational Choice," in R. Gore and H. Dyson, eds., *The Making of Decisions* (Glencoe, Ill.: Free Press, 1964), p. 119.
10. Ibid., p. 122.
11. Ibid., p. 119 (italics added).
12. Charles Lindblom, "The Science of Muddling Through," *Public Administration Review,* 19 (1959), Reprinted in Gore and Dyson, *Making of Decisions.*
13. Charles Lindblom and David Cohen, *Usable Knowledge* (New Haven, Conn.: Yale University Press, 1975), p. 10.
14. Ibid., p. 160.
15. Ibid., p. 155.
16. Ibid., p. 166 (italics added).
17. Ibid., p. 162.
18. For an illuminating discussion of the social purposes of infanticide, see Jermine Teichman, *Illegitimacy* (London: Erwin, 1978).

Chapter 5: Information and Data for Analysis

1. *Toward a Social Report* (Washington, D.C.: Department of Health, Education and Welfare, 1969), pp. 57-112.
2. Duncan MacRae, *Policy Indicators: Links Between Social Science and Public Debate* (Chapel Hill: University of North Carolina Press, 1985), pp. 127-28.
3. David Greenberg and Philip Robins, "The Changing Role of Social Ex-

periments in Policy Analysis," in Robert Aiken and Paul Keher, eds., *Evaluation Studies,* vol. 10 (Beverly Hills, Calif.: Sage, 1985), p 23.

4. Aiken and Keher, "Introduction," *Evaluation Studies,* p. 12.

5. Harold Linestone and Murray Turoff, eds., *The Delphi Method: Techniques and Applications* (Reading, Mass.: Addison-Wesley, 1975), ch. 6.

6. An excellent beginning text is Robert Weinbach and Richard Gunnell, *Statistics for Social Workers* (New York: Longman, 1987).

7. This brief discussion follows the organization of statistical analysis in *Statistical Analysis Systems* (Apex, N.C.: SAS Institute, 1989), one of the most widely used systems for computer analysis of data.

Chapter 6: Income Maintenance

1. For purposes of consistency and comparisons, all data referenced in this and subsequent chapters are drawn from U.S. Bureau of Census, *Statistical Abstract of the United States (1987)* and *(1994)* unless otherwise noted. This makes it possible to compare data from one chapter to the next. Although more current data sets may exist in specific cases, the U.S. Census provides one of the most reliable and universal data bases. See chapter 4 for a discussion of issues involved in data collection and analysis. The value of in-kind benefits is reported in U.S. Bureau of Census, "Estimates of Poverty Including the Value of Non-Cash Benefits," *Technical Paper No. 91,* Feb. 1984. Vee Burke, "Cash and Non-Cash Benefits for Persons with Limited Income: Eligibility Rules, Recipient and Expenditure Data, FY 1990–92" (Washington, D.C.: Congressional Research Service, September 1993), p. 18.

2. Ibid., p. 18.

3. Programs available to persons who do work or have worked are: (1) Social Security, (2) Unemployment Compensation, (3) Railroad Employees Retirement Insurance, (4) Veterans' Disability Pension, (5) Medical Hospital and Medical Insurance, and (6) federally assisted home loans. Programs for those who do not work are: (1) Supplemental Security Income, (2) AFDC (3) general assistance, (4) veterans' pensions and (5) Job Training Partnership Act.

4. Harold Watts and Albert Reece, eds, *Final Report of the New Jersey Graduated Work Incentive Experiment,* vol. 1 (Madison: University of Wisconsin Press, 1974), pp. 78-235.

5. See also Leonard Goodwin, *Causes and Cures of Welfare* (Cambridge, Mass.: D.C. Heath, 1982), p. 87.

6. Robert Greenstein, *Smaller Slices of the Pie* (Washington, D.C.: Center for Budget Policy, 1986), p. 1

7 U.S. Department of Commerce, Bureau of the Census, "Estimates of Poverty Including the Value of Non-Cash Benefits," *Technical Paper No. 91*, pp. 22-23. Vee Burke, p. 21.

8. See *Social Security and the Changing Roles of Women* (Washington, D.C.: Department of Health and Human Services, 1979). U.S. Congress, Committee on Ways and Means, *Overview of Entitlement Programs (The Green Book)* (Washington, D.C.: Government Printing Office, 1993), p. 488.

9. *The Green Book* (Washington, D.C.: Government Printing Office, 1993), pp. 501-2.

10. These data were drawn from Carmen Solomon, *Aid to Families with Dependent Children, Report No. 83-1* (Washington, D.C.: Congressional Research Service, 1983), pp. 194-206.

11. Ruben Snipper and Carol Wilkins, *Issues in Work-Welfare Policy* (Washington, D.C.: Congressional Budget Office, 1984), pp. 16, 66.

12. John Palmer and Isabel Sawhill, eds., *The Reagan Record* (Cambridge, Mass.: Ballinger, 1984), p. 192.

13. Data on the Child Support Enforcement Program were taken from Ron Haskins, Brad Schwartz, John Akin, and Andrew Dobelstein, "How Much Child Support Can Absent Fathers Pay?" *Policy Studies Journal*, 6:6 (Dec. 1985), pp. 201-23.

14. Data in this section are taken from *The Budget for Fiscal Year 1988*, vol. 1 (Washington, D.C.: Office of Management and Budget, 1987), table 107.

Chapter 7: Health

1. David Mechanic, *Medical Sociology: A Selective View* (New York: Free Press, 1968), p. 16.

2. U.S. Congress, Committee on Ways and Means, *The Hospital Cost Containment Act of 1977* (Washington, D.C.: Government Printing Office, 1977), p. 3.

3. Data in this discussion are taken from *Statistical Abstract of the United States (1988)* unless otherwise noted.

4. Odin Anderson, *Blue Cross Since 1929: Accountability and the Public Trust* (Cambridge, Mass.: Ballinger, 1975). See ch. 3 in particular.

5. Andrew Dobelstein, "Impact of Behavioral Sciences in Medical Practice," in Robert Cheshire, ed., *The Environment Affecting Health Science*

Behaviors (Cleveland, Ohio: Case Western Reserve Press, 1978), pp. 115-66.

6. C. Arden Miller, "The Cost Effectiveness of Pre-natal Care," unpublished, University of North Carolina, Department of Maternal and Child Health, 1989.

7. Jack Meyer, *Incentives Versus Controls in Health Policy* (Washington, D.C.: American Enterprise Institute, 1985), pp. 3-4.

8. Congressional Budget Office, *Containing Medical Care Costs Through Market Forces* (Washington, D.C.: Government Printing Office, 1982).

9. Karen Davis and Cathy Schoen, *Health Care and the War on Poverty: A Ten Year Appraisal* (Washington, D.C.: The Brookings Institution, 1987), ch. 2.

Chapter 8: Housing

1. See Department of Housing and Urban Development, *Environmental Review Guide for Community Development Block Grant Programs* (Washington, D.C., Department of Housing and Community Development, 1986).

2. See Anthony Downs, *Federal Housing Subsidies: How Are They Working?* (Washington, D.C.: The Brookings Institution, 1973), pp. 30-33.

3. Office of the President, "Report of the Commission on the Causes of Racial Disorder" (Washington, D.C., 1968).

4. U.S. Congress, Senate, Subcommittee on Housing and Urban Affairs, *Hearings* (Washington, D.C.: Government Printing Office, 1970).

5. See George Von Furstenberg, "The Distribution of Federally Assisted Rental Housing Services by Regions and States," in R. Sternlieb and H. Paulus, eds., *Housing* (New York: Aims Press, 1974), pp. 9-45.

Chapter 9: Child Welfare

1. Joseph Chepaitis, "Federal Social Welfare Progressivism in the 1920s," *Social Service Review,* 45:2 (June 1971), pp. 213-28.

2. R. Takamishi, "Childhood as a Social Issue: Historical Roots of Contemporary Child Advocacy Movements," *Journal of Social Issues,* 35 (1978), pp. 8-28.

3. Olin A. Wringe, *Children's Rights: A Philosophical Study* (Boston, Mass.: Routledge & Kegan Paul, 1981), p. 88 (emphasis added).

4. Norman Polansky et al., *Damaged Parents* (Chicago: University of Chicago Press, 1981), ch. 1.
5. U.S. Bureau of the Census, *County Statistics* (Washington, D.C.: Bureau of the Census, 1994), tables 142, 143.
6. Ron Haskins, Andrew Dobelstein, John Akin, and Brad Schwartz, "Estimates of National Child Support Collections," Grant No. 18-P-00259-4-10 (Washington, D.C.: Office of Child Support Enforcement, 1985).
7. Ron Haskins, Brad Schwartz, John Akin, and Andrew Dobelstein, "How Much Child Support Can Absent Fathers Pay?" *Policy Studies Journal,* 14:2 (Dec. 1985), pp. 201-22.
8. Gunnar Myrdal, *An American Dilemma* (New York: Harper & Row, 1962).
9. Office of Policy Planning and Research, *The Negro Family: The Case for National Action* (Washington, D.C.: Department of Labor, 1965).
10. Kenneth Clark, *The Negro American* (Boston, Mass.: Houghton Mifflin, 1966).
11. See Andrew Billingsley and Jeanne Giovannoni, *Children of the Storm* (New York: Harper & Row, 1975).
12. Lee Rainwater, ed., *Black Experience* (New York: Transaction Books, 1970), p. 6.
13. See Gilbert Steiner, *The Abortion Dispute and the American System* (Washington, D.C.: The Brookings Institution, 1983).
14. Gilbert Steiner, *The Children's Cause* (Washington, D.C.: The Brookings Institution, 1976), p. 255.
15. Gordon Blackwell, *Future Citizens All* (Chicago, Ill.: American Public Welfare Association, 1952).
16. P.L. 87-543 (Public Welfare Amendments of 1962), Title I, Part A, Sec. 101.
17. Gilbert Steiner, *The State of Welfare* (Washington, D.C.: The Brookings Institution, 1971).
18. Council of Economic Advisors, *Economic Report to the President* (Washington, D.C.: Government Printing Office, 1987).
19. Manpower Demonstration Research Corporation, *Summary and Findings of the National Supported Work Demonstration* (Cambridge, Mass.: Balinger, 1980).
20. U.S. Congress, House of Representatives, Committee on Ways and Means, *Overview of Entitlement Programs (The Green Book)* (Washington, D.C.: Government Printing Office, 1993), pp. 889–91.
21. Frank Bolton, Jr., *The Pregnant Adolescent* (Beverly Hills, Calif.: Sage Publications, 1980), ch. 7.

22. Andrew Dobelstein, "The Bifurcation of Social Work and Social Services," *Urban and Social Change Review,* 18:1 (1985), pp. 9-13.
23. Comptroller General of the United States, *Report to Congress: States Use Several Strategies to Cope with Funding Reductions under the Social Services Block Grant,* Washington, D.C., GAO, Aug. 1984.
24. Carol Stack, *All Our Kin: Strategies for Survival in a Black Community* (New York: Harper & Row, 1974), chs. 3 and 4.
25. Harold Watts and Albert Reece, eds., *Final Report of the New Jersey Graduated Work Incentive Experiment,* vol. 1 (Madison: University of Wisconsin Press, 1974).
26. Haskins et al., "Absent Fathers," p. 27.

Chapter 10: Older Adults

1. Quoted in Andrew Dobelstein, *Politics, Economics and Public Welfare,* 2d ed. (Englewood Cliffs, N.J.: Prentice Hall, 1985), p. 81.
2. See, for example, Rosabeth M. Kanter, *Work and Family in the United States* (New York: Sage, 1977), p. 18 ff.
3. For example, Robert Finch, who was at the time secretary of health, education and welfare, complained that "federal benefits and services of all kinds in 1970 will average about $1,750 per aged person and only $190 per young person." *Parade Magazine,* Nov. 27, 1970.
4. U.S. Congress, House of Representatives, Committee on Ways and Means, *Overview of Entitlement Programs (The Green Book)* (Washington, D.C.: Government Printing Office, 1993), pp. 889–91, pp. 1559–60.
5. U.S. Congress, Committee on Ways and Means, *Background Material and Data on Programs Within the Jurisdiction of the Committee on Ways and Means* (Washington, D.C.: Government Printing Office, 1986), pp. 60 and 68.
6. *Statistical Abstracts (1994),* table 715.
7. Ibid., tables 1283 and 1285.

Chapter 11: A Foundation for Public Policy: Analysis and Choice

1. George Gilder, "Women in the Work Force," *Atlantic Monthly* (Sept. 1984), p. 24.

2. Robert Eyestone, *From Social Issues to Public Policy* (New York: Wiley, 1978), p. 104.

3. Charles Murray, *Losing Ground: American Social Policy, 1950–1980* (New York: Basic Books, 1984).

4. Richard Epstein, *Takings: Private Property and the Power of Eminent Domain* (Cambridge, Mass.: Harvard University Press, 1985).

5. Ibid., p. 318.

6. Peter O. Steiner, "The Public Sector and the Public Interest," in R. Haverman, ed., *Readings in Economics* (New York: Holt, Rinehart, and Winston, 1984), pp. 22-30.

7. Robert Morris, *Rethinking Social Welfare* (New York: Longman, 1986), p. 5.

8. Alvin Schorr, *Common Decency: Domestic Policies after Reagan.* (New York: Yale University Press, 1986), p. 5.

9. Ibid., p. 216.

10. Jeffrey Galper, "Social Work, Public Welfare and the Limits of Liberal Reform," *Public Welfare* (Spring, 1973), p. 34.

11. Theodore Lowi, *The End of Liberalism* (New York: W.W. Norton, n.d.), p. 85.

12. John Locke, *Two Treatises of Government* (London: Black Swan, 1698), II, ch. 5,5. (Locke's original title was "Two Treatises of Government: In the Former the False Principles and Foundation of Sir Robert Filmer, and his Followers are Detected and Overthrown.") Italics in original, unless specifically stated otherwise.

13. Ibid., II, ch. 7, 87.

14. Ibid., II, ch. 5, 50.

15. Ibid., I, IV, 42.

16. James Tully, *A Discourse on Property, John Locke and His Adversaries* (Cambridge: Cambridge University Press, 1982), pp. 61, 63.

17. Ibid., p. 138.

INDEX

INDEX